Descriptive, informational, enjoyable, memor[...]
Land of the Book. This is my friend Charlie Dye[...]
you need to read this book. If you have, it is [...]
memories, it will be a great refresher course in [...]
that effectively links the Land with the Book.

MARK L. BAILEY
Chancellor and Sr. Professor of Bible Exposition, Dallas Theological Seminary

I know of no better guide to the Holy Land than Dr. Charlie Dyer. His many decades of leading thousands of pilgrims to Israel combine with his wit, wisdom, and winsome way to produce a virtual tour so descriptive you'll feel like you're on the bus touring the Holy Land! Many guides can point to piles of rocks, or spit out dates for archaeological digs, but Charlie guides us a step further by connecting it all to Scripture—and to our lives. *Experiencing the Land of the Book* is a life-changing journey through Israel because it combines the very best of Charlie's expertise and passion: the land of Israel and the Word of God.

WAYNE STILES
Host, Walking the Bible Lands

There is not a better guide to take you on a tour of the Holy Land than Dr. Charlie Dyer. In the book, Charlie combines his knowledge of the Bible with his extensive experience to make each site along the way come alive. As I read, I visualized each site in my mind, and even though I've visited these sites many times, I learned something new at each one. This work is insightful, practical, and extremely helpful. You will find yourself immersed in the Bible, laughing at Charlie's humorous traveling anecdotes, while also being deeply challenged in your walk with God. I heartily recommend this book for anyone seeking to explore the land of Israel and link "the land" with "the Book."

DOUGLAS M. CECIL
Life Stage Pastor, Christ Chapel Bible Church, Fort Worth; adjunct professor, Dallas Theological Seminary

Charlie Dyer has been a faithful guide for decades. When I was a student at Dallas Theological Seminary, he faithfully guided me and many other students through the Old Testament prophets and the land of the Bible. I've used his teaching as a reliable resource for tours I've led to Israel. There's no better guide to lead you through the Holy Land. I hope you will join him on the journey of a lifetime as the Bible comes alive to you like never before.

MARK HITCHCOCK
Senior Pastor, Faith Bible Church, Edmond, OK; Associate Professor of Bible Exposition, Dallas Theological Seminary

Dr. Charlie Dyer changed my life when he said "Mark, don't forget . . . it IS the Lord's will for you to go to Israel!" From that point forward, I have followed his love for the land, the people, and the biblical narrative. Charlie's passion for Israel is unmatched. In *Experiencing the Land of the Book*, he guides the reader from Dan to Beersheba, noting what we should see along the way. Read this book! Don't miss the tour. Not only will you learn about the Promised Land, but about the promised Savior!

MARK M. YARBROUGH
President and Professor of Bible Exposition, Dallas Theological Seminary

My life was transformed by going to Israel with Charlie Dyer in 1995! I've never been the same, and neither will you as you travel alongside this renowned Bible teacher and professor. Charlie has taken pastors and leaders on high-level, meaningful, spiritually fulfilling, once-in-a-lifetime Bible tours. And now you can have that same unforgettable journey. Go with Charlie to Israel through the pages of this outstanding book. You'll never be the same!

TOM DOYLE
CEO, Uncharted Ministries

How do you take the stories, lessons, and laughter from more than a hundred trips to Israel and jam them between two book covers? I have no idea. But Charlie Dyer has done it! In this one unique volume, Charlie has bought your plane ticket, reserved your bus seat, and booked the hotels. He's even packed along some tasty humor. So, there's no excuse for not traveling to the Holy Land with him. As you do, you're sure to encounter the hilarity of a Mark Twain, the humility of a pastor, and the heart of Jesus. That's Charlie Dyer, your guide. And your adventure is about to begin!

JON GAUGER
Cohost, The Land and the Book *radio program; Special Projects | Programming, Moody Radio*

Having taken numerous trips to Israel with Dr. Charles Dyer, I can affirm that his grasp of biblical history and ability to share it are one of a kind. His passion for knowing deeply this coveted land soon captivates seasoned scholars and Bible newcomers alike. In this latest book, Charlie has managed to put a journey through Israel into writing and pictures like no other. Anyone unable to experience the biblical enrichment a trip to Israel brings now has the next best thing! For an insider's view of Israel, then and now, open this book!

ED CANNON
President/CEO, Far East Broadcasting Company

You haven't visited Israel? Or you have, and would like to return without the hassle of tickets, airports, passports, and bus schedules? Then find a comfortable chair and take a guided, pictorial tour with Charlie Dyer, who has personally introduced thousands of people to "the land of the Book." My wife and I have visited Israel several times but are delighted that we can return once more to relive the memories, enjoy the scenery, and be reminded that our faith is rooted in the soil of history and actual events. Thanks, Charlie, for the gift you have given to the body of Christ by producing a book that will be treasured by all who rejoice that God chose this land to visit our planet and that, in His good time, these places will still have a glorious future.

ERWIN W. LUTZER
Pastor Emeritus, The Moody Church, Chicago

Charlie Dyer's guide to exploring Israel is quite unique and helpful. For a person who will never travel to Israel, this volume provides scores of insights, explanations, and encouraging devotionals. It also represents a great resource to equip a believer preparing to travel to Israel (or to read during their time in the land). In this helpful resource, Charlie superbly combines humor, clear explanations, interesting side stories, and insightful connections between biblical history, the land of the Bible, and scores of biblical passages. I have numerous resources that I draw on as I prepare for trips I lead to Israel, but will happily add this warm-hearted, clearly written, well-illustrated, and impactful guide for exploring and benefiting from the important connection between God's sacred Word and the land where the biblical events took place.

MICHAEL GRISANTI
Director of Israel Studies and Distinguished Research Professor of Old Testament, The Master's Seminary

With a tinge of Mark Twain humor, a ton of biblical scholarship, and a true passion to know the Lord and His Word through His land, Charlie Dyer has logged a written journey through the Holy Land sifted from his extensive experience of leading groups to Israel. Having been to Israel many times with Charlie, he brings a unique flavor grounded in the Scriptures and expressed colorfully through many first-time pilgrims' experiences. You will learn and laugh your way through each site while at the same time falling deeper in love with the Lord, the Land, and His Book. Thank you, Charlie, for sharing these treasures of truth in a personal way!

GREG HATTEBERG
Executive Director of Alumni Services and Assistant Professor for Educational Ministries and Leadership, Dallas Theological Seminary

Drawing from his extensive travels in the land of Israel, Dr. Charles Dyer has written a book that is destined to become a cherished classic. Following the enduring style of Mark Twain's *The Innocents Abroad* (1869), Charlie has written an account of his own travel adventures in Israel. This book is loaded with interesting and helpful information about the biblical sites and stories. The extensive use of photographs will help readers visualize the landscapes and features Charlie so well describes. Having guided over one hundred tour groups through Israel, Charlie has had many surprising and humorous adventures, which he recounts as he leads readers on a riveting tour of the land. Readers will have a hard time putting this book down. I loved it! And I'm sure that you will too.

J. CARL LANEY
Professor Emeritus, Western Seminary

In my role at Dallas Theological Seminary, it is one of my greatest joys to host tours of pilgrims in Israel and watch as the Bible comes to life in their lives. Charlie Dyer led many of our tours and designed a unique, life-changing journey through the land that put the pieces together in a way few others can. I'm excited that he has put this special journey into a narrative so everyone can have this experience, even if they never have the opportunity to travel to Israel.

KIM TILL
Vice President for Advancement, Dallas Theological Seminary

EXPERIENCING the LAND of the BOOK

A Life-Changing Journey through Israel

CHARLES H. DYER

MOODY PUBLISHERS

CHICAGO

Unless otherwise indicated, all Scripture quotations are taken from the Holy Bible, New Living Translation, copyright © 1996, 2004, 2015 by Tyndale House Foundation. Used by permission of Tyndale House Publishers, Carol Stream, Illinois 60188. All rights reserved.

Scripture quotations taken from the (NASB®) New American Standard Bible®, Copyright © 1960, 1971, 1977, 1995, 2020 by The Lockman Foundation. Used by permission. All rights reserved. www.lockman.org

All emphasis in Scripture has been added.

Edited by Elizabeth Cody Newenhuyse
Interior design: Puckett Smartt
Cover design: Erik M. Peterson
Cover photos of Israel by Charles H. Dyer
All photos by Charles H. Dyer

Library of Congress Cataloging-in-Publication Data

Names: Dyer, Charles H., 1952- author.
Title: Experiencing the land of the book : a life-changing journey through
    Israel / Charles H. Dyer.
Description: Chicago : Moody Publishers, [2022] | Includes bibliographical
    references. | Summary: "Blending history, rich biblical teaching, and an
    illustrated travelogue, this book connects its travelers to fifty
    highlights. Dyer brings travelers into contact with the land and "living
    stones"-people. You'll connect with the biblical story. And you'll laugh
    and learn from the vast collection of tales Dyer has accumulated over
    the years"-- Provided by publisher.
Identifiers: LCCN 2022014788 (print) | LCCN 202201 (ebook) | ISBN
    9780802428882 | ISBN 9780802474988 (ebook)
Subjects:
Classification: LCC DS103 .D944 2022 (print) | LCC DS103 (ebook) | DDC
    915.694/04--dc23/eng/20220427
LC record available at https://lccn.loc.gov/2022014788
LC ebook record available at https://lccn.loc.gov/2022014789

Originally delivered by fleets of horse-drawn wagons, the affordable paperbacks from D. L. Moody's publishing house resourced the church and served everyday people. Now, after more than 125 years of publishing and ministry, Moody Publishers' mission remains the same—even if our delivery systems have changed a bit. For more information on other books (and resources) created from a biblical perspective, go to www.moodypublishers.com or write to:

Moody Publishers
820 N. LaSalle Boulevard
Chicago, IL 60610

1 3 5 7 9 10 8 6 4 2

Printed in the United States of America

CONTENTS

GALILEE TO THE DEAD SEA

GOING UP TO JERUSALEM

AROUND JERUSALEM

As one of those who likes to say I was "raised in the church," I still recall my impressions of Israel from decades ago in Sunday school. Despite our teachers' (who had never visited the Holy Land themselves) attempts to impress us with how small Israel was compared to the United States, I still envisioned a vast expanse I would likely never visit either—a land boasting the history and stories of all my heroes from the Bible.

Little did I know that my blessed career would afford me the opportunity to visit Israel not once but four times—which my friend Charlie Dyer would refer to as "a good start."

I was pleased to see in my wife's high school yearbook—from several years before we even met—that her "life goal" was to someday visit the Holy Land. What a thrill to be able to help her fulfill that dream. And how fortunate for us that one of our trips was hosted and led by none other than Dr. Dyer himself. Our memories of that adventure remain vivid, as Charlie evidenced more than just encyclopedic knowledge of the Land of the Book. His almost childlike enthusiasm translated to an unforgettable experience.

Yes, it was exhausting. And no, I can't improve on the old adage of feeling as if we were drinking from a fire hose—desperately trying to take in everything he showed and taught us. We shot pictures galore and took notes so quickly we can hardly make them out now. But that's the beauty of this book. It took me back to every site and reminded me that, despite Charlie's unparalleled scholarship, he is somehow able to keep the cookies on the lower shelf where we mere laypeople can reach them.

You'll find this book, like Charlie himself, human, relatable, and accessible. If you've been to Israel with him, you'll relive every moment. If you haven't been there with him, you'll feel as if you have. And if it's at all within your power, you'll go with him someday.

JERRY B. JENKINS
Novelist and biographer

Mark Twain

INTRODUCTION

In 1867, Mark Twain traveled on an "Excursion to the Holy Land, Egypt, the Crimea, Greece, and Intermediate Points of Interest." The entire journey lasted almost five months. Before the ship docked at Jaffa to tour the Holy Land, Twain had already chosen a more adventuresome route. As the original brochure described it, "Those who may have preferred to make the journey from Beirout [sic] *through* the country passing through Damascus, Galilee, Capernaum, Samaria, and by the River Jordan and Sea of Tiberius can rejoin the steamer."[1] For twelve days Twain rode through the Holy Land on horseback, carefully picking his way down dusty, rock-strewn trails as he visited the various sites.

During his time in the Holy Land, Mark Twain felt the group was moving too fast, especially when they reached Jerusalem. "Our pilgrims compress too much into one day. One can gorge sights to repletion as well as sweetmeats. Since we breakfasted, this morning, we have seen enough to have furnished us food for a year's reflection if we could have seen the various objects in comfort and looked upon them deliberately."[2]

I wonder how Twain would react to a typical visit to the Holy Land today. Most trips only last ten to twelve days, and that includes the travel time over and back. In less than nine days the typical traveler is whisked around the land—from Dan to Beersheba—on an air-conditioned tour bus, pausing along the way to snap photos of different sites and visit the ever-present souvenir shops. On the first day, these modern pilgrims say to themselves, as they reach for their phones to take photographs, "This is unforgettable!" By the third day, many are starting to mutter, "Where are we again?" as the bus stops at still another site. This is when Mark Twain's words can come back to haunt the tired traveler. "The sites are too many. They swarm about you at every step; no single foot of ground . . . seems to be without a stirring and important history of its own."[3]

Having traveled to Israel over a hundred times (I lost count!), I've seen tours that are the religious equivalent of the Bataan Death March. Obsessed tour leaders and jaded guides march weary pilgrims up and down countless hills to see yet another forgettable ruin. Many of these weary travelers would benefit from having their own modern-day Mark Twain sitting near the back of the bus, providing a running commentary *sotto voce* on the people, places, and peculiarities being encountered each day.

Several years ago, my friend Greg Hatteberg and I wrote *The Christian Traveler's Guide to the Holy Land* to help prepare people for a trip. The purpose for the guide was to give each traveler a brief overview of the sites they would be visiting. A thumbnail map showed the site's location, followed by a synopsis of what happened there biblically, along with selected pictures. Our desire was to have the trip become more than just a fuzzy collection of disjointed memories and photos. The book's success has reinforced our belief that the more someone knows about the different sites before visiting the Holy Land, the more he or she will remember and appreciate the trip later.

However, I always felt the book lacked one thing—a Mark Twain–like sense of personality and humor that could help someone connect to the different sites emotionally as well as intellectually. Over the years I've gathered stories linking many sites to events our groups have experienced. These funny-but-true tales help anchor those sites in my mind. For example, I can't talk about the Jordan River baptismal site at Yardenit without remembering the lady who was baptized wearing purple underwear. Over the years thousands of others who've traveled with me have also gotten to experience that event vicariously. You will as well, when you reach that chapter!

That brings me to the purpose for this book. This is a travelogue of sorts that will take you on a journey through Israel. Along the way you will visit the sites seen by most pilgrims. And we *will* focus on the biblical events that make each site so special. But you will also be introduced to fellow travelers who, over the decades, have made an unforgettable impression on me. And through the retelling of those stories, I trust you will also become emotionally connected to the different sites.

The Holy Land is full of rocks and stony ruins. But a successful trip to Israel will also bring the traveler into contact with the "living stones" we call humanity. By introducing you to both kinds of stones, I'm confident you will come to love the land of Israel as much as I do.

So, lace up your sneakers, slather on the sunblock, and hang on to your hat as we embark on this unique tour to Israel. We'll visit many unforgettable sites and gaze out over some incredible vistas. And along the way we'll also meet some amazing individuals. Through it all, we'll open God's Word to explore how a journey through this land can bring the message of His Book to light!

The author with a "modern" Roman soldier

The First Day

MOUNT ARBEL
NAZARETH
MOUNT CARMEL
MEGIDDO
CAESAREA
BEN GURION AIRPORT

The Theater at Caesarea

CHAPTER 1

Caesarea:
The City Built on Sand

After a long flight—with little sleep but several movies—our planeload of pilgrims finally lands in Israel. Some tour groups head immediately to Jerusalem, but our plan is to drive north along the coast toward Galilee, saving Jerusalem until the end of the trip. After a short night's rest, our first stop is Caesarea, the seaside city built by Herod the Great.

THE EXCITEMENT OF THE FIRST STOP

As the bus stops at the entrance, excited tourists grab their hats and cellphones, adjust the headsets to their listening devices, and walk into the site. The guide tries to lead everyone toward the theater, but the tourists seem to scatter in all directions, snapping soon-to-be-forgotten pictures of every nondescript rock and broken statue. The wayward lambs finally enter the seaside theater and gaze in awe at their first authentic "ancient ruin" rising up from the surrounding sands.

Though restored by archaeologists—and used today for musical performances—the theater retains the well-worn look of a structure that has faced the Mediterranean Sea for twenty centuries. The scarred and pocked sandstone hints at the storms that have lashed it through the years. For the jet-lagged tourists their initial drowsiness gives way to a sense of excitement. But this emotional reaction is *not* from the height, or grandeur, or intricate workmanship of this theater. Rather, it comes from being face-to-face with the first visible, tangible link to the past. This is the group's first gateway back to the time of the Bible.

The tourists suddenly realize that Herod the Great might have walked across the same stones they are now treading, his hands could have brushed against the very walls they are touching. The remains of Herod's palace—the very palace where the apostle Paul was imprisoned for two years—stands a scant few hundred yards away. Before the group leaves Caesarea they will also visit the hippodrome, where chariot races were held, the ancient harbor—built by Herod and later rebuilt by the Crusaders—and the Roman aqueduct that brought water from Mount Carmel, six miles away.

One of the guide's many responsibilities on the tour is to keep the group moving. They want to slow down, breathe in the history, and populate the ruins with people from the Bible—Herod the Great, Herod Agrippa I, Peter, Cornelius, Philip the evangelist, Paul, Felix, Festus, and Herod Agrippa II. But the guide knows all the other sites the group must cover during this day. Like the White Rabbit in Walt Disney's *Alice in Wonderland*, they are all but shouting, "We're late, we're late! For a very important date! No time to say 'hello, goodbye,' we're late, we're late, we're late!"

The hippodrome next to Herod's palace

For most visitors to Caesarea, walking through the ruins is emotionally impactful, the first of many such experiences during the trip. But those who are able to look beyond the impressive ruins—and who aren't distracted by the guide's impatience—will sometimes spot the fatal flaw in Herod the Great's grand design for Caesarea. The city's foundations didn't rest on solid rock like that in the hills off to the east. Instead, the city spread out along the shifting sands of the Mediterranean coast. Herod's original harbor is gone . . . sunk beneath the sea. The aqueduct that brought Caesarea its life-giving water now stands in majestic isolation from the rest of the city. The aqueduct's northern edge disappeared beneath the sand that has relentlessly reclaimed its territory, and its southern end has been torn away by the Mediterranean—leaving a gap between the aqueduct and the city it was built to serve. Vast parts of the ancient city itself still remain covered by sand.

Remains of the Roman aqueduct

What Herod thought was permanent was only temporary. The city— named after Caesar, built with Roman technology, and intended as a monument to Herod's greatness—couldn't endure. The buildings may have been grand, but their foundations were supported by nothing more than shifting sand.

Leaving the theater, the group passes through a small forest of pillars and sarcophagi on its way to Herod's palace. The palace itself juts out into the Mediterranean, along with a freshwater pool extending out into the sea—perhaps the world's first infinity pool. On the north side of the palace, the group walks in the foundations of the assembly hall built by Herod the Great to receive important visitors. This is almost certainly the room where the apostle Paul stood before Festus and Agrippa. In Acts 25, Luke reported that Agrippa and his wife entered the auditorium "with great pomp, accompanied by military officers and prominent men of the city" (v. 23). Imagine the scene. Rome's provincial governor entertaining royalty, the grandson of King Herod, along with all the prominent citizens of Caesarea.

And then Paul was led into the assembly hall, the iron chains on his wrists and ankles clanking and scraping across the mosaic floor. To those gathered in the room, Paul must have seemed little more than a common prisoner brought in to satisfy the curiosity of this visiting dignitary.

But when Paul was invited to speak, the scene changed. Paul shared his personal testimony, including his encounter with the resurrected Jesus of Nazareth. But Paul wasn't done. Speaking directly to these leaders who thought they held his life in their hands, Paul presented the claims of Jesus and called on them to respond to *Him*. Jesus was to "suffer and be the first to rise from the dead, and in this way announce God's light to Jews and Gentiles alike"

The site of Herod's palace and assembly hall

(Acts 26:23). Agrippa the Jew and Festus the Gentile understood that Paul was speaking directly to them!

Festus cried out, "Paul, you are insane. Too much study has made you crazy!" (Acts 26:24). But Paul wouldn't back down. "I am not insane, Most Excellent Festus. What I am saying is the sober truth" (v. 25). And then pointing to King Agrippa he said, "King Agrippa knows about these things. I speak boldly, for I am sure these events are all familiar to him, for they were not done in a corner! King Agrippa, do you believe the prophets? I know you do" (vv. 26–27).

Agrippa interrupted Paul and responded, somewhat defensively, "Do you think you can persuade me to become a Christian so quickly?" But Paul refused to be silenced. "Whether quickly or not, I pray to God that both you and everyone here in this audience might become the same as I am, except for these chains" (vv. 28–29).

The apostle Paul passed through Caesarea, his two-year imprisonment likely little more than a footnote in the ledgers of the Roman rulers who governed Judea from here. But the mission to which Paul had committed his life was not built on shifting sand. It was anchored on the solid rock of Jesus. Paul himself reminded the church at Corinth of this truth. "For no one can lay any foundation other than the one we already have—Jesus Christ" (1 Cor. 3:11).

Paul's words raise an important question for any group about to begin its journey through the Holy Land. In what should we place our trust? It's the same question that some who listened to Paul's message two thousand years ago must have asked themselves. They could see the visible might of Rome. Could such might and power somehow be less significant than the promise of salvation offered through the death and resurrection of Jesus Christ? To many in Paul's day, such a choice must have seemed absurd. The Roman ruler of Caesarea, after hearing Paul's impassioned message, cried out, "Paul, you are insane" (Acts 26:24). He could see the impressive buildings already standing, hear the clank of hammers hitting chisels to fashion still more monuments to Rome's greatness. To Festus, *this* was reality. How could Paul believe that the power of God through Jesus Christ was greater than this?

Two millennia have passed since these men met in this very audience hall in Caesarea. Only fragments of the palace remain. The city built to honor the name of Caesar—and promote the greatness of Herod—is nothing more than an archaeological curiosity. Worn, weathered, world-weary. But the message announced by the apostle Paul has spread with power around the globe. That's an important lesson to carry from this first stop on this journey through the land!

FUN WITH SEMINARY STUDENTS

I love beginning a tour at Caesarea. Unfortunately, the extensive archaeology and amazing work of preservation have taken away the ability to pull a practical joke on guests. Before much of the restoration had been completed, parts of the excavation were reburied beneath the sand to prevent damage or looting. On some of my early trips with seminary students we would take them on a walk between Herod's palace and the harbor area. At one key spot we would stop and say, "Imagine what else might be buried here in the sand, right under our feet!" And then we would begin scraping the sand away with our feet.

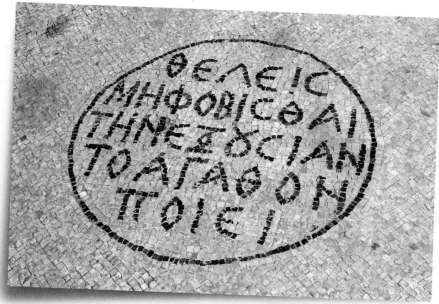

Mosaic with quotation of Romans 13:3

As Greek letters started coming into view, the students would get excited and drop to their knees to help brush away more sand. Soon the group had uncovered an entire inscription. And then the budding Greek scholars would translate, with a little help from the professors, "Would you like to live without fear of the authorities? Do what is right, and they will honor you." Why, that's a direct quotation of Romans 13:3!

And indeed it was. This Byzantine-era inscription, one of two actually, was discovered on the floor of a large public building. The inscription is now completely uncovered, but the "joy of discovery"—and the practical joke—are forever gone!

Take some time to explore on your own. Make sure to get all your pictures. And don't forget to use the restrooms on your way back to the bus. But don't dawdle! The bus will be leaving in fifteen minutes. "We're late, we're late, we're late!"

Looking out over the Jezreel Valley from the top of Mount Carmel

CHAPTER 2

Mount Carmel:

Elijah's Mountaintop Experience

The road to the summit of Mount Carmel—the traditional site of Elijah's contest with the prophets of Baal—is paved, but fairly narrow. Two small cars can pass one another going in opposite directions without difficulty, but not two tour buses. Thankfully, there are multiple spots along the road where one bus can ease over to the side, allowing another to squeeze by. Passengers learn to appreciate the skilled drivers who pass within mere inches of each other while keeping their side mirrors unscathed.

The road to the top of Mount Carmel wasn't always so nice. On my early trips to Israel there were places where the road was barely wide enough for one bus. If two buses met unexpectedly at one of those narrow spots, one was forced to back up until the driver could pull to the side and allow the other to squeeze by. I never heard any reports of accidents on that road, but I'm sure the experience tested the nerves of new drivers.

The road finally snakes its way up to a monastery on one of the tallest peaks of the Mount Carmel range. The monastery is named Muhraqa, which in Arabic means "place of burning" or "place of the fire." It was built by the Discalced Carmelite Order. Of course, the average visitor to the Holy Land has never used the word "discalced" in a normal conversation, which shows how this trip can add greatly to one's vocabulary. The word comes from the Latin word for shoes—*calceare*. To be "discalced" was to be without shoes! Somehow the word never caught on with most people, probably to Shoeless

Joe Jackson's everlasting relief. Thankfully, pilgrims today can keep their shoes on at the site. There's no need to be shoeless on Mount Carmel!

Some guides don't like bringing their groups to Muhraqa. It's an out-of-the-way drive to reach the site, and apart from the monastery's tiny gift shop there are no stores in the immediate vicinity. Tourists seldom realize that many stores offer guides and drivers a commission for bringing their busloads of tourists in to shop. Some less-than-honorable guides would prefer to skip sites like Muhraqa to give their people more time for shopping at "my friend's very special olive wood shop" in Nazareth.

I was once leading a group in Israel at the same time as my brother-in-law. After our tours, we remained in Israel and had a few free days to do some exploring on our own. As we talked about our most recent trips, he mentioned how sad it was that the road up to Muhraqa had been washed out. "But I was just there with our group. The road wasn't washed out," I said.

Over the years my brother-in-law led several other tours to Israel, but he never used that guide again!

After paying the entry fee, the guide leads the group across a plaza toward the main building. Some stop to take a picture of the statue of Elijah who is glaring menacingly down at them, sword in hand, threatening to slay any remaining prophets of Baal who might be hidden among the group. On reaching

Statue of Elijah on Mount Carmel

the building, the pilgrims climb a set of stairs to the rooftop viewing platform for a spectacular view of the Jezreel Valley.

I love Mount Carmel, in part, because of this grand view. On most days the Jezreel Valley is covered in a light blanket of haze, but a visitor can still see enough to appreciate the strategic significance of this valley, also known as the Valley of Esdraelon or the Valley of Armageddon. This rooftop perch helps a person visualize how much history God has packed into such a small country. The modern state of Israel has conveniently built a military airfield in the valley, and its two runways form a giant V that can be used to help orient the group geographically. The left runway is pointing toward a ridge that has a town on top. The ridge is the Nazareth Ridge, and the town is the modern city of Nof HaGalil ("the Galilee View"). The original city of Nazareth is right next to it, and it's hard to tell the two apart from here. People can mentally place Jesus, Joseph, and Mary on that hill.

The same runway is also pointing to a rounded hill sticking up just *behind* the Nazareth Ridge. That's Mount Tabor. A later tradition associates this mountain with the Transfiguration, though Mount Hermon is a better candidate for that event. But two spiritual giants from the Old Testament *did* stand on the summit of this mountain—Deborah and Barak. Mount Tabor is the mountain in Judges 4–5 where they led an army of ten thousand Israelites against the chariots of Canaanite general Sisera.

The right runway is pointing to still another hill, the Hill of Moreh. The name doesn't bring a glimmer of recognition to most in the group until they populate the hill with other notable characters from the Bible. At the base of the hill is the modern town of Afula. It's the location of the Old Testament town of Ophrah—the hometown of Gideon! On the right (south) side of the hill was the Old Testament town of Shunem. Elisha stopped off at the home of a Shunammite woman and announced she would give birth to a son (2 Kings 4). Later, Elisha raised that child to life following the boy's tragic death.

On the left (north) side of the hill was a town from New Testament times called Nain. In Luke 7 Jesus raised back to life a son belonging to a widow from Nain. The people responded by saying, "A mighty prophet has risen among us" (Luke 7:16). Why did they respond to this miracle by calling Jesus a prophet? Perhaps because the greatest miracle that ever took place in the area happened just three miles away, on the other side of the hill, when the prophet Elisha raised that young boy to life!

From the hill where Jesus grew up, to the hill where Deborah and Barak led Israel in a great victory, to a hill where two young boys were raised from the dead—by Elisha and Jesus. And we're not yet done with this visual sweep of history. Just to the right of the Hill of Moreh, off in the distance, is Mount Gilboa. That's the hill where Gideon chose his three hundred men to defeat the Midianites, where Saul and his sons died fighting the Philistines, and where Ahab and Jezebel built a palace . . . and a man named Naboth refused to sell them his nearby vineyard.

Thirteen hundred years of Bible history unfold in the valley below. And we haven't included the hill on which we're now standing! Mount Carmel is actually a range that extends for twenty-four miles. Below us in the valley our tourists can just make out a green ribbon of vegetation that marks the twisting course of the Kishon River—really nothing more than a small rivulet for most of the year. Somewhere on this hill is where Elijah fought his contest with the prophets of Baal and the prophets of Asherah, and way down there at the Kishon is where Elijah had the people put these false prophets to death.

Today, groups wearing headsets are able to spread out along the railing here on the monastery roof and take in the panorama while Bible teachers speak into a microphone. But in earlier days, groups needed to huddle together around the teacher if they wanted to hear. This was especially true if there were multiple groups sharing the rooftop at the same time.

On one occasion, I had just started speaking when a large group came up on the roof. I motioned to our party to gather around me in the corner. I told them I would need to talk softly because I didn't want to disturb the other group. Meanwhile that group began to huddle in the center of the roof around a hand-drawn compass showing the direction to various sites. I didn't know exactly what the leader was saying, but at one point he must have described the fire that fell from the sky following Elijah's prayer. He evidently associated it with the "cloven tongues of fire" that fell in Jerusalem on the day of Pentecost, because the group suddenly came alive with wild shouts and ecstatic utterances! Thankfully, no physical fire fell from the cloudless sky that day, and no prophets of Baal wandered onto the roof.

On most occasions the weather on Mount Carmel has been nice, though somewhat hazy, for our late morning visit. When sharing the story of Elijah's encounter with the prophets of Baal, I usually focus on the drought. I want the group to imagine what it would have looked like when, after a three-and-a-half-year drought, a cloud no larger than a human fist finally appeared to the west, over the Mediterranean. Sometimes there will even be a cloud that I can use as an illustration. But there was one time on Mount Carmel when I had to focus on the downpour rather than the drought!

It was early spring, and the weather had been threatening all morning. But as we neared the top of Mount Carmel, the heavens let loose. We learned later that up to eight inches of rain fell on Mount Carmel that day, causing severe flooding in Haifa. We sat on the bus for a short time waiting to see if the storm would end. It didn't, so I retold the story of Elijah and the prophets of Baal, focusing on the great storm God sent after the contest. The rain was so heavy we couldn't even see the monastery from the parking lot, less than a hundred yards away. The people all knew the story, but the special effects were spectacular.

There's much Bible history that can be seen from the summit of Carmel, but there are also some profound lessons every visitor should carry

> **The events in the Bible are real events that took place in real locations and impacted the lives of real people.**

away from the site. The first is the reminder that the events in the Bible are real events that took place in real locations and impacted the lives of real people. The tangibility of those stories makes a profound impression on most visitors. A second lesson is the reminder that anyone choosing to stand with God need not fear the opposition. Whether it's Elijah, Deborah and Barak, or Gideon, the victory came when faithful men and women chose to follow and obey Him. And finally, we need to drive off this mountain with a caution. Whenever we have what some describe as a "mountaintop experience," like the one Elijah had here on Mount Carmel, no matter which way we head, we need to be prepared to face the spiritual valley that inevitably follows. Elijah's mountaintop in 1 Kings 18 was followed by his fearful flight into the wilderness just one chapter later. Life is a series of spiritual peaks and valleys. Enjoy the peaks, but always remain prepared for the valleys. Just ask Elijah!

Remains of Bronze Age gate at Megiddo

CHAPTER 3

Megiddo:
The Site of Armageddon

Walking across the site of ancient Megiddo is a good early test of a group's physical abilities. The previous sites only involved relatively short walks, but the hike across the summit of Megiddo is more taxing. It's longer. It requires walking over some irregular ground. And it ends by descending 180 steps into the town's water tunnel, followed by a climb of eighty steps to get back out.

The group is ready to take a short break by the time we reach the first stop, the Late Bronze Age city gate. This gate was in use when Joshua led the children of Israel into the promised land, and it helps explain why Israel failed to occupy the land fully. In fact, Megiddo is specifically singled out in this regard. "The tribe of Manasseh failed to drive out the people living in . . . Megiddo, and all their surrounding settlements, because the Canaanites were determined to stay in that region" (Judg. 1:27). Standing by this gate, that makes great sense. The defenses would have looked quite imposing to a group of desert nomads. That doesn't *excuse* Manasseh's failure, but it does help explain it.

During Mark Twain's visit to the Holy Land, he stood at ancient Megiddo and reflected on all the armies that had gathered in the Jezreel Valley over history.

The Plain of Esdraelon—"the battlefield of the nations"—only sets one to dreaming of Joshua and Benhadad and Saul and Gideon; Tamerlane, Tancred, Coeur de Lion, and Saladin; the warrior kings of Persia, Egypt's heroes, and

Napoleon—for they all fought here. If the magic of the moonlight could summon from the graves of forgotten centuries and many lands the countless myriads that have battled on this wide, far-reaching floor, and array them in the thousand strange costumes of their hundred nationalities, and send the vast host sweeping down the plain, splendid with plumes and banners, and glittering lances, I could stay here an age to see the phantom pageant.[1]

Until someone has visited Israel, Megiddo and the Jezreel Valley are simply names from the Bible with little historical significance. Yet for those like Twain, who've stood on the summit and gazed out across the valley, the strategic location becomes clear. To the west, the valley reaches to the Mediterranean at modern-day Haifa, and to the east it connects with the Jordan Valley. Near where we're standing, the International Highway passed by Megiddo connecting the two great civilizations of Egypt and Mesopotamia. A parade of cars and trucks can still be seen traveling along the modern road that follows the pathway used by the Egyptian army 3,500 years ago.

Carl Rasmussen has described the Jezreel Valley as "the stage on which the armies of the world have made their entrances and exits."[2] And certainly that's what Mark Twain must have had in mind as he stared out over the same vista. The spot where we're standing, the hill of Megiddo, has more than just *historical* significance. The word "hill" in Hebrew is *har*, and in the book of Revelation *har Megiddo* gets transliterated as *Armageddon*. Its very name points to a still-future gathering of armies at this site.

When most hear the word Armageddon they think of the final battle of the ages, the ultimate spot where good will triumph over evil. But as we stand here I want our group to walk off the site with a slightly different perspective. To me, the hill of Megiddo marks the spot where evil—at least temporarily—seems to triumph over good. To understand why I say this, we need to visit Megiddo on two separate occasions.

The first visit takes place near the end of the kingdom of Judah. Judah's last good king, Josiah, ruled on the throne, but the dark clouds of war were gathering on the horizon. To the northeast, Assyria and Babylon were fighting for control over Mesopotamia. The once-great Assyrian empire was on the ropes. The army of Babylon had already destroyed the city of Nineveh and was advancing to attack what was left of the Assyrian forces. To Josiah's southwest, Egypt was on the rise, hoping to benefit from this power struggle. The mighty army of Egypt began marching north to rescue the Assyrian army, stop the Babylonians, and expand its power and influence along the way.

Good King Josiah saw the Egyptian advance as a mortal threat to his kingdom. Though the Egyptians marched up the International Highway and away from Jerusalem, Josiah mobilized his army and rushed north to stop them at the only spot where his smaller force might have a strategic advantage—at Megiddo. He hoped to bottle up the Egyptian army in the narrow pass nearby that carved its way through Mount Carmel.

Josiah's ill-fated military campaign ultimately cost him his life. The Bible describes the encounter this way: "King Josiah and his army marched out to fight him, but King Neco killed him when they met at Megiddo. Josiah's officers took his body back in a chariot from Megiddo to Jerusalem and buried him in his own tomb" (2 Kings 23:29–30). Megiddo is the spot where Josiah lost his life, and the kingdom of Judah lost its independence.

If this first stop at Megiddo takes us back in time 2,600 years, the second takes us to a time that's still future—a time when it seems as if all the world will fall under the control of Satan and the forces of evil.

What many call the "battle of Armageddon" is not actually described as a battle in the Bible. The book of Revelation pictures it as a staging area for the armies of the world. Satan, the Antichrist, and his false prophet send their demonic emissaries into all the world "to gather them for battle against the Lord on that great judgment day of God the Almighty . . . And the demonic spirits gathered all the rulers and their armies to a place with the Hebrew name *Armageddon*" (Rev. 16:14, 16). Armageddon is the *gathering place*, the spot where the armies join forces for their final campaign against Israel . . . and eventually against God Himself.

Megiddo represents the high-water mark of Satan's plan for global conquest. The armies of the world ultimately unite behind his false messiah at Megiddo for a series of military campaigns that will end in Jerusalem. But just when victory seems within his grasp, Jesus will descend from heaven to the Mount of Olives to destroy the invaders and rescue His followers. An army that appears unstoppable when it gathers at Megiddo will ultimately be vanquished by the true King and Messiah when He returns from heaven.

Knowing how the story ends gives our band of pilgrims a different perspective as we get ready to continue our exploration of Megiddo. Directly behind where we're standing, archaeologists uncovered a large altar built from fieldstones. Though we're looking down at the altar, it was once the "high place" for those living here just before the time of Abraham.

One of my most unique memories from Megiddo is of a time when we weren't able to go up on the site. Clouds had skittered across the sky all morning, threatening rain. For a while we had been fortunate, but that all changed as our bus rolled into the parking lot. The clouds opened up and a driving rain soaked the group as we ran to the building entrance. While waiting for the rain to stop, we used the indoor model to explain the details of the site. It was still raining, so we sent the group to the restrooms. Little did we know that our time at the site was just about over.

As the group started gathering near the pathway to walk up on the site, we saw a stream of water rushing down toward the building. Within just a few minutes the pathway was completely flooded, the water several inches deep. And the rain hadn't slowed down one bit. We waited a few more minutes, but it became obvious that we wouldn't be able to go up on the site without becoming completely soaked. We finally gave up and ran back to the bus.

As we drove toward the Sea of Galilee and our hotel, we passed Mount Tabor. The bus splashed through deep puddles on the road while we talked about how God enabled Deborah and Barak to defeat the forces of Sisera by sending a massive rainstorm at just the right moment. No one in the bus had any doubts such a storm could turn fields into a quagmire and make the chariots

Canaanite altar discovered at Megiddo

useless as the iron-rimmed wheels sank into the mud. The group never got to see Megiddo, but they also never forgot the story of Deborah and Barak!

HIKING ACROSS MEGIDDO

The overlook at Megiddo is a wonderful spot to talk about the role Megiddo plays in history and in prophecy, but it's also an excellent spot to rehearse the key hills that frame the Jezreel Valley—Mount Carmel, the Nazareth Ridge, Mount Tabor, the Hill of Moreh, and Mount Gilboa are all clearly visible from this overlook. (Well, as long as it's not raining!) Next to the overlook is a cut taken from the ancient hill—the archaeological equivalent of taking a slice out of a layer cake. And in one of those remarkable accidents of discovery, the archaeologists just happened to pick a spot where there was a Canaanite altar—a high place made of rounded stones.

As we begin our trek across the top of the hill, we come to a spot where the

39

less mobile "sheep" can separate from the more sure-footed "goats." And as if to follow Jesus' command in Matthew 25, the sheep head off to the right for a downhill walk back to the Visitor Center where the bus is waiting. The sure-footed goats take the pathway to the left heading across the rest of the site.

Grain storage silo built into the ground

Stone manger with sculpture of a horse

After stopping at a large grain storage silo dug into the ground, we reach the stables. During the time of King Ahab, these held the horses that pulled Israel's chariots. But what's perhaps even more interesting for our group are the stone mangers. Some are ancient, and some are new. These new ones were added, along with the artistic horses, to help visualize the ancient ruins.

Those mangers also help bring the story of Jesus' birth into sharper focus. Most churches have some sort of manger or crèche that they bring out at Christmas. The manger is usually made of wood and stuffed with straw, into which is placed the blond-haired, blue-eyed Jesus. But while a manger made of wood might look nice, it would have been quickly gnawed to bits by hungry animals. A more logical choice for a manger was the limestone that formed the backbone of the hill country. It was cheap, plentiful, and durable. Once it had been chiseled into shape it would last indefinitely. Here at Megiddo are 2,600-year-old mangers still holding their shape.

> A manger made out of wood may look nice, but it would have been quickly gnawed to bits by hungry animals.

Of course, I haven't yet had any churches adopt my suggestion.

The final destination on our journey across Megiddo is the tour of the water tunnel. Walking down more than 180 steps is difficult for anyone with knee problems. But imagine how difficult it would have been before the modern OSHA-approved, seven-inch steps were installed. The original steps were carved from limestone, varied in height, and were usually wet and slippery from the water spilled from the jars of the women who were carrying them up from the spring.

At the bottom of the steps is the passageway carved through bedrock. The builders needed to get the depth, direction, and distance just right to have the tunnel end just below the original spring. Then they diverted the spring so that it flowed down into the tunnel. Finally, they blocked off all outside access to the spring so no enemy would know the location of this secret entrance into the city.

The cool dampness inside the tunnel is a welcome relief on a warm day.

The water tunnel at Megiddo

Unfortunately, the tunnel ends all too soon, and we now have to climb the equivalent of eight flights of stairs to exit the water system. If our timing is right, the bus *should* be waiting for us at the end of the pathway. One more site checked off our itinerary!

Looking down into Nazareth from the Mount of Precipice

CHAPTER 4

Nazareth:

Jesus' Hometown

In Jesus' day, Nazareth was a tiny village with just a few hundred residents. Like many of the small towns scattered throughout the hills of Judea and Galilee, it was remote and hard to reach. Few outsiders would ever go out of their way to reach the village. Nathanael's words echoed the common sentiment of the day: "Can anything good come from Nazareth?" (John 1:46).

Though Nazareth was less than five miles as the crow flies from the International Highway that connected Egypt to Mesopotamia, a visitor had to climb a steep ridge to reach the town. After making it to the top of the hill, the would-be visitor discovered that the village itself was situated in a natural depression just below the top of the ridge. It was nestled in this bowl because that's where a natural spring—the town's water supply—was located. Nazareth was just a small village hidden away on top of the hill. The Old Testament passes by without a single reference to Nazareth. And even though it was Jesus' hometown, it's still only mentioned seventeen times in the New Testament.

But because of its association with Jesus, Nazareth became a major pilgrim stop and tourist destination. Over time, the town also grew in size. By the 1950s, Nazareth had nearly 20,000 inhabitants. Today, the town has grown to over 80,000 people. But the same two-lane road that snaked its way through the small village is still the main route through the center of town. The busloads of tourists arriving to visit the churches, shrines, and stores of Nazareth must work their way along this narrow road that is choked with cars, delivery vans, street vendors, and shops selling genuine hand-carved olive wood and religious souvenirs.

The best place to view Nazareth today is from the Mount of Precipice, a spot on the edge of the hill. Standing here and looking down at Nazareth, it's easy to see the natural bowl in which the town started. The gray, cone-shaped roof of the Basilica of Annunciation is located at the bottom of the bowl in the center of town. From this vantage point we can also see why Nazareth today is a victim of its own success. The original road to the town twisted its way up the hillside from the Jezreel Valley before descending into the bowl and through the center of town on its journey north.

THE RIOT IN NAZARETH

Here on the Mount of Precipice we can also look down into the Jezreel Valley and see the new highway that tunnels its way through the rock, making the ascent to the top much easier than it was a few decades ago. But as the group looks down at the valley and roadway below, the story of Jesus returning to Nazareth in Luke 4 also comes into clearer focus. Jesus had returned to

Looking down into the Jezreel Valley from the Mount of Precipice

Nazareth and was invited to read and expound the Scriptures in the synagogue. The people appreciated the hometown boy until He began talking about Elijah and Elisha and their ministries to Gentiles. Luke records the chaotic end to this synagogue service. "When they heard this, the people in the synagogue were furious. Jumping up, they mobbed him and forced him to the edge of the hill on which the town was built. They intended to push him over the cliff" (Luke 4:28–29).

Turn and look back at Nazareth. The Basilica is about a mile away. Then turn and look down the side of the steep cliff toward the Jezreel Valley. The worshipers in the synagogue that Sabbath day were so angry they pushed Jesus out of the synagogue . . . and out of the village . . . and all the way out to the edge of the cliff where we're now standing. And then they planned to shove Him off the side of the cliff! The words in Luke 4 take on greater force and impact when you understand how far the people were willing to go to show their rejection of Jesus' ministry.

> The words in Luke 4 take on greater force and impact when you understand how far the people were willing to go to show their rejection of Jesus' ministry.

WHAT SHALL WE VISIT?

For Roman Catholic and Greek Orthodox pilgrims, no trip to the Holy Land would be complete without a visit to the Basilica of the Annunciation and the Virgin's Fountain, along with several other holy sites. But many Protestant groups avoid the city because of all the traffic congestion. Historically, the Roman Catholic and Orthodox groups have sought to find the actual spot where events in the life of Christ took place, and then build a shrine and hold religious services there. Protestants are more interested in seeing the vistas and trying to imagine what the scene looked like when the events in the Bible took place.

Mark Twain noticed the difference and wrote about the grotto and basilica in Nazareth with his tongue firmly embedded in his cheek. "It is an imposture

Basilica of the Annunciation

—this grotto stuff—but it is one that all men ought to thank the Catholics for. Wherever they ferret out a lost locality made holy by some Scriptural event, they straightway build a massive—almost imperishable—church there, and preserve the memory of that locality for the gratification of future generations. If it had been left to Protestants to do this most worthy work, we would not even know where Jerusalem is to-day, and the man who could go and put his finger on Nazareth would be too wise for this world."[1]

Stonemason at work in the Nazareth Village

Since this is a Protestant tour, the Protestant "holy site" in Nazareth is the Nazareth Village—and that's our next destination. Nazareth Village is a re-creation of what Nazareth might have been like in the time of Jesus. Tourists visit houses, a farm, and a synagogue set up as they would have looked during Jesus' day. Visitors can watch a farmer plowing his field with an iron-tipped plow, or see a carpenter crafting furnishings and tools, or view a stonemason chiseling a stone to be used in a building, or sit inside the replica of a first-century synagogue. This outdoor museum is a highlight for many because it allows them to visualize how Nazareth might have been in the time of Jesus.

WHERE ARE YOU FROM?

Nazareth Village also brings back memories of a special trip to Israel with my radio cohost. We were in Israel recording for a Moody Radio Christmas special. This type of trip is fairly intense. The two of us, along with our wives, traveled at breakneck speed through the land to record as many interviews and sounds as possible in the limited time we had.

We somehow managed to schedule our visit to Nazareth Village at a time when there were no other groups. The director gave us a personal tour while we took time to record the sounds of bleating sheep, grain being winnowed, and olives being crushed in a press.

The highlight of our time there came when two young shepherds approached leading a small flock of sheep and goats. The older of the two appeared to be in his late teens or early twenties, and he watched with interest as we recorded. Finally, my cohost went over to see if he could speak with, and perhaps interview, this young shepherd.

The Nazareth shepherd from "Goshen"

49

"WHERE–ARE–YOU–FROM?" he asked. He was very careful to speak slowly and to enunciate clearly, hoping the shepherd would have enough of a grasp of English to understand his question. The shepherd paused, looked carefully at my cohost, and then said, slowly and distinctly, "GO–SHEN, IN–DI–AN–A!" It turned out that he was an American college student doing a service project overseas!

That encounter was a great reminder that not everything in the Holy Land is what it might seem to be on the surface. And that's a good lesson for every pilgrim to remember as they travel through the land hoping to somehow connect to the days of David, Elijah, and Jesus.

The Sea of Galilee from Mount Arbel

CHAPTER 5

Mount Arbel:
Galilee's Scenic Panorama

Most pilgrims traveling to Israel have never heard of Mount Arbel. It's never mentioned in the Bible, and until fairly recently it wasn't included in most tours. Before being made into a National Park, the site could only be accessed by driving through an agricultural community and then hiking nearly a mile up a dirt road and rocky pathway. No food kiosk. No bathroom facilities. And almost no visitors. But for those who *did* hike up, the view was breathtaking.

During the rainy season, the dirt road could become a muddy quagmire. We hiked to the summit with one group of pastors only to discover that low clouds obscured all visibility. By the time we made it back to the bus, our hiking boots and sneakers were coated with red-tinted mud. Our driver made us take off our shoes before allowing us back onto his bus, and we spent most of the evening trying to scrape off thick clumps of *terra rosa* soil.

Walking to the top of Mount Arbel in the summer was almost as bad, especially when the hot afternoon sun beat down from a cloudless sky. A pilgrim on one of my earlier trips was convinced I was trying to kill her by taking her on a five-mile hike. In those early years I resorted to telling anyone who asked that the walk was "only three kilometers." In reality the walk was about half that distance. But it didn't matter because most Americans can't visualize how far a kilometer really is.

The nearby *moshav*, the local farming co-op, saw a business opportunity in the increasing number of buses driving through their community to walk up Mount Arbel. They purchased a herd of donkeys and offered to rent them to individuals wanting to ride to the top. The business didn't last too long because younger visitors wanted to walk while older visitors were afraid to ride.

And for good reason!

On one occasion, we saw an older rabbi rent a donkey so he could ride to the top while his pupils walked. But the small donkey wasn't happy carrying the portly rabbi. Partway up the hill the donkey bucked, and the unfortunate rabbi tumbled off, landing on his own backside. The young students had a good laugh at the rabbi's expense, and so did the group of foreigners following along behind.

Hiking to the top of Mount Arbel

Today, the walk to the top of Mount Arbel is much easier. Tourists can take advantage of restrooms, fill their water bottles from the fountain, and even buy an ice cream bar for a quick burst of energy. It's still an uphill walk, and the group quickly spreads out along the path. But those in front don't mind waiting because the view from the summit is so amazing.

MOUNT ARBEL'S UNFORGETTABLE VIEW

The moment a pilgrim reaches the summit of Mount Arbel, all thoughts of sore feet, burning lungs, or achy knees vanish. They're replaced with a view of the Sea of Galilee 1,250 feet below. And unlike the sloping pathway taken to reach the top, a sheer cliff provides a dramatic vista of nearly the entire lake. It's like viewing a giant 3D map of the sea in vivid color!

Looking down at the Sea of Galilee from Mount Arbel

Standing on the edge of the cliff, one can trace the life of Christ that unfolded along its shores. Just below are the ruins of Magdala, the hometown of a woman named Miriam. Miriam of Magdala—better known to most as Mary Magdalene. A little further up the shoreline is a group of red-roofed buildings. That's Tabgha, the spot where Jesus likely first called His disciples and then appeared again to them following the resurrection. The hill just behind it is the Mount of Beatitudes.

Continue following along the shore and you will spot the village of Nahum. The Hebrew word for village is *kephar*, so the town was known as Kephar Nahum. We know it in the Bible as Capernaum. A little beyond that is where the Jordan River enters the Sea of Galilee, and beyond that lie Bethsaida and Gergesa—the areas where Jesus fed the five thousand and where the swine ran down into the sea.

From this vantage point, tourists discover that most of Jesus' ministry took place in a small triangle-shaped area along the very northern tip of this small lake. The points of the triangle are the three cities in which the gospel writers say Jesus performed most of His miracles—Bethsaida, Chorazin, and Capernaum.

I love standing here on Mount Arbel because it reminds me of God's words in Isaiah 55:8. "'My thoughts are nothing like your thoughts,' says the LORD. 'And my ways are far beyond anything you could imagine.'" If *we* had been in charge of sending the Messiah, this is *not* where we would have sent Him. It's too small, too remote, too insignificant. We would have chosen Rome, or maybe Jerusalem. But *not* the northern shore of a small lake in Galilee.

Yet God did send Jesus to this out-of-the-way patch of the Roman Empire . . . to the district of Galilee . . . to an obscure corner of a freshwater lake in a region that even the Jews of Judea looked down on. What was God thinking? Again the words of Isaiah come to mind: "My thoughts are nothing like your thoughts."

Earlier in the book of Isaiah God let us know why He selected the very spot of land that lies below us now. Right after Jesus' forty-day temptation in the wilderness, Matthew writes, "When Jesus heard that John had been arrested, he left Judea and returned to Galilee. He went first to Nazareth, then left there and moved to Capernaum, beside the Sea of Galilee, in the region of Zebulun and Naphtali. This fulfilled what God said through the prophet Isaiah" (Matt. 4:12–14). Matthew then quotes Isaiah 9:1–2. "Nevertheless, that time of darkness and despair will not go on forever. The land of Zebulun and Naphtali will be humbled, but there will be a time in the future when Galilee of the Gentiles, which lies along the road that runs between the Jordan and the sea, will be filled with glory. The people who walk in darkness will see a great light. For those who live in a land of deep darkness, a light will shine."

Jesus had to go to the land of Zebulun and Naphtali because God told Isaiah the prophet this would be the area He would honor. Now, most people don't know what area was promised to the tribes of Zebulun and Naphtali. So pause for a moment and look at the maps in the back of your Bible. Or, if you're using an electronic Bible, then Google both names. Here's what you'll discover. The region around Nazareth was part of the area given to the tribe of Zebulun, and the northwest corner of the Sea of Galilee belonged to the tribe of Naphtali. Jesus went to the very area where God said the light of His Messiah would shine!

Isaiah actually tells us quite a bit about this predicted ministry. He says God had originally humbled the area, calling it "Galilee of the Gentiles." By that he meant the area had come under God's judgment to the point where God allowed the Gentiles to dominate and control the region. In Isaiah's day, it was taken over and controlled by the Assyrians. In Jesus' day, it was the Romans. But it was Galilee "of" or "controlled by" or "belonging to" the Gentiles. Foreigners controlled the fate of God's people.

Isaiah also identifies Galilee with the Jordan River and "the sea." You might never have thought about it, but to what "sea" was God referring? We usually think of the Mediterranean Sea, but Isaiah connects the sea with the Jordan River, and the tribal allotment of Zebulun and Naphtali. It's the Sea of Galilee! Isaiah announced that this was the place God would select to throw the switch on the floodlight of His glory.

One final time, look back down at the lake. Focus on that tiny triangle of land where Jesus performed so many of His miracles. What lesson

> What lesson can we take away from this lofty perch overlooking a small lake in an out-of-the-way area in Galilee?

can we take away from this lofty perch overlooking a small lake in an out-of-the-way area in Galilee? Here's the lesson that strikes me with incredible force every time I come to this spot: *nothing is ever insignificant if God is in it.* All too often we're guilty of using the wrong yardstick to measure importance. We mistakenly assume that if something is bigger, and flashier, and more prominent, then it must be more significant. But think about Isaiah's prophecy. God chose this most insignificant area to do some of His most significant work. Jesus taught, healed, and fed multitudes here. He also gathered a small group of disciples here. And His ministry to that seemingly insignificant group of fishermen and tax collectors ultimately turned the world upside down.

MOUNT ARBEL'S UNMISTAKABLE PROFILE

Whenever possible, I want our group to visit Mount Arbel *before* they journey around the Sea of Galilee. Arbel provides a panorama that puts the individual sites around the Sea in perspective. Its vista gives pilgrims a visual framework in which to place the different locations. But it does one more thing. Mount Arbel's unmistakable profile provides a visual point of reference for us as we travel on and around the Sea of Galilee. It gives people a spot to which they can align the many sites they will soon visit. Just keep watching for Mount Arbel along the western shore.

A view of Mount Arbel from the Sea of Galilee

As groups are driving toward the Sea of Galilee, Mount Arbel is hidden. When the Sea of Galilee finally comes into view, I like to direct everyone's attention out the left side of the bus toward a tiny tree perched atop a small hill in the distance. For the next several minutes I keep pointing to the tiny tree to remind them it is our next stop—Mount Arbel! Let's just say most passengers are underwhelmed, and perhaps just a bit annoyed that I keep pointing to that tiny tree from every conceivable angle.

Once we get off the bus and start up the hill, I again point out the lone tree. But now I tell them our destination is just slightly beyond the tree. The tree is a carob tree—of "fake chocolate" fame—which produces pods like those fed to the pigs by the prodigal son in Jesus' parable. But that silly tree suddenly takes on new meaning when the group reaches the top of Mount Arbel. Many a tourist has had his or her picture taken beside that tiny carob tree!

Sadly, something happened to the tree. It's still there, but it's now only a shadow of its once beautiful self. I hope the tree recovers and thrives once

The lone carob tree atop Mount Arbel

more. It's a great visual marker to help people pinpoint the destination as they climb the back side of Mount Arbel. And once they've been on top, the tree also becomes a reference point, letting them know where they stood when they gazed out across the Sea of Galilee for the first time!

Around the
Sea of Galilee

CHORAZIN
BETHSAIDA
MOUNT OF BEATITUDES
CAPERNAUM
TABGHA
MAGDALA
KURSI
YARDENIT

The Sea of Galilee from the bow of the boat

CHAPTER 6

The Sea of Galilee:
The Little Lake with a Big History

Mark Twain never had the opportunity to sail on the Sea of Galilee. When his band of fellow pilgrims reached the lake, they spotted a boat and asked their guide to find out how much the boatmen would charge for an extended excursion. The captain said it would cost two Napoleons—eight dollars. "Too much!" they responded, "we'll give him one!" Twain recorded the sad but humorous response.

> I never shall know how it was—I shudder yet when I think how the place is given to miracles—but in a single instant of time, as it seemed to me, that ship was twenty paces from the shore, and speeding away like a frightened thing! Eight crestfallen creatures stood upon the shore . . . Instantly there was wailing and gnashing of teeth in the camp. The two Napoleons were offered—more if necessary—and pilgrims and [guide] shouted themselves hoarse with pleadings to the retreating boatmen to come back. But they sailed serenely away and paid no further heed to pilgrims who had dreamed all their lives of some day skimming over the sacred waters of Galilee and listening to its hallowed story in the whisperings of its waves, and had journeyed countless leagues to do it, and—and then concluded that the fare was too high.[1]

Thankfully, the opportunity to sail on the Sea of Galilee is now included as a part of virtually every tour. For almost an hour, today's pilgrims get to imagine what it must have been like for Jesus and His disciples to sail on this storied lake. Of course, today's boats are much larger than those in the time of Jesus. And they come equipped with a powerful engine, sound system, emergency flotation devices, and relatively comfortable seats. But once the group is out on the water, it's easy to imagine what it must have been like two millennia ago. Well, that is until someone zooms past on a jet ski.

The Sea of Galilee actually surprises many visitors because of its small size. When people think of a "sea," they envision a large, salty body of water like the Atlantic or Pacific Oceans. But the Sea of Galilee is simply a freshwater lake, and a relatively small one at that. It's seven miles wide, thirteen miles long, and encompasses sixty-four square miles. Yellowstone Lake, in Yellowstone National Park, is twice the size of the Sea of Galilee, while Lake Tahoe, which straddles the border between California and Nevada, is three times its size. And Lake Champlain, which straddles New York and Vermont, is seven and a half times as large!

Those from the Midwest might want to know the size of the Sea of Galilee in comparison to one of the Great Lakes. Unfortunately, such a comparison is virtually meaningless. The surface area of Lake Erie, the smallest of the Great Lakes, is 155 times the size of the Sea of Galilee. And the entire nation of Israel would fit quite comfortably into Lake Michigan—with enough space left over for an additional 216 lakes the size of the Sea of Galilee!

It's hard for most tourists to imagine such a small lake having such a large history. Of course, its claim to fame comes primarily from the gospel accounts of Jesus' ministry along its shores. That's what makes the time spent here so special. Visitors are also surprised to discover the Sea of Galilee is seven hundred feet below sea level. It has a tropical climate, with groves of bananas and date palms growing in the fertile soil ringing the shoreline.

By Western standards, the Sea of Galilee is still relatively undeveloped. If the lake were in the United States it would be encircled with condos and covered with ski boats and other watercraft. The number of hotels and other attractions along the shore is growing, and so is the number of powerboats skimming across its waters. But a boat ride on the lake remains a very spiritual, and pleasurable, experience.

Several decades ago, one boat operator had the brilliant idea of modifying his boats to make them look more like those that would have been on the lake in the time of Jesus. Two companies tried to market their boats as Jesus boats, and in the mid-1990s that led to a lawsuit. We weren't aware of the legal wrangling at the time but were pleasantly surprised when a television crew for ABC News asked if they could accompany our group out on the lake. A seminary colleague was with us, and he spoke to the group as the cameras rolled. That night we excitedly called home to tell our families to watch the evening news.

But nothing happened!

Family members watched every night for weeks, but the story never appeared. A year later, on the Saturday before Easter, my wife and I were cleaning up after supper. We had the news turned on, and the anchor gave a tease before breaking for a commercial. "Next up, the legal fight among Jewish tourist boat owners over the exclusive right to the name Jesus." That had to be it! We grabbed a tape and slammed it into the VCR. That's when we learned about the lawsuit over the right to claim the name of Jesus. And we were able to catch brief glimpses of our group on the boat!

My favorite trip out on the lake took place on a cold, blustery January morning with a group of pastors. For a number of years, the Alumni Director of the school where I was serving would invite a small group of pastors to travel to Israel with us. We would take them to the sites during the day, and then at night we would talk about the logistics involved in leading a group from their church on a trip. It was also a good time for the pastors to get together and decompress, especially after the hectic holiday season. But in January the days are short, and the weather can be very unpredictable.

As we got to the dock and boarded the boat for our morning excursion, the day didn't look too promising. Dark clouds were scudding low across the sky, and a breeze from the west had already started to roil the lake. But it was still relatively calm, and the captain felt he could take us out and back without too much difficulty. He guided the boat out into the lake and started heading north. Finally, he cut the engine so we could share lessons from the life of Jesus out there on the lake. But our time of quiet reflection was cut short when a sudden storm, with a blast of wind, swept across the lake from the south. The boat began bobbing and rocking from side to side like a giant cork.

Usually, an afternoon breeze from the Mediterranean will sweep in over the Sea of Galilee from the west. If you can imagine blowing on a hot bowl of soup, you can visualize the effect that the wind has on the lake as it comes down off the hills. However, when a storm hits, the wind can come from any direction. And the waves can quickly grow in height and intensity.

Before we could finish our time of study, the captain fired up the engine and turned his launch back toward Tiberias and the safety of its harbor. We were now sailing directly into the face of the storm as wind-whipped waves broke over the bow. That was the first time I saw how suddenly, and violently, a storm could arise on the Sea of Galilee. And where were the pastors as the ship struggled to make it back to shore? They were all at the front of the boat, being pelted by the rain and drenched by the breaking waves, as they shouted into the teeth of the storm, "Peace! Be still!"

That storm brought the reality of Mark 4:37–39 into perspective. Some translations say "a furious squall came up" or "a fierce storm arose," and we picture a massive thunderstorm, with driving rain and jagged bolts of lightning, followed by ominous claps of thunder. But Mark, who based his gospel on the testimony of Peter, provides a far more accurate description. He literally wrote that the boat encountered "a great whirlwind of wind." While this storm might have been accompanied by rain and lightning, that's *not* what frightened the disciples. They focused instead on the wind-whipped waves that were "breaking into the boat" so that it "began to fill with water." I imagine Peter using violent hand gestures as he shared the story with Mark to emphasize how the boat was being tossed about as the water poured in over the side.

That's the only real storm I've ever encountered on the Sea of Galilee, though we've had our share of choppy water. On one occasion we were leading a large, multi-bus trip. We arranged to have the group board several different boats to go out on the lake. We then rendezvoused and lashed the boats together with the bows facing the same direction. This allowed all the participants to see the speaker and the musicians who were located at the front of the center boat.

When I was a young child I loved playing in the swimming pool. One amusing pastime involving placing my hand on the surface of the water and curling my fingers into a loose grip—as if holding an imaginary baseball bat in my hand. Then I would squeeze my fingers together, forcing the water inside to shoot out like a fountain. I mention that because that's the image that came to mind as I stood in the back of the center boat and watched the scene unfold. As the speaker continued, the wind and waves would push bows of the different boats together like a giant hand, forcing the water between them to shoot up like a small geyser. The speaker was oblivious to what was happening just behind him until the alignment of the boats shot one of those geysers of water directly down on top of him. It was the Holy Land equivalent of dumping a cooler of Gatorade on the coach!

Over the years, a boat ride on the Sea of Galilee has become quite sophisticated. From a simple excursion from Point A to Point B, the entire experience has now evolved into an emotionally and spiritually rewarding adventure. It begins with the hoisting of the flag of the pilgrims' home country and the playing of their national anthem,

Hoisting the flags

followed by Israel's national anthem. Tasteful but contemporary Christian music is then played as the boat glides out into the sea. The engine is shut off for a brief devotional time, which might be followed by either a demonstration of casting a net into the water or a lesson in how to dance the Horah to the music of "Hava Nagila." Then it's time to open up the boat's gift shop and sell "I Sailed on the Sea of Galilee" shirts, stone-and-seashell necklaces, and placemats featuring key sites around the Sea of Galilee.

As soon as the boat docks, our happy bunch of pilgrims disembarks for the next stop on our itinerary, while another group of travelers lines up to board.

The chapel on the Mount of Beatitudes

CHAPTER 7

The Mount of Beatitudes:
Blessed Are the Flexible

The Mount of Beatitudes sits on a hill overlooking the Sea of Galilee. The site is beautiful, and so is the chapel. Antonio Barluzzi, the architect, designed the building in the shape of an octagon. In part, his design mimicked the style of the earliest churches built in the land. In fact, just a mile away, in the ruins of ancient Capernaum, a visitor can gaze on the foundations of an octagonal Byzantine-era chapel built by Queen Helena, Constantine's mother.

But Barluzzi had a second reason for designing his chapel with eight sides. On each of the sides he placed one of the Eight Beatitudes spoken by Jesus in His Sermon on the Mount. I'm not impressed by many of the church buildings in the Holy Land. They're either dark and cramped—and in desperate need of a deep spring cleaning—or they're over the top in gaudy ornamentation, drawing attention to themselves rather than to the people or events they're commemorating. One pilgrim described such churches as being full of "smells and bells"—all decked out and painted up, with no place to go.

The churches designed by Barluzzi are different. Each is appropriate to the site it commemorates, focusing a visitor's attention on the event being remembered rather than trying to draw attention to itself. As our busload of travelers drives up to the Mount of Beatitudes, I'm reminded of the Ninth Beatitude—the one never found in the Bible or even in Barluzzi's chapel, but which is important for every traveler to the Holy Land.

"Blessed are the flexible, for they will not get bent out of shape."

True, Jesus didn't include that beatitude in His Sermon on the Mount, but then as the Son of God nothing ever took Him by surprise. The same thing can't be said for many of the pilgrims packed into the scores of buses now stopping at the entrance. For example, most groups set a wake-up call at the front desk each morning, but hotels will invariably miss one room. At the end of each day I remind everyone on our bus what they need to bring along the next day, but invariably someone forgets and has to run back to the room, holding everyone up. And no matter what time we tell everyone to be back at the bus, there always seems to be at least one person who lingers too long in the gift shop—or who loses track of time while taking photos.

I suppose it would have been too difficult for Barluzzi to design his chapel as a nonagon rather than an octagon, but I still think this would have been a good site to somehow slip in that Ninth Beatitude. After all, many of the

The wordless warnings to all visitors

other signs posted at the site don't exactly match the sermon preached by Jesus! For example, the sign on the previous page was posted by the *Associazione Nazionale per Soccorrere i Missionari Italiani*—the National Association to Help the Italian Missionaries. Check out their wordless list of warnings!

This sign is posted at the entrance to the site. It doesn't matter what language you speak, you know immediately that pets, shorts, talking, food or drink, guns, and smoking are *not* allowed.

Do not drink the living water!

A fountain was added to the site some years ago. On the left is a quotation from John 7:37. "Let anyone who thirst[s] come to me." But then you notice the sign just to the right: "Water not for drink." Thankfully, those words were *not* spoken by Jesus!

In spite of these somewhat crazy signs, and the many busloads of pilgrims who often pack the site, the Mount of Beatitudes is a wonderful place for quiet reflection. However, that wasn't always the case.

SISTER HELLFIRE AND DAMNATION

For many years the chapel was overseen by a rather diminutive nun. But though she was a modern-day Zacchaeus in her physical stature, she ruled with her own rod of iron, putting the fear of God into many guides and group leaders. One guide actually nicknamed her "Sister Hellfire and Damnation" for the way she enforced the regulations at the site.

On one occasion, this particular guide brought a Brazilian church group to the site. He was so busy leading the group in that he didn't notice one of them carried along a guitar case. The guide gave his explanation and then turned the group loose for a time of reflection and sightseeing while he walked back toward the entrance.

He hadn't gone very far before he heard a group singing loudly to the beat of a guitar. He paused, thinking to himself how unusual it was to have a group singing so loudly. Then he noticed that they seemed to be singing in . . . was that Portuguese? He turned and started running back to warn his group. But before he could reach them, a voice was screeching over the loudspeaker system, "STOP THAT SINGING! AND GET OFF THE GRASS!"

Sadly, Sister Hellfire and Damnation is no longer at the chapel overseeing visitors. Several years ago she was killed in an unfortunate automobile accident on her way to Bethlehem for Christmas celebrations. She was replaced by another nun who tries to enforce all the regulations in a kinder, gentler fashion. I'm hoping the new approach works, because she's so much easier to work with.

But just in case, when you are at the site, read the signs . . . and make sure you don't drink the water!

The synagogue at Capernaum

CHAPTER 8

Capernaum:
The Village of Nahum

Welcome to the Village of Nahum!

I see from the puzzled looks on your faces that you don't remember reading about this village in the Bible. Certainly that's true of the Old Testament, but the town plays a very important role in the life of Christ. Still unsure? Perhaps it would help if I use the English transliteration of its name—Capernaum! Now I see heads nodding in agreement! You see, the name Capernaum is a transliteration of two Hebrew words, *Kefar Nahum* which mean "the village of Nahum." We don't know if the town was named after the Old Testament prophet Nahum, or after some otherwise unknown individual. But we do know that, over time, this small village had become a major commercial hub.

Located along the northwestern edge of the Sea of Galilee, the town had achieved a level of importance in Jesus' day because of its location near the border of the land of Galilee ruled by Herod Antipas. Less than three miles away the Jordan River divided Herod Antipas's kingdom from the land ruled by Herod Philip. The Romans saw the strategic importance of the town. That's why they posted a garrison of soldiers and established a tax collection office there.

But for the common laborer in Capernaum, life revolved around the lake . . . and the fertile soil along its shores. Fishing must have been the primary occupation, but the dark volcanic rock in the area had weathered into a rich soil that also made farming an attractive option. The Jewish historian Josephus put it this way: "Their soil is universally rich and fruitful, and full of the plantations of trees of all sorts, insomuch that it invites the most slothful to take pains in its cultivation by its fruitfulness: accordingly, it is all cultivated by its inhabitants, and no part of it lies idle."[1] Little wonder that Capernaum had such an abundance of millstones for grinding grain. We'll view some of these millstones later.

Our tour begins with a look at what is traditionally considered to be Peter's house. Actually, there isn't much to see. On my early visits to Capernaum we could look at the foundations of his house, and of an ancient church built on the site. But then a modern church was built above the ruins. In some ways it resembles a giant crab that might have crawled out of the lake, or perhaps a flying saucer that chose this exact spot to land. The church is not architecturally beautiful. But what it lacks in beauty it makes up for in thoughtfulness for those who visit. Throughout history, most churches commemorated a significant site by wiping it out and replacing it with a massive stone edifice.

Entrance to the church built over the traditional house of Peter

Thankfully, this chapel was built on stilts, so to speak, to allow visitors to view the ruins underneath.

PETER'S INSURANCE CLAIM

Over the years, I've had to replace two roofs on two different houses. In both cases the roof was damaged by violent storms with hail the size of golf balls. The insurance company calls such storms "acts of God." Thankfully, within a few weeks we were able to get a roofing company to come and repair the damage. And insurance covered most of the cost!

In the time of Jesus, at least one resident of Capernaum had to have his roof repaired. Matthew, Mark, and Luke all record the basic story, though each focuses on different details of what took place. But by putting all the accounts together, we have a good idea who owned the house that needed a new roof. Since Jesus was a guest at the house of Simon Peter, the roof in question must have been the one on Peter's house! If there had been homeowners insurance in Peter's day, I imagine he still would have had trouble getting the company to pay for his damage, because in his case the "act of God" took place *after* the roof was damaged.

Capernaum was abuzz about Jesus. He had already healed many who were sick and cast out demons from those who were possessed. A short trip across the lake and back brought additional stories of the sudden calming of a storm and a dramatic encounter with demons and a herd of swine. And now Jesus was back in town, and the frenzied mob pushed and shoved their way forward to try to squeeze into the presence of this suddenly popular rabbi.

Unfortunately, the scene was very discouraging for a group of men who arrived in Capernaum right then. They had walked for miles carrying a paralyzed friend on a wooden pallet. They wanted to bring him to Jesus to be healed. But Capernaum's narrow streets, and the throngs of people filling them, brought this band of brothers to a screeching halt. The way to Jesus was blocked. And that's when one of the friends had a brilliant idea. If we can't get in through the door, let's try the roof!

Inside and outside views showing the construction of a typical roof

This is where our cultural background can create problems. We read about a house and picture a pitched-roof house covered with shingles. We then envision men with hatchets and saws up on the roof cutting through the plywood decking and rafters while trying to keep their friend from rolling off his pallet. But the typical first-century house in Capernaum was built of rock with wooden beams stretched across the top to support a flat roof. Smaller pieces of wood were then spread diagonally across the beams, and these were covered with plaster. A small wall or parapet extended around the edge of this flat roof to keep someone from accidently falling off, while an outside staircase provided access.

Archaeologists have discovered that in some cases these roofs were then covered with clay tiles, similar to roofing tile still used today. Installing clay tile on the roof definitely made it stronger and more durable. But it also added weight, requiring more structural support, and it increased the cost. Tiled roofs were more rare, suggesting that a house with a tiled roof was a more luxurious home.

The three gospel accounts all tell the story of the paralytic man who was brought to Jesus by his friends. Mark says the friends had to dig through the roof to lower the paralytic down to the spot where Jesus was seated in the home. But Luke adds one additional detail. He says they "went up to the roof and took off some tiles. Then they lowered the sick man on his mat down into the crowd, right in front of Jesus" (Luke 5:19). These friends had to pull off the heavy roof tiles first and then dig through the plaster and wood underneath to create a space large enough to lower this paralytic down through the opening. Their hard work left a gaping hole in Peter's roof.

Now as I said before, when we have to repair our roof, it's often because of some "act of God," like a hailstorm. But in this story the damage to the roof preceded the act of God!

Leaving the shaded patio below the church hovering over Peter's house, the next stop on our tour is the synagogue. The white limestone structure isn't the synagogue that stood in Capernaum in Jesus' day. These are the remains of a synagogue built several hundred years later. But the black basalt base on which this synagogue rests *is* the foundation of the synagogue that stood here during the time of Jesus.

The synagogue in the time of Jesus was a much simpler, less expensive structure. This isn't surprising because it had taken the financial assistance of a

The interior of the synagogue

Roman centurion to help build it. When the servant of the Roman centurion stationed in Capernaum fell ill, the centurion "sent some respected Jewish elders to ask him to come and heal his slave. So they earnestly begged Jesus to help the man. 'If anyone deserves your help, he does,' they said, 'for he loves the Jewish people and even built a synagogue for us'" (Luke 7:3–5).

The sun is beating down and there is very little shade, so we won't stay inside the synagogue long. But have a seat on one of the stone benches lining the walls while we look back at all the miracles that happened in Capernaum. This is the town where Jesus healed Peter's mother-in-law, and where He healed the paralytic lowered down through the roof of Peter's house. It's also the place where Jesus healed the centurion's servant. In addition, Jesus raised to life the synagogue ruler's daughter, and healed a sick woman with an issue of blood. While these are the stories specifically singled out by the gospel writers, Matthew adds that many who were sick and demon-possessed came to Him in Capernaum and Jesus "healed all the sick" (Matt. 8:16).

> The synagogue in the time of Jesus was a much simpler, less expensive structure.

More of Jesus' recorded miracles take place in Capernaum than in any other city, including Jerusalem. This was the base of operations for His ministry in Galilee, and the people living here saw and heard it all. We might think of the citizens of Capernaum as being exceptionally blessed by having a front row seat to so much of Jesus' ministry. But the reality is that even though they saw the miracles, most never responded in faith to the claims made by Jesus. They liked the excitement and activity, but they never let the truth of what He was saying and doing penetrate their hearts. And the final results were catastrophic.

Jesus finally rebuked the three cities in Galilee that saw more miracles than any others. And the city receiving the greatest judgment was Capernaum. "And you people of Capernaum, will you be honored in heaven? No, you will go down to the place of the dead. For if the miracles I did for you had been done in wicked Sodom, it would still be here today. I tell you, even Sodom will be better off on judgment day than you" (Matt. 11:23–24). As we sit here in these skeletal remains of a synagogue we come face-to-face with a sobering reminder. Just like the people of Jesus' day, we're coming face-to-face with the historical reality that Jesus walked these streets and made these claims. And the ultimate eternal issue is this: What will you do with Jesus? Will you accept and acknowledge Him as Savior and Lord? Or will you choose to continue living your life without bending your knee to His claims? The lifeless ruins of Capernaum today remind us that such choices have eternal consequences.

A MILLSTONE TURNED BY A DONKEY

All along the perimeter of Capernaum are other "less important" archaeological remains. At least many guides think they are less important as they hustle their tourists out of the synagogue and on toward the exit. But we're heading into the shade just beside the synagogue because there's one particular find I want you to see. And on our way, let me share another story from Capernaum.

In Matthew 17:24 we're told that Jesus and His disciples arrived back in Capernaum. Chapter 18 then begins with "about that time," suggesting the events that follow happened at the same time as those in the previous chapter. The disciples ask Jesus to answer a question: "Who is greatest in the Kingdom of Heaven?" (Matt. 18:1). Jesus responded by calling a small child to use as an illustration. "So anyone who becomes as humble as this little child is the greatest in the Kingdom of Heaven" (v. 4).

But then Jesus issued a warning against those who might try to cause a childlike follower of Him to stumble and sin. He said it would be better for such a person "to have a large millstone tied around your neck and be drowned in the depths of the sea" (Matt. 18:6). What exactly is a "large millstone"? In the original language it literally says a "millstone of a donkey"—that is, a large millstone that would be turned by a donkey. So what does a millstone of a donkey look like? Right in front of us is the answer!

See that large, hourglass-shaped basalt stone? That's an upper millstone.

A large basalt millstone at Capernaum

Grain was poured into the top while animals like donkeys were attached to the connections on either side to turn it. This upper millstone sits on a cone-shaped lower millstone. As the upper millstone turned around the lower one, the grain passing through the opening inside would be crushed. But now back to Matthew 18.

Jesus said it would be better for an individual to tie a large, heavy millstone around his neck and be "drowned in the depths of the sea" than to cause one of His followers to sin. Again, location is everything. Jesus spoke these words as He stood beside the Sea of Galilee. It's easy to visualize Jesus pointing to one of the many millstones being turned by donkeys in the area and then, in a sweeping gesture, turn and point toward the Sea of Galilee. It's as if Jesus said, "You want to put a snare or trap in the way of My young followers to trip them up? I've got a suggestion that will actually be more beneficial for you. See that large basalt millstone over there? Take a rope and fasten the millstone around your neck. Then drag it over to the Sea of Galilee and jump in! Bringing about your own physical death would be better for you than the eternal judgment you will receive from Me for harming My young followers."

MOSES AND THE TORAH ARK

It's almost time for us to leave Capernaum, but we have one more stop to make on our way out. A row of carved limestone decorations is on our right as we head toward the exit. One particular carving stands out from the rest. It depicts a box on wheels with doors on one side. Stand here long enough and you might hear a tour guide come by and say something like this: "And here you see one of the most magnificent carvings from the synagogue, which shows Israel's ark of the covenant in the wilderness."

Carving of the Torah ark at Capernaum

If you're confused, don't be. This is *not* the ark of the covenant. That ancient box had two golden cherubim with outstretched wings on top. And it had long poles on two sides because it was to be carried by the Levites, not placed on a cart (Ex. 25:14; Num. 4:15). There are only two times the ark of the covenant was placed on a cart—once when it was returned to Israel by the Philistines (1 Sam. 6), and once when David first tried to bring it up to Jerusalem (2 Sam. 6). Neither incident ended well!

This stone carving represents the Torah ark, a moveable box in which the scrolls of the Law, the Prophets, and the Writings were kept. The box was wheeled into place in the synagogue for Sabbath services and then returned to a place of safety and protection between services.

The misidentification by some guides reminds me of Mark Twain's experience in Jerusalem. While visiting the Dome of the Rock, which he called the Mosque of Omar, he reported that "Just outside the mosque is a miniature temple, which marks the spot where David and Goliah [sic] used to sit and judge the people." He included a footnote, which, in typical Twain fashion, is as significant as the initial statement. "A pilgrim informs me that it was not David and Goliah, but David and Saul. I stick to my own statement—the guide told me, and he ought to know."[2] All I can say is yes he *should*!

The ruins of ancient Chorazin

CHAPTER 9

Chorazin:

Capernaum with a View

Jerome Murphy-O'Connor referred to Chorazin as "Capernaum with a view,"[1] and that's a good description of the site. Nestled in the hills about three miles from the Sea of Galilee—and a thousand feet higher in elevation—the inhabitants of ancient Chorazin enjoyed a wonderful view of the lake while avoiding the oppressive heat and humidity along its shore.

Chorazin was built from the black basalt rock that covers the northern edge of the Sea of Galilee. As a result, the site is virtually invisible until the bus is almost on top of the ruins. Unlike some of the other sites in the area, relatively few tour groups stop at Chorazin. But for the groups that do, Chorazin's solitude is a welcome break from the convoys of buses and hordes of tourists at the other religious sites.

And yet, as the travelers climb off the bus at Chorazin, a hint of boredom can be spotted in glazed-over eyes. "Here we are at *another* forgettable stop! It's hot, and I'm tired and thirsty. And besides, I don't recall *any* events from the Bible that took place in Chorazin. Is it okay if I just stay on the bus and sit out this site?"

And the answer that helps these pilgrims perk up and quicken their step is this: "If you want to miss one of the towns where Jesus did more miracles than virtually any other place in the land, then by all means stay here on the bus. But if you want to know more about Jesus and His miracles, then follow me." That usually gets the crowd moving. And by the time the group reaches the synagogue, they are revived and ready to listen.

THE SYNAGOGUE

The synagogue at Chorazin is the perfect complement to the one in Capernaum. Both are from after the time of Jesus, and both are oriented so the entryways face Jerusalem. But the synagogue at Chorazin better illustrates the synagogue that stood in Capernaum during the time of Jesus. It's smaller and less ornate. And it was constructed from nearby basalt stone rather than white limestone transported from a greater distance. This synagogue, along with the one uncovered at Magdala, helps travelers visualize what a synagogue might have been like when Jesus ministered in the region.

Interior of the synagogue

But what makes Chorazin so special? The town is only mentioned twice in the Gospels—once by Matthew and once by Luke. And in both passages it's only mentioned in passing as one of three towns cursed by Jesus. But it's *how* the three towns are introduced in those passages that gives Chorazin its special status. "Then He began to reprimand *the cities in which most of His miracles were done*, because they did not repent. 'Woe to you, Chorazin! Woe to you, Bethsaida! For if the miracles that occurred in you had occurred in Tyre and Sidon, they would have repented long ago in sackcloth and ashes'" (Matt. 11:20–21 NASB).

Matthew and Luke both singled out three cities that experienced more miracles of Jesus than anywhere else. And Chorazin—along with Bethsaida and Capernaum—is one of the cities on that list! Now, name a single miracle Jesus performed in Chorazin. If none come to mind, don't let it bother you. The Bible doesn't record *any* of the miracles Jesus performed at Chorazin. Apart from the single reference to the town in the two gospels, we know nothing else about Jesus' ministry here. And yet, that reality helps us understand a key truth about the ministry of Jesus. What we have recorded for us in the Bible is only a small sampling of the many things Jesus taught and did during His time on earth. Chorazin saw many miracles, but none are recorded in the Bible.

The fact that we don't have every single miracle performed by Jesus doesn't discourage me or cause me to doubt the Bible. No, just the opposite. If Jesus ministered for over three years in the Holy Land, He *must* have done more than what's recorded in the Gospels. In fact, the apostle John tells us this is the case. "The disciples saw Jesus do many other miraculous signs in addition to the ones recorded in this book. But these are written so that you may continue to believe that Jesus is the Messiah, the Son of God, and that by believing in him you will have life by the power of his name" (John 20:30–31). And then one chapter later John reminded his readers once again that his account was only a *partial* record of all Jesus did. "Jesus also did many other things. If they were all written down, I suppose the whole world could not contain the books that would be written" (John 21:25).

The Gospels are a selective account of Jesus' life and ministry. God had the writers record everything we needed to know to be convinced of His life, His ministry, and His claims. Jesus did many miracles in Chorazin, but none were essential to our understanding of His person and work, and so none were included.

THE SEAT OF MOSES

Standing here in the synagogue helps us visualize a number of events in the life of Jesus, but my favorite is the account in Luke 4. That chapter describes an event that happened in the synagogue in Nazareth, but we can use this synagogue to illustrate what took place. In that account, the attendant handed Jesus the scroll of the prophet Isaiah. Jesus unrolled it to the portion we know as Isaiah 61, and then He began to read. Very likely, the scroll was taken from the Torah ark, the moveable box containing the Scriptures, that would have been placed in the open space between two of the entryways.

See that flat stone on the ground, just inside the center door? That could be the base of the podium or lectern on which the scroll was placed while being read. In a modern synagogue it's called the *bimah* or *bema*. Jesus would have stood at the *bimah* in Nazareth as He read from the book of Isaiah. Then Luke says Jesus rolled the scroll back up, handed it to the attendant to be placed back in the Torah ark, "sat down," and began to teach (Luke 4:20–21). But where did Jesus sit?

In the "seat of Moses."

On the other side of the Torah ark, by the center doorway, is a stone chair or seat. This chair is carved from the same volcanic rock that covers the area. The one here in the synagogue is actually a reproduction. The original is in the Israel Museum in Jerusalem. If you look carefully at the front you can see writing. The inscription is in Aramaic, and it identifies the person who had the chair carved for the synagogue. "Remembered be for good Judah ben Ishmael who made this stoa and its staircase. As his reward may he have a share with the righteous." The stoa that's mentioned isn't the Greek word for a colonnaded porch, but refers instead to the platform on which the chair sat.

I love it! Judah ben Ishmael paid to have the chair, the platform on which it rested, and the stairs up to it carved for the synagogue. Then, of course, he decided to have his name placed on the gift so everyone could remember how generous he was. We still do the same thing today!

The chair in which Jesus sat to teach in Nazareth was likely similar to

Replica of the Seat of Moses in the synagogue

Chorazin. This was the spot where the teacher would sit to expound on the Scriptures. This chair also helps explain one other passage of Scripture. In Matthew 23:2 Jesus said, "The scribes and the Pharisees have seated themselves in the chair of Moses" (NASB). His meaning is clear. This was the spot where these religious leaders would sit and expound on the Scriptures. Just as Moses had led Israel and taught them God's precepts, so the person sitting in this chair was leading those in the synagogue. And to the extent those seated in this place of authority were expounding on God's commands, Jesus said, "So practice and obey whatever they tell you." However, He then added, "But don't follow their example. For they don't practice what they teach" (v. 3). Jesus follows this with a scathing rebuke on the hypocrisy of the religious leaders in His day.

Exciting stuff for an out-of-the-way town that few today bother to visit!

After taking some time to explore the restored houses just beyond the synagogue, it's time to head back toward the entrance. But there's still one stop remaining.

COME LIVE IN MY SHADE

Throughout Chorazin are wonderful shady places to rest and picnic. The *Ziziphus spina-christi* tree, which gets its name from the tradition that the crown of thorns placed on Jesus was made from its branches, provides the shade for these spots. These trees, with their dense roots that choke off other plants, keep the shaded area underneath relatively free of weeds. They also produce a fruit of sorts that can be eaten, though it's not very tasty. Our final stop is in the refreshing shade of one of these large *Ziziphus spina-christi* trees.

Heading to the shade of a Ziziphus spina-christi tree

Most groups simply ignore the trees on their walk to the synagogue, but there's a great story to tell in the shade of this tree. It's the parable told by Jotham, the one son of Gideon who survived the massacre of all his other brothers by Abimelech and the men of Shechem. The story is found in Judges 9. As the people of Shechem gathered to anoint Abimelech king, Jotham stood on top of Mount Gerizim and cried out to the people below. He told them the story of the trees that gathered to anoint for themselves a king.

The trees first asked the olive tree to be king, but the olive declined. They then asked the fig tree, followed by the grapevine, but they too declined the offer. Finally, perhaps in desperation, they asked what our Bibles call the "thorn-bush" or "bramble" to be king. In Hebrew it is the word *'atad*. The problem is that the details of the story don't really fit a tangled thornbush. Nogah Hareuveni, the founder of Neot Kedumim, Israel's Biblical Landscape Reserve, believes the *Ziziphus spina-christi* tree is a better candidate.[2] Like the other trees, it produces a fruit, though not nearly as useful. And it can offer the other trees an opportunity to "take shelter in my shade" (Judg. 9:15). Unfortunately, if they do, they will die, since the roots of this tree steal all the nourishment underneath its leafy canopy. So this tree could be the *'atad* tree of Judges 9—the worthless tree that will destroy anything trying to thrive under its "protection."

Our now-energized pilgrims reach into their pockets and purses for their smartphones to record still another aha moment.

THE CONEY

On the way back to the bus, watch for a brown, furry animal about the size of a groundhog. This animal lives in the rocks, and Chorazin is one place where it can often be spotted. It's known as a rock badger or hyrax, but my favorite name is the one given to it in the King James Version of the Bible—the coney!

Leviticus 11:5 labeled coneys as unclean animals, meaning they couldn't be eaten. But Proverbs

A coney rests on a pile of rocks

30:24–28 sheds a more positive light on these furry mammals. The passage identifies coneys as one of four "small but unusually wise" animals from whom humans can learn valuable life lessons. So what lesson can they teach us? "Hyraxes—they aren't powerful, but they make their homes among the rocks."

As we watch these creatures scamper among the rocks, the words of that proverb come to life. These animals are relatively defenseless. If they were to be caught out in the open, they could easily be taken by predators. But coneys don't live out in the open. To spot them, you look for rocks—rock ledges along cliffs, or rocks piled up into stone fences . . . or in ancient ruins like here in Chorazin.

What's the lesson we're to learn from this insignificant animal? Coneys, though small and relatively defenseless, have wisely sought out places of safety. They illustrate the importance of not living foolishly, of making sure not to expose themselves to threats or dangers unnecessarily. Exercising care and caution in threatening circumstances is wise. Just ask these animals scampering over the rocks.

Sign at the entrance to Bethsaida

CHAPTER 10

Bethsaida:

The City That Went Missing

The average person might think losing an ancient city would be a hard thing to do. After all, it's not like misplacing a pair of glasses or a cellphone. Cities were built of brick and stone, two materials that survive for long periods of time. Those living in the cities dropped coins, threw away broken pots, and buried their dead—in short, they left things behind that ought to make it obvious that people had lived there at some point in the past.

But it seems that finding the city of Bethsaida has always been elusive. Part of the problem in locating an ancient city is knowing what the city was named. And names could change over time. In the New Testament the gospel writers talk about a city named Bethsaida. The name means "house of fishing" or "house of hunting." According to John 1:44, Bethsaida was the original hometown of Philip, Peter, and Andrew. And their connection to Bethsaida shouldn't come as a surprise because Peter and Andrew were both fishermen. But where exactly was this city, and what was its official name?

The Jewish historian Josephus provides some clues that help in the identification of Bethsaida. He said the city received a physical makeover and a new name by Herod the Great's son Philip, who "advanced the village Bethsaida, situate[d] at the lake of Gennesareth, unto the dignity of a city; both by the number of inhabitants it contained, and its other grandeur, and called it by the name of Julias; the same name with Caesar's daughter."[1] In other words, Philip renovated the city and changed its name to honor the family of the king who placed him in power. Josephus also tells his readers that the Jordan River "first passes by the city Julias, and then passes through the middle of the lake Gennesareth"[2]—that is, the Sea of Galilee. So the city was situated on the north side of the Sea of Galilee, by the Jordan River.

And yet, until recently no one knew exactly where Bethsaida was located. Many scholars now believe a site call Et-Tell is the likely location of Bethsaida. However, others doubt the connection between Et-Tell and Bethsaida. They have suggested at least two other alternative locations for the town. Why do they not believe this site is Bethsaida? Just as in real estate, the key issue is location, location, location.

If the name Bethsaida means "house of fishing," where's the water? Et-Tell is located a *mile* north of the Sea of Galilee. To the skeptics, identifying this spot as Bethsaida requires a marketing ploy worthy of a slick real estate developer trying to entice people to buy into a "fishy" development. "Have I got a deal for you! You can get in on the ground floor of our latest seaside

Archaeological excavations at Et-Tell

development in Galilee—House of Fishing! Located *almost* on the shore of the beautiful Sea of Galilee!"

There is a solution to this problem. The city might be a mile away from the Sea of Galilee today, but it could have been much closer in antiquity. It's possible that sediment rushing down the Jordan River filled in the area around Bethsaida, creating a delta that pushed the shoreline further south. So even though the site today is no longer on the water's edge, it could very well have been by the Sea of Galilee two thousand years ago. And as if to help support this fact, archaeologists even uncovered a house at the site where they found fishing hooks, anchors, and lead weights for nets.

But students of the Bible might discover a second fishy fact about Bethsaida. No town by that name can be found in the Old Testament. And yet, archaeologists have uncovered remains of a major Old Testament city at Et-Tell. So what was the name of this town before it became Bethsaida? We don't know for certain, though archaeologists have suggested it might be identified with the city of Zer mentioned in Joshua 19:35. Many believe that the city, whatever its name, was the capital city of a kingdom called Geshur. This kingdom stretched from the Sea of Galilee northeast almost to Damascus, and the king who ruled there during the time of David was named Talmai. David even entered into an alliance with this king by marrying Talmai's daughter.

THE BIGGEST FISH STORY OF ALL

Perhaps the biggest fish story of all from this town is the one about the slimy son who got off the hook. Don't remember that story? I think you will once I fill in some of the details!

The story begins at this very site, but a thousand years *before* the time of Jesus. That's when the town was the capital of the kingdom of Geshur. It was early in David's reign, and he was still working to secure his throne. The Bible describes it as a time when there was "war between those who were loyal to Saul and those loyal to David" (2 Sam. 3:1). We know the outcome of the story, but at the time other nations didn't know who would come out on top.

And in those situations it was always better to hedge one's bets. That's what makes the historical footnote found in 2 Samuel 3 so important. The writer notes the rise in David's strength, and illustrates it by naming the six *sons* born to David during this period (vv. 2–5).

Each son was born to a different wife, sadly reflecting the reality of marriage in that day. But the writer pauses at the third son to provide one additional detail to set that son apart from the others. The third son was "Absalom, whose mother was Maacah, the daughter of Talmai, king of Geshur" (2 Sam. 3:3). During that historical period kings would form alliances through marriage. We don't know if David approached Talmai or if Talmai approached David, but in either case David married the daughter of the king of Geshur, cementing the relationship between the two nations.

It's possible that David visited this site—and walked on its streets. We simply don't know. But we do know David's son Absalom spent time here. In 2 Samuel 13 we're introduced to the treacherous nature of Absalom as he plotted the murder of his brother Amnon. It was a sordid period in David's family history. Amnon had raped Absalom's sister Tamar, and Absalom wanted revenge. David failed to act against Amnon, which was wrong, but so was Absalom's deceit and desire to seek vengeance. Absalom murdered his older brother, who was first in line to the throne, and then Absalom "fled to his grandfather, Talmai son of Ammihud, the king of Geshur" (2 Sam. 13:37).

For three years, Absalom lived in exile in the kingdom of Geshur. He spent three years thinking about all he had done, and all he'd left behind. But instead of softening his heart, the time here seemed to have hardened Absalom even more. He was eventually allowed to return to Jerusalem, and after two additional years was reconciled to David. Or at least David thought they had reconciled. David forgave Absalom, but Absalom never forgave David. Eventually, Absalom traveled to Hebron and announced *he* was now king. What followed was still another sad chapter that marred the final part of King David's reign, and it cost Absalom his life.

During the excavations at the site, archaeologists discovered a shrine

Reproduction of the shrine to the moon god

dedicated to the moon god. The shrine was located just outside the city gate. The horns of the bull form a crescent that symbolizes the crescent moon. Sadly, the shrine at the site was damaged by vandals. But thankfully, the original stone had already been taken to the Israel Museum in Jerusalem, where it's on display.

RENAMING THE CITY

By the time of Jesus the city had been renamed Bethsaida, at least until Herod's son Philip decided to rename it again. Philip rebuilt two cities in his kingdom—one in the north at the base of Mount Hermon, and this one in the south by the Sea of Galilee. He renamed both cities to honor Caesar, the Roman emperor who helped secure his position as king.

The stone picturing the moon god

He renamed the northern town of Panias "Caesarea Philippi" ("Philip's Caesarea," to distinguish it from the town of the same name built on the Mediterranean coast by his father). Philip also renamed the town of Bethsaida "Julias" in honor of Caesar's daughter. However, the local population continued calling both cities by their original names.

THE FISHY MIRACLE

Matthew 11 lists Bethsaida as one of the three towns where Jesus performed most of His miracles. And yet, can you name a miracle performed *in* Bethsaida? If you're good at Bible trivia you might eventually come up with Mark 8. That's the account of Jesus' healing of the blind man where Jesus had to perform the miracle twice. But in the passage it says Jesus led the man *outside* Bethsaida before performing the miracle. So technically Jesus was in the city when the blind man was brought to him, but the man wasn't healed *in* Bethsaida. And apart from that one miracle we don't know any of the other miracles Jesus actually performed *in* this town. As we said earlier, something fishy is going on.

In Mark 8, a group of people brought a blind man to Jesus to be healed. After leading the man outside town Mark records Jesus "spitting on the man's eyes, [and then] he laid his hands on him and asked, 'Can you see anything now?'" (Mark 8:23). The man answered, "I see people, but I can't see them very clearly. They look like trees walking around" (v. 24).

That's where many have a problem with this story because it looks at first as if Jesus were having an off day. He tried to heal the man, but the miracle came up just a little short. Jesus had to put His hands on the man's eyes a second time before the man could finally see everything clearly.

Is this a case where Jesus had to redo the miracle to get it right? Thankfully, the answer is no!

This two-stage miracle wasn't for the benefit of the town or the man being healed. Rather, it was an illustration—an object lesson—for Jesus' disciples. They had some insight into who Jesus was, but there was still much for them to learn. Just like this blind man, the disciples had only partial sight when it came to their understanding about Jesus. More work was needed before they could see clearly.

LESSONS FROM BETHSAIDA

What lessons can we take with us from our time here inside this fishy "house of fishing"? Let me suggest two—one from the Old Testament and one from the New. First, Absalom reminds us of the need to keep short accounts with God. Absalom's bitterness against his brother, and then his bitterness against his own father, led to his downfall. The writer of Hebrews says it this way: "Watch out that no poisonous root of bitterness grows up to trouble you, corrupting many" (Heb. 12:15).

Second, Bethsaida reminds us of the warning attached to every stock prospectus: "Past performance is not a guarantee of future results." In the New Testament, Bethsaida was an important city, the capital of the region ruled by Herod Philip. It was one of the top three cities where Jesus performed miracles, and a quarter of Jesus' key disciples came from this town. Sounds impressive, doesn't it? But look at the site today. Bethsaida is a cautionary reminder not to drive

> God is infinitely more concerned about our future than He is with our past. And to forget that is to become like Bethsaida is today— a mere shadow of what it once was.

through life with our eyes focused on the rearview mirror. It's not what we've already done that's important; it's what lies ahead. God is infinitely more concerned about our future than He is with our past. And to forget that is to become like Bethsaida is today—a mere shadow of what it once was.

Mosaic at Tabgha with a basket of bread and two fish

CHAPTER 11

Tabgha:
Site of the Misplaced Miracle

Tabgha is a deceptively confusing but beautiful site on the shore of the Sea of Galilee a mile and a half southwest of Capernaum. Virtually all Catholic pilgrims visit the site, while many Protestant groups do not. The name of the site itself seems cloaked in mystery. Tabgha is actually the Arabic name of the site, which was a corruption of the Greek name Heptapagon—"seven springs" —because seven freshwater springs feed into the Sea of Galilee at the spot.

But perhaps the most confusing thing of all about the site is the reason for its religious significance. Church tradition identifies the site as the place where the feeding of the five thousand took place. The mosaic with the depiction of two fish and a basket of loaves is seen as proof that this is indeed the site. Unfortunately, the discovery of another mosaic with loaves and fish at Hippos, on the other side of the lake, casts doubt on the identification. This might be a wonderful place to remember that miracle, but it's *not* the spot where the miracle occurred.

Matthew provided a good summary of the events surrounding that miracle. In Matthew 13:54, Jesus visited His "hometown" of Nazareth. He was in the region of Galilee, an area ruled at that time by Herod the tetrarch—a son of Herod the Great who was also known as Herod Antipas. Matthew 14 reports that Herod became alarmed when he heard about the miracles Jesus performed. He thought Jesus might be John the Baptist returning from the dead, which was upsetting since he's the one who had John put to death!

Then Matthew writes, "As soon as Jesus heard the news [that John had been put to death], he left in a boat to a remote area to be alone" (Matt. 14:13). When Jesus heard Herod Antipas was focused on His ministry, He sailed to the other side of the Sea of Galilee. The Jordan River was the boundary of Herod's kingdom. By sailing to the eastern side of the lake, Jesus left Herod's jurisdiction. Matthew then records that the feeding of the five thousand happened in a "remote area" somewhere on that side of the lake.

After the miracle, Jesus commanded the disciples to "cross to the other side of the lake" (Matt. 14:22) while He stayed on the mountain to pray. This is when Jesus then walked on water. But as amazing as that story is, jump ahead to the end of the account. Matthew concludes the story by saying, "After they had crossed the lake, they landed at Gennesaret" (v. 34). Gennesaret is the Greek transliteration of the Hebrew word Kinneret. That's the name of the lake, but it was also the name of a city on the lake that was about a half mile south of Tabgha.

Bear with me here! Jesus started in the region of Herod Antipas and crossed over the Sea of Galilee to leave Herod's jurisdiction. The feeding of the five thousand took place somewhere on the other side of the Sea of Galilee, east of the Jordan River. After the miracle, the disciples got in a boat to head back across the Sea, and they end up at Gennesaret, near Tabgha. So the feeding of the five thousand couldn't have taken place at Tabgha because it's on the wrong side of the lake.

Some of the confusion has risen because Mark's gospel says that when Jesus dismissed the crowd, He "insisted that his disciples get back into the boat and head across the lake to Bethsaida" (Mark 6:45). But how could they get in a boat and head *to* Bethsaida if they were already on that side of the lake to begin with? When you read that verse in Mark, it sounds like Bethsaida is on the opposite side of the lake from where the miracle occurred, but this would seem to contradict all the other gospel accounts.

The answer is found in the original Greek wording. In giving directions, Mark used two different Greek prepositions. First, Jesus gave the disciples orders literally to go "across the lake." Mark used the preposition *eis* which indicates direction to a place. The destination to which they were heading was "across the lake." Then, much like a modern GPS, Jesus clarified the specific *route* they were to take to reach that destination. They were to travel *pros* Bethsaida. That is, they were to go along the northern edge of the lake—by or toward or around Bethsaida—rather than try to take a shortcut directly across the lake. The windstorm that follows indicates Jesus was giving wise advice. Mark 6:45 implies the feeding of the five thousand took place further to the east of Bethsaida, on the very northeastern edge of the Sea of Galilee, because they had to go past Bethsaida on their journey west. The miracle *didn't* happen at Tabgha.

BEST FISHING SPOT ON THE SEA OF GALILEE

For seventy years Mendel Nun was a member of Kibbutz Ein Gev on the eastern shore of the Sea of Galilee. For decades, he worked as a fisherman on the lake, becoming the recognized expert on fishing these waters. In 1989, he wrote *The Sea of Galilee and Its Fishermen in the New Testament*. When describing Tabgha, he wrote, "The springs of Tabgha have great economic importance. In the winter, the warm water draws schools of warmth-loving musht, tropical in origin, to the vicinity. . . . The Capernaum fishermen stayed in this area during winter and early spring, making Tabgha an important industrial suburb of Capernaum."[1]

When Jesus first called Peter, Andrew, James, and John, it was while they were fishing (Matt. 4:18–22). Following His resurrection, when He appeared again to the disciples in Galilee, it was while they were fishing (John 21:1–14). Very likely, as Nun concludes, "Most of the events in the Gospels connected with fishing therefore took place at Tabgha."[2] No wonder the site had religious significance for early Christians! The Church of the Primacy of Peter commemorates the spot where Jesus said to Peter three times, "Simon son of John, do you love me? . . . Feed my sheep" (John 21:15–17).

It is perfectly clear why Catholics stop at this site. They revere Peter as

Church of the Primacy of Peter from the Sea of Galilee

the first pope, and they believe Jesus' multiplication of the loaves and fishes took place here as well. But why do Protestants tend to avoid the site? Probably because we *don't* revere Peter as the first pope, and because we believe the feeding of the five thousand took place on the *other* side of the lake. Yet if we're not careful, we can miss out on a very significant site. If Mendel Nun was right—and as a secular Jew he had no denominational axe to grind—this site bookends Jesus' ministry with His disciples.

> **How would you respond to Jesus if He were to come, say your name, and then ask, "Do you love Me?"**

It's nearly impossible to shoehorn in all the religious sites on a whirlwind tour through Israel. Even running from sunup till sundown, there are still more sites to see than time available to see them. But Tabgha is worth visiting. Take a brief tour of the church. Get your photo of the mosaic of the fish and loaves. But then head down to the seaside. Find a spot along the shore and read John 21. How would you respond to Jesus if He were to come, say your name, and then ask, "Do you love Me?"

Looking out onto the Sea of Galilee

The site of Magdala, just below Mount Arbel

CHAPTER 12

Magdala:
Miriam of Migdal

O ur next stop on this whirlwind tour around the Sea of Galilee is the Jewish village of Migdal, nestled at the base of Mount Arbel. Until recent archaeological discoveries brought new interest to the site, its greatest claim to fame was a woman named after Moses's sister. This woman from the time of Jesus was named Miriam of Migdal, but you probably know her best from the way her name is written in the New Testament—Mary Magdalene.

Did you ever wonder why there were so many women named Mary in the New Testament, even though no women named Mary are found in the Old Testament? It's because the Hebrew name Miriam was transliterated into Greek as *Mariam*, and then that was transliterated into English as Mary. The thirteen times Miriam appears in the Hebrew Bible, the Septuagint (Greek translation of the Old Testament) transliterates her name as *Mariam*. Anyone named Mary in the New Testament was named after Moses's sister. That's why there are at least six different women in the New Testament named Mary, including Jesus' mother, Mary the sister of Martha who lived in Bethany, and Mary Magdalene.

If Mary's actual name was Miriam, the name of her hometown was Migdal or Magdala. *Migdal* is the Hebrew word for tower. In the Babylonian Talmud the town was known as Magdala Nunayya, the "tower of the fishes." Apparently it was also known in Greek as Tarichaea ("place for processing fish") and Dalmanutha (Mark 8:10).

Until 2009, few tours stopped at Magdala because there was almost nothing to see. But that year the town's synagogue from the time of Jesus was uncovered, and the site suddenly became a popular stop.

THE SYNAGOGUE

A visitor to the synagogue at Magdala comes away with two distinct impressions. The first is how small the synagogue really was. We somehow envision Jesus preaching in arena-sized synagogues packed to the rafters with thousands of worshipers. But a hundred individuals sitting side by side in this small space would have filled the building to overflowing, bringing down the wrath of the local fire marshal—had such an official existed at the time. Other synagogues, like the one in Capernaum, were larger; but this building represents a typical village synagogue in the time of Jesus. It's a good reminder not to despise small congregations. Jesus certainly didn't.

Mark 1:39 says Jesus "traveled throughout the region of Galilee, preaching

The synagogue at Magdala

in the synagogues and casting out demons." That raises an interesting possibility. Could Miriam of Migdal—Mary Magdalene—have first encountered Jesus when He came to preach in this synagogue? This is her hometown. And while we hear more about her during the events of the crucifixion and resurrection, Mark 16:9 also provides a glimpse into Mary that seems to point back to the time of her first encounter with Jesus. There, Mark describes her as "the woman from whom [Jesus] had cast out seven demons." Mary was one of those who experienced Jesus' miraculous power over Satan's demonic forces. And from that initial encounter she became a follower of Jesus. Luke specifically mentions her as one of the women who traveled with Jesus' entourage and who "were contributing from their own resources to support Jesus and his disciples" (Luke 8:3).

The second impression one gets from the synagogue comes from a close inspection of the stone pedestal found inside the ruins. Actually, today's visitors can only view a replica of the original pedestal, which is safely locked away. The pedestal was used to hold a scroll as it was rolled out and read during a service.

The pedestal itself is only about eighteen inches high, so unless it rested on a table, someone needed to sit or kneel in front of it to read. That tiny detail is a good reminder that styles of worship in the past were never as two-dimensional or rigid as we might suppose. In Luke 4:16, Jesus went to the synagogue in Nazareth on the Sabbath,

Stone pedestal in Magdala synagogue

115

and He "stood up to read." That was the normal custom, going back to the time of Ezra when he stood on a platform to read the Word of God while the people stood to listen (Neh. 8:2–5). However, in Magdala, if the stone pedestal rested on the floor, it required the reader to sit or kneel to read as the scroll was unrolled.

The most interesting elements of the pedestal are the carvings along the sides and top. In the front of the pedestal, where the person reading would sit, is a carving of a seven-branched menorah. It's likely a representation of the one found in the temple in Jerusalem. It's almost as if the person seated in front of the pedestal could imagine himself looking through the doors of the temple into the Holy Place.

The sides of the pedestal have pillared archways, while the back has carvings of wheels and fire. The elements on the back could represent the wheels and fiery angelic beings connected with the throne-chariot of God in Ezekiel 1. If so, then that side of the pedestal represents the holy of holies, the very spot where the shekinah glory of the Lord dwelt. On top, where the scroll would rest, is a large carved rosette.

Could this pedestal be designed to represent the temple in Jerusalem? If so, it was a reminder every Sabbath that the God of Israel visibly dwelt among His people in Jerusalem. The synagogue was never intended to replace that reality.

THE ENCOUNTER CHAPEL

It's only a short walk from the synagogue down toward the shore of the Sea of Galilee. By the shore, the Catholics have built a spiritual center called Duc In Altum, which comes from the Latin translation of Jesus' words to Peter in Luke 5:4: "Put out *into the deep* water" (NASB). Inside is a replica of a first-century boat with the Sea of Galilee in the background.

But as impressive as that photo op might be, we're heading down the stairway to the lower level of the building to visit the Encounter Chapel. The floor in that chapel is part of the original first-century marketplace of Magdala, just beside the ancient port. The mural on the wall, which is amazing in its detail, depicts the moment when the woman with the issue of blood touched the hem of Jesus' garment and was healed.

I do need to confess that the mural causes me a small amount of angst. It has nothing to do with the mural itself; it's the *location* that bothers me. The woman with the issue of blood was healed in Capernaum as Jesus was on His way to the home of Jairus, the synagogue official. My sense of geographical authenticity wants to pull the mural from the wall at Magdala and physically carry it up to Capernaum to the spot where that event actually happened. But then I remind myself that the Franciscans at Capernaum have been there since 1894. They've had more than enough time to paint their own mural. Their Catholic brothers at Magdala gave them a 115-year head start. And frankly, the folks at Magdala can be forgiven for appropriating some of the stories from Capernaum. After all, Capernaum has more than its share of great stories about Jesus. Magdala has only the name of a single citizen. Granted, she is a noteworthy individual, but she can hardly be expected to carry the site all by herself.

No, those in charge of Magdala should be applauded for their passion and for their creativity.

And I promise I won't tamper with the mural.

Mural showing encounter between Jesus and the woman with the issue of blood

The Jordan River baptismal site of Yardenit

CHAPTER 13

Yardenit:

The Lady in Purple Underwear

Yardenit illustrates the reason so many visitors to Israel get confused. It's a beautiful baptismal site at the northern end of the Jordan River, just below the Sea of Galilee, even though Jesus was baptized at the southern end of the Jordan River near Jericho. And this "Christian holy site" is run by a Jewish kibbutz! But while those facts might cause confusion, they don't take away from the special beauty of the site, or its significance for those who choose to be baptized here.

In my younger days I hesitated to bring groups to Yardenit. My youthful idealism said this wasn't the *authentic* site, that it only operated to make a profit, and that most of those seeking to be baptized here had already "taken the plunge" back home. Thankfully, my youthful zeal gave way to an older and wiser approach. For many, being baptized in the Jordan River is a spiritual and emotional highlight of their trip to the Holy Land. It's an opportunity to publicly identify with the Lord while following Him in a very tangible act of obedience.

And yet spiritual experiences can sometimes collide with the humorous side of reality.

The day before we actually visit the baptismal site at Yardenit, I explain to the people the opportunity they will have to be baptized in the Jordan River. I ask those who want to be baptized to meet with the pastor who will be doing the baptizing to talk through both the spiritual significance of baptism as well as the practical logistics. I also remind anyone wanting to be baptized to bring something to wear on their feet as well as a bathing suit or shorts and T-shirt to wear underneath the baptismal robe. And I share the story of the lady who wore purple underwear!

THE LADY WHO WORE PURPLE

It happened several years ago when I was co-leading a group of friends and supporters for the school where I was teaching. The president of the school was in the group and would be doing the baptizing. He was getting up in years, so we had another staff member in the water to assist. The day before, I gave the reminder to bring along footwear and something to wear under their robes, and I foolishly assumed everyone was paying attention.

The kibbutz that operates the baptismal site provides (for a fee) a robe, towel, baptismal certificate, and access to the changing area for everyone being baptized. I went down with the rest of the group to secure one of the baptismal areas. It was a beautiful day, warm but not oppressively hot. The water level in the Jordan was higher than normal thanks to heavy winter rains. What we didn't know was that Israel was about to release some water into the Jordan River from the dam just upstream. Nor did we know that one of the ladies wanting to be baptized had forgotten to bring along her bathing suit.

The group gathered at the water's edge as the president and the assistant led the procession of those being baptized out into the water. Thinking back on it, I'm amazed at how rapidly the water seemed to rise. By the time the lady in question had reached the president, the water had already risen up to his chest. As she bent her knees, he held her arms and placed her on her back under the water.

That's when things started to go wrong.

The woman was somewhat large, and as she bobbed back to the surface her feet floated out from under her. The beautiful white gown, made from thin cotton, became totally translucent. That's when it quickly became apparent that she had forgotten her bathing suit and had decided to be baptized in her purple underwear. Unfortunately, she also began floating out of the president's tenuous grasp, beginning her own personal pilgrimage down the Jordan River. The president called for help, and the assistant went sloshing through the water as fast as he could to reach her before she broke completely free of her moorings and started drifting toward another baptismal spot. Those of us standing on shore were transfixed by the entire affair.

That dear saint, and the president who was baptizing her, have since passed on into glory. I wonder if they've met up somewhere in the New Jerusalem, perhaps along the shore of the river of life, and chuckled as they reminisce over the "baptizee in the purple underwear" who almost got away. They might be gone, but the story lives on with every group I take to Israel.

ADDITIONAL FACES

Most of the time, the one doing the baptizing knows those who are being baptized. But every so often we pick up some extras. Usually they are people living in Israel who have come to faith. Their friends encourage them to visit the baptismal site and ask someone to baptize them. Of course, language can be a problem. The first time this happened, the leader looked puzzled because the person at the end of the line didn't look familiar. So the leader asked him, "Are you here to be baptized?" The response, in Russian, wasn't helpful.

The conversation brought the message of salvation down to its most basic level. The leader held up his two index fingers to form a cross and then pointed to his heart. And then he pointed to the person wanting to be baptized. The man responded with a hearty "Da!" And with that basic affirmation of faith, this young Russian was baptized by an American pastor, at a Christian holy site run by a Jewish kibbutz!

Baptismal services at the Jordan River are also memorable for the one doing the baptizing. On one occasion we had a Christian leader who was so caught up in the moment that he started preaching a sermon right in the middle of the baptism . . . while still holding the fellow being baptized *under* the water! As the seconds ticked off, giggles from the group on shore turned to gasps.

They were concerned that the symbolism of baptism—dying to sin and being buried with Christ—might send the senior saint still under the water straight from the Jordan to heaven. Thankfully, the extemporaneous sermon ended and the leader pulled the man up out of the water . . . more "baptized" than most.

Thousands are baptized every year at Yardenit. The water in the Jordan possesses no unique qualities that set it apart from the water in church baptistries back home, except perhaps the fact that the water is colder and has fish swimming around that nibble on the toes of those being baptized. So what is

A pilgrim being baptized

it that makes the site so special? It's the visible reminder that the Jordan River is where Jesus was baptized, and baptism is something Jesus commanded of His followers. "Therefore, go and make disciples of all the nations, baptizing them in the name of the Father and the Son and the Holy Spirit. Teach these new disciples to obey all the commands I have given you. And be sure of this: I am with you always, even to the end of the age" (Matt. 28:19–20).

As if to emphasize the universality of Jesus' command, the walls along the perimeter of Yardenit are covered with scores of ceramic tiles featuring the account of Jesus' baptism from Mark 1. My personal favorite is the one in Hawaiian Pidgin. You might need to read it aloud, but it's worth the time and effort.

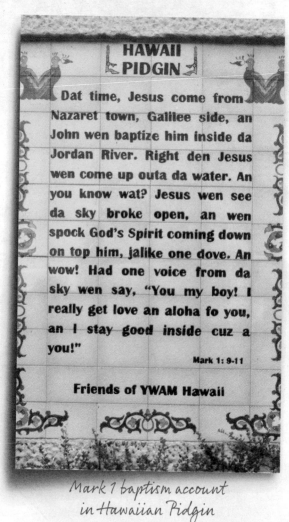

Mark 1 baptism account in Hawaiian Pidgin

Looking down at the monastery from the chapel on the hillside

CHAPTER 14

Kursi:

Site of the Demon-Possessed Swine

Kursi is a throwaway stop on most tours. The guide might mention the site as the bus zooms past on the highway, but few bother to stop. Part of the reason is that the exact location where Jesus cast the demons into the herd of swine is disputed. Matthew 8 reports that Jesus cast the demons out of two men into a herd of swine. However, Mark 5 and Luke 8 only describe *one* demon-possessed man, and they place the event at a different location. Thankfully, the apparent contradictions are easily resolved.

I like visiting Kursi because it helps clear up all the confusion. Matthew, writing to a Jewish audience, records the *exact* location where the event took place. Mark and Luke, writing to audiences less familiar with the geography, record the nearest large city they would be familiar with. We do the same thing all the time. Depending on how familiar you are with Pennsylvania, I might say I grew up north of Philadelphia, near Bloomsburg, or in Almedia. All are equally true, but they are not equally helpful. The more familiar you are with the area, the more specific I can become.

Matthew supplies the exact location where the event took place, though the spot is still debated. Some believe it's at the southeastern end of the Sea of Galilee, while others—including me—believe it's farther north, halfway up the eastern shore. The Arabic name of the site farther north is Kursi, which preserves the earlier Greek name Gergesa. The discovery of a Byzantine monastery at the site, with a small chapel on the hillside above, suggests that the early church also viewed Kursi as the site of the miracle.

I have several friends who disagree with me on the identification. We can "agree to disagree" on the matter since it's not crucial to one's faith. But on one student trip the debate got a little intense. At Kursi I explained why I felt it was the most reasonable choice. As we drove south my friend tried to present his arguments for the alternative site. I must have been pushing back a little too forcefully because he finally said, "All right, let's stop the bus and hike to the other site!" I agreed, and our group of students started on an impromptu field trip.

The dirt roadway zigzagged through banana groves, and I sensed my friend wasn't quite as confident as he was at first that we were really heading in the right direction. The road ended at a fence, and inside was a flock of ostriches being raised by a local kibbutz. I couldn't let the opportunity pass. "Not only do you have the wrong location, you have the wrong animal as well!"

Most people who read the story about the demon-possessed men and the herd of swine imagine the herd tumbling off a cliff into the Sea of Galilee.

The "steep bank" leading down to the Sea of Galilee

However, there is no cliff overlooking the Sea on the eastern shore. (The only cliff fitting that description is Mount Arbel, and it's on the other side of the lake.) Matthew 8:32 says the herd "plunged down the steep *hillside* into the lake." Standing here on the roadway, our group can match up all the details of the story.

We first need a "steep hillside" that leads down to the Sea of Galilee. Actually, there's only one spot matching that description on the entire eastern side of the lake. It's about a mile south of Kursi and the monastery. A finger of land drops down from the top of the Golan Heights all the way to the water's edge. Head north or south of that finger of land and the area along the lake flattens out onto a plain before reaching the water. But at that one spot the slope descends from top to bottom, only broken today by the notch carved out of the hillside for the highway.

Our very first stop is at that notch in the hillside. Off to the north we can make out the spot where the ancient village of Gergesa was situated. Matthew says the herd of swine were feeding "at a distance from them" (Matt. 8:30 NASB). We can easily see from one site to another, though the two spots are about a mile apart.

The tombs—where the two demoniacs lived—would have been carved into the hillside just to the east of the town. That's where the ancient monastery, with its separate chapel on the hillside, is located. And that's where Jesus and the disciples would have encountered these two demon-possessed men. Some see a problem with Matthew recording the presence of two men while Mark and Luke describe only one. But that's not really a problem. Matthew records the exact number of demoniacs for those who were familiar with the location, and who might even have heard fearsome tales of these dangerous men. Mark and Luke focus on the more prominent of the two—the one through whom the demons actually spoke.

For many years, a yellow sign with a red triangle and warning written in Hebrew, Arabic, and English was affixed to a barbed wire fence next to the pathway on which we're standing. The sign was a reminder that from 1948 until 1967 this area was the border between Israel and Syria . . . and that we were now on the edge of a minefield. Many a pilgrim stood next to the sign to try to frighten family and friends back home with vague hints of actual danger during the trip. Alas, the days of such trickery are now over. Israel has removed all the mines along these former border areas. And the sign is now gone as well.

The sign warning against land mines

We're not quite done with our visit to Kursi. Having seen the spot where the pigs rushed headlong into the sea, let's visit the spot where Jesus encountered the demon-possessed men. It only takes a few minutes for the bus to reach the monastery, designed in typical Eastern Orthodox fashion. The monastery was obviously built to commemorate some religious event. And the only event that took place in this area is Jesus' encounter with these men and their legion of demons. The addition of a small chapel on the hillside suggests the tombs themselves were carved into the mountain in that area. They were outside the village, but not at too great a distance since the townsfolk would have had to carry the bodies of those who died out to the tomb for burial.

Inside the ruins of the Byzantine monastery

It's almost time to head to the bus, but I have one last story to share. We first need to walk back to the entrance of the monastery. Years ago I was invited to visit Israel with a large group of pastors and Christian leaders. The trip was sponsored by the Israel Government Tourist

Office, and the purpose was to encourage us to bring groups to Israel. Had that been my first experience in Israel I'm not sure I would have returned. The trip turned out to be a logistical nightmare. A convoy of buses rolled through the land, bringing hundreds of pastors and religious leaders to locations with insufficient restaurants . . . and bathrooms. We began the day in Tel Aviv, and our final stop was at Kursi—Gergesa. It was almost sunset, and we still had to drive back to our hotels in Tel Aviv for the night. But the Tourist Office wanted to show us a special option for Christian pilgrims now available at this site.

Just beside the entrance was what looked like a stepped shrine. The tourism official then told the group this was to be a spot where Christian pilgrims could light a votive candle and receive a certificate acknowledging their act of pious devotion. All for a price, of course. It was too much to resist. I didn't light the

The "stepped shrine" at the entrance to the monastery

candle, but I did get one of the certificates, which I later mailed to a friend with this note: "I was at Gergesa. I thought of the swine . . . and I thought of you!"

That particular marketing pitch landed with a thud. I never saw any groups pause to light candles at the place of the swine. Eventually the shrine itself became a dilapidated planter holding a few anemic pots of plants. Some religious rituals are just not well-suited to archaeological sites.

North to
Mount Hermon

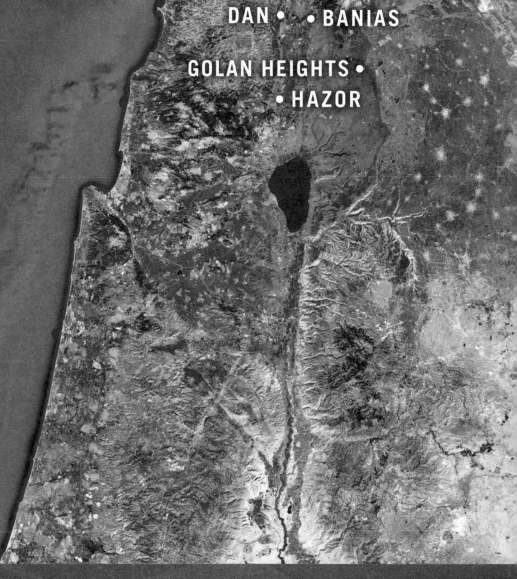

MOUNT HERMON

DAN •   • BANIAS

GOLAN HEIGHTS •

• HAZOR

The acropolis of Hazor with Mount Hermon in the background

CHAPTER 15

Hazor:

Controlling the International Highway

Today's journey is a road trip to the far northern edge of Israel. Our drive takes us first to a narrow strip of land perched between the mountains of Upper Galilee on the west and the Jordan Valley on the east. Just beyond the hills to our west is the present-day border between Israel and Lebanon. The Jordan Valley to our east looks rather beautiful today, with its patchwork of fields and orchards. Come at the right time of year and you can watch as millions of birds stop off at Huleh Lake on their migration between northern Europe and Africa. This lake is a mere fifteen miles north of the Sea of Galilee.

But what looks beautiful today was a great danger in the past. Until just over a century ago this northern extension of the Jordan Valley was what we might euphemistically call wetlands—though where I grew up the more common word was *swamp*. Trekking through the valley in the past brought travelers face-to-face with the three "Ms"—mud, mosquitoes, and malaria. As a result, the International Highway—the unofficial roadway that stretched between Egypt and Mesopotamia—went along the narrow strip of tableland between the high mountains and the swampy valley. And standing guard over that strip of land was the ancient city of Hazor.

Before we reach Hazor we must first drive by the modern town of Rosh Pina. On my very first trip to Israel this little town made a big impression on me. It was the summer of 1982, and Israel, the PLO, and Syria were at war. Most of the actual fighting took place in Lebanon, though Katyusha rockets were fired at several communities in northern Israel. Just a few days after the fighting began, our busload of students followed the Israeli army north into Galilee. Late on the afternoon of the second day, we pulled into a youth hostel at Rosh Pina to spend the night.

As we climbed out of the bus and lined up to check in, the lady behind the desk distributed our bed sheets and towels. We were the only group there, so she gave us a very basic tour of the facilities. "Here are your rooms. Here is the lavatory and shower area. Here is the dining hall. Here is the bomb shelter . . ."

"Wait! Hold it just a second! Slow down. What was that?" Very matter-of-factly, she stopped and repeated herself, as if we must simply be hard of hearing. "I said, 'This is the entrance to the bomb shelter.'"

I felt a sudden urge to turn to one of my fellow travelers and say, "Toto, I've a feeling we're not in Kansas anymore!" In reality, we were less than ten miles from the border with Lebanon, and the PLO's Katyusha rockets had an effective range of thirteen miles. But what seemed so surprising—well, actually shocking—to us was simply the reality of everyday life for this woman at the reception desk. It was definitely a new perspective on what it was like to live in Israel.

We're not stopping at Rosh Pina today, but seeing the town is a reminder that our first stop of the day will soon be coming into view. It's time to open my Bible and read from Joshua 11 and Judges 4. Both chapters describe battles between Israel and a Canaanite leader named Jabin. Since the events in these two accounts took place nearly a century apart, the name must refer to two different individuals. Jabin, which means "perceptive" or "discerner," was likely a throne name, or royal description, used by the king. Much like "Pharaoh" was used to refer to the different kings of Egypt, Jabin might have been the Canaanite equivalent of referring to the ruler as "wise one" or "your Excellency."

The ruler of Hazor certainly seemed to match his title. The city he controlled was the largest in the country at the time of Joshua. It sat on this narrow strip of land between the mountains and the swamp land and guarded the major trade and travel route connecting the two great civilizations of the day.

According to Joshua 11, this king ruled over all the kings in the immediate area. His influence stretched from the foot of Mount Hermon southward to the Sea of Galilee and then westward to the Mediterranean.

On a clear day my favorite view of Mount Hermon is the one rising up as we approach ancient Hazor. Though Mount Hermon is still thirty miles away, it rises majestically in the distance. In the early spring the top of Mount Hermon can still be covered in snow, contrasting beautifully with the green foliage covering the hillside of Hazor.

As we drive along the road skirting ancient Hazor, the site doesn't look that impressive, at least not at first. But that's because the hill beside us isn't the whole city. It's only the acropolis. The true size of Hazor becomes clear as the road climbs up onto the site itself. The ancient town now extends across both sides of the highway. And as we drive off the hill, we can trace the outline of the city as it extends out to the left. Hazor was a large city.

SERVING THE MOON GOD

Excavations at Hazor are still ongoing. The city gate and part of the city wall from the time of Solomon were uncovered in the mid-1950s by Israeli archaeologist Yigal Yadin. The most recent excavations have extended for more than thirty years, focusing on the Canaanite palace on the acropolis. The hope is to someday uncover the royal archive of ancient Hazor. That will be a discovery that could rival the Dead Sea Scrolls.

The early excavators at Hazor also uncovered a shrine to the moon god, *Yerah* or *Yarikh*. The room contained a row of standing stones with an offering table in front and a carving of an individual carrying a bowl in outstretched hands. Carved onto the chest of the man, perhaps a priest, was a crescent moon. A crescent moon can also be seen at the top of the center standing stone. The stone has two hands apparently raised in worship to the moon.

The worship of the moon god occurred throughout the ancient Near East. One of the major centers of worship was Ur, the city from which God called Abraham. As Joshua said in his final message to the people of Israel, "Long ago

Row of standing stones found in a room in Hazor

your ancestors, including Terah, the father of Abraham and Nahor, lived beyond the Euphrates River, and they worshiped other gods" (Josh. 24:2). One of the gods Terah worshiped must have been the moon god.

When Israel came into the land, the first major city captured was Jericho and the last major city captured was Hazor. Both were totally destroyed by fire. And both were centers of worship for the moon god. How do we know this? Jericho's name comes from the name for the moon god, *Yerah* or *Yarikh*. And the discovery of the shrine to the moon god at Hazor makes it clear that the moon god was venerated there as well. It's almost as if God ordered the destruction of both cities to make sure Israel never reverted back to the worship of the moon.

Viewing the ruins of Hazor and recognizing that the city was a center of moon worship helps illustrate God's direct command in Deuteronomy 4. "And when you look up into the sky and see the sun, moon, and stars—all the forces of heaven—don't be seduced into worshiping them. The LORD your God gave them to all the peoples of the earth . . . So be careful not to break the covenant the LORD your God has made with you. Do not make idols of any shape or form, for the LORD your God has forbidden this. The LORD your God is a devouring fire; he is a jealous God" (Deut. 4:19, 23–24).

The worship of the moon god

The stream from the Spring of Dan,
one of the sources of the Jordan River

CHAPTER 16

Dan:

Ancient Israel's Northern Border

As the bus pulls into the parking lot at the site of ancient Dan, one thought dominates every pilgrim's mind: Where are the bathrooms? The hour-long bus ride, coupled with that extra cup of coffee at breakfast, has given even the most spiritually minded of the group a laser-like focus on the basic necessities of life. Thankfully, the Israel Nature and Parks Authority has taken that into consideration and installed very nice restroom facilities. Once everyone has taken advantage of those amenities, we're ready to begin the hike into the nature reserve.

THE SIN OF THE DANITES

The first part of the journey through the site follows the stream that flows from underneath the hill on which the ancient city of Dan was built. The word *refreshing* always comes to mind as I begin this hike. This is not what visitors to Israel expect to see. The rushing water reminds me of the streams I saw growing up in the hills of northeastern Pennsylvania.

> The word *refreshing* always comes to mind as I begin this hike. This is not what visitors to Israel expect to see.

Pausing at one bend along the pathway, I pull out my Bible to talk about the decision made by part of the tribe of Dan to relocate to this area. The story is recorded in Judges 18, and it's a preacher's dream of a message, with appropriate applications on the dangers of disobedience, deception, and idolatry. The tribe of Dan had been given an inheritance by God Himself in Joshua 19:40–48. But instead of taking that land by faith, they hid in one tiny corner and complained that "an inheritance had not been allotted to them as a possession" (Judg. 18:1 NASB). They then sent out their own team of spies to improve on God's revealed will for their lives. Along the way they connected with a young Levite who had hired himself out as a false priest to a rich man with a collection of idols. The spies located some unclaimed land, convinced the tribe to move, and brought along the priest who helped lead them into idolatry, until they were eventually taken into captivity.

But now that our group is actually standing in the land discovered by the five spies, the black-and-white moral of the message becomes a little fuzzier. Was it wrong to leave their inheritance? Well yes, but look at all this water! And see how fertile the land is. Our band of travelers hasn't yet visited the territory God originally promised to Dan, but they can't imagine it being as nice as this piece of real estate. And the quietness and security are big selling points. You can almost hear the five spies selling the rest of the tribe on the move. It was all about "location, location, location!" Or, as they put it, "When you get there, you will find the people living carefree lives. God has given us a spacious and fertile land, lacking in nothing!" (Judg. 18:10).

So was it wrong for the Danites to seek an "upgrade" on God's original plan? Standing here, some might be tempted to side with the Danites. But that's where history helps provide perspective. When God parceled out the land, He knew what was over the chronological horizon. By moving from their original inheritance to this area, the Danites jumped out of the proverbial frying pan into the fire. The Philistines controlled part of the land God had originally assigned to the tribe of Dan. But in relocating here, the tribe became the bull's-eye—the center of the target—for every major nation that invaded the land from the north. The Syrians. The Assyrians. The Babylonians. The first stop on their journey of conquest through the promised land was always Dan.

Hundreds of years after the time of the Judges, Jeremiah the prophet predicted the impending invasion of the Babylonians against Jerusalem. Here's how he pictured the approach of the Babylonian army. "The snorting of the enemies' warhorses can be heard all the way from the land of Dan in the north" (Jer. 8:16). Long before they reached Jerusalem, the enemy had already reached Dan. Walking through the nature reserve here is a reminder that God's revealed will is always best, even if it might not look that way at the time. Any attempt to bypass God's plan will always bring greater heartache.

SKINNY-DIPPING

Midway through the hike, our group is faced with a choice. Most can follow me on a beautiful walk right beside the stream. Unfortunately, this also means walking on round, wobbly stones. And if we're following a group of school children on an outing, the stones will almost always be wet and slippery. The rest of the group can follow my wife, who will lead them on a smooth and quiet path through the woods. The two routes eventually rejoin, but most of the adventure—and danger—is on the path I've chosen.

Stepping from stone to stone along the rushing stream reminds me again of my very first trip to Israel. When our group reached Dan, the only people here, besides us of course, were the Israeli army. They were using the nature reserve as a place where soldiers could step away from the fighting in Lebanon for some rest and recreation. As we walked along the stream on that trip we had to be very careful where we stepped because the rocky pathway wasn't as well maintained as it is today. But at one spot the brush and trees had been cut away to reveal a beautiful view of the rushing water. Unfortunately, it was also the spot where some Israeli soldiers had decided to go skinny-dipping! They looked up, saw us, and simply waved as we walked on by. I'm sure we are one of the few groups who can ever say we surprised the Israeli army and caught them with their pants down!

CONCUSSION COMING THROUGH

Today, the pathway along the stream isn't too difficult, though during the winter months the volume of water can increase. Small rivulets of water seem to seep out at different places and cascade over the rocks on their way to the stream. And after the occasional winter rainfall, even the dirt pathway between the areas of rock can become quite muddy. That mud eventually ends up on the rocks, making them very slippery. Hikers must pay careful attention or their feet can slip off the rocks and into the cold water.

Unfortunately, always looking down also has its disadvantages. Some of the trees in the nature reserve have low-hanging branches extending across the pathway, waiting to club any unsuspecting hiker in the forehead. I try to warn our travelers about this danger, but it's easy to forget between the excitement of taking pictures and the fear of slipping and falling into the water. One hiker was so intent on her feet that she banged her head hard against one of these branches. The rest of the hike she was shouting, "Concussion coming through!"

Eventually, we reach the Spring of Dan, the spot where the main spring of water flows out of the ground. This spring is one of the largest in the Middle East, sending out eight and a half billion cubic feet of water annually. And all of that water comes from the rain and snow that falls on Mount Hermon.

It's now time to climb up the hill on which the ancient city of Dan was built. The refreshing sound of rushing water will soon be only a fond memory.

THE HIGH PLACE OF DAN

The walk to the top of the hill is relatively easy and brings us to the high place at Dan. Here we encounter the first of many religious counterfeits we'll see on our journey through Israel. The shrine brings to mind my short career in banking. During my first eighteen months in graduate school I worked as a teller in a local bank. I managed to give away an additional $1,000 in currency in that short time. (I hated the fifteenth and thirtieth of each month—and most Fridays—because people came to make deposits and get cash. This was *before* the advent of direct deposit and ATM machines.) It became clear my calling wasn't in banking.

One enjoyable lesson I did learn while working at the bank came when they asked a Secret Service agent to come and teach us how to spot counterfeit money. I pictured the agent bringing samples of the different counterfeit bills circulating in the area. But to my initial disappointment he didn't display a single counterfeit bill. Instead, he spent the time focusing on those items that are especially difficult for forgers to reproduce. The lesson turned out to be extremely valuable: the more you know the original, the easier it is to spot *any* counterfeit.

That life lesson unfolded as we explored the temple complex at Dan. It had an outer courtyard with an altar, similar to what was in Solomon's Temple in Jerusalem. From the aluminum frame marking out the size of the altar, the original must have been quite impressive. But it was counterfeit. Those who walk over and explore the remaining stones of the ancient altar discover they were chiseled into rectangular blocks. But God's command for an altar was

The high place at Tel Dan

very clear. "Then build an altar there to the LORD your God, using natural, uncut stones. You must not shape the stones with an iron tool. Build the altar of uncut stones, and use it to offer burnt offerings to the LORD your God" (Deut. 27:5–6).

Just beyond the altar was where the temple itself stood. Stone steps led up to the entrance, just like in Jerusalem. This temple also would have had a Holy Place and a holy of holies, just like the temple in Jerusalem. But look closely enough and you can spot the counterfeit. God commanded Israel to worship Him at the place He would choose, and God ultimately chose Jerusalem (Deut. 12:5, 11). But King Jeroboam, the first king of the northern kingdom of Israel, "made two gold calves. He said to the people, 'It is too much trouble for you to worship in Jerusalem. Look, Israel, these are the gods who brought you out of Egypt!' He placed these calf idols in Bethel and in Dan—at either end of his kingdom. But this became a great sin, for the people worshiped the idols, traveling as far north as Dan to worship the one there" (1 Kings 12:28–30). This religious temple was built to house one of the two golden calves. From the very beginning, it was a poor counterfeit that tried to resemble the genuine temple in Jerusalem.

WAVING TO HEZBOLLAH

Just beyond the high place of Dan is an observation spot where groups can stand on the northern border of Israel and look into Lebanon. Two miles away is a small Arab village named Ghajar. Part of the village is in Israel, but part is in Lebanon. It's hard for Americans to imagine being able to stand on the border with Lebanon in total peace and safety, but that's the reality of a tour to Israel.

To help put the situation in perspective, I encourage the group to wave toward the village. "It's possible that someone from Hezbollah will be watching and see you." To help set the mood for the group I turn toward the village and wave heartily. Though the group is behind me, I assume they are waving as well. However, on one trip I turned around in time to notice that one member of our

The village of Ghajar on the border between Israel and Lebanon

group had decided to take a different approach. He was only using one finger on each hand, and he was definitely *not* waving. Thankfully, everyone else was!

THE GATES OF DAN

As we continue our tour of ancient Dan, we eventually rendezvous with those who didn't walk along the stream. It's now time to visit the two ancient gates that have been uncovered. The first is a mud brick gate from the Bronze Age. Though it's sometimes called Abraham's Gate, it was probably placed into use several hundred years after the time of Abraham. Abraham did pass by this area when he attacked the kings who had captured his nephew Lot (Gen. 14:14–15), but he didn't see this gate.

The mud brick gate was constructed with an arched opening. Many students are incorrectly taught that the Romans invented the arch. This gate clearly shows that the use of the arch as a building technique was around long before the Roman Empire. However, the Romans did perfect the technique.

The mud brick gate at Dan survived because at some point in history the people living there decided to bury it. Perhaps the gate had been placed at too vulnerable a location, or perhaps it was in too inconvenient a spot for trade and traffic. Whatever the reason, the gate was buried and incorporated into the city's walls. Otherwise, the mud brick would have dissolved long ago.

A few hundred yards beyond the mud brick gate is the gate complex constructed during the period of Israel's divided monar-

The mud brick gate at Dan

chy. Inside the outer doorway is a courtyard with the remains of a platform. The platform marked the spot where the governor would sit to judge cases brought before him. It was the courthouse of the day. On occasion we've used this spot when couples have asked to renew their marriage vows. And we actually had one marriage proposal made here. (She said yes!)

To reach the inner gateway that led into the city, those entering the outer gate had to turn to the left. Are you right-handed or left-handed? If you're right-handed, then I'm sorry to have to tell you that you're now dead! A right-handed soldier carried his sword or spear in his right hand, and his shield

Passageway through the outer gate into the courtyard

in the left. As he entered the outer gate and turned left to head toward the inner gate, those guarding the wall would be shooting at him. The unfortunate right-handed soldiers would be holding their protective shields in the wrong hand. No wonder prominence was given to left-handed soldiers (Judg. 20:16)!

One of the greatest archaeological finds from ancient Dan was uncovered in the plaza just outside this gate complex. Archaeologists uncovered pieces of a stone monument that contained a commemorative inscription. This *stele* was carved and set up by the king of Damascus following his defeat of Israel and capture of the city. Later, Israel recaptured the city, smashed the monument, and buried the fragments.

What makes the inscription on the *stele* so significant is that it can be dated to a specific time in Israel's history. The king claims, incorrectly, to have "killed Jehoram son of Ahab king of Israel and . . . Ahaziah son of Jehoram king of the House of David." Those two kings were killed in 841 BC, and at the time they were fighting against Hazael king of Damascus (2 Kings 8:28–29). But perhaps most significant is Hazael's boast that he killed the "king of the House of David." Until the discovery of this monument, many believed David was nothing more than a myth, an Israeli legend something like King Arthur, invented a thousand years later to glorify Israel's early history. But here's an inscription made less than 130 years after King David's death announcing that the ruler of the kingdom of Judah reigned over the "House," or dynasty, of David. Archaeology scores another victory for the reliability of the Bible!

Inscription mentioning the "House of David"

Water flowing from the base of Mount Hermon at Banias

CHAPTER 17

Banias:

Site of Peter's Great Confession

WHAT'S IN A NAME?

It's only a short bus ride from Dan to Banias, but it's enough time for someone to do a quick Bible search and discover there is no town in the Bible
named Banias. So how does this next site connect to the Bible? That's easy!
Modern Banias is really a place named Panias—only it was called Caesarea
Philippi in the Bible. Confused? Then follow me out onto the site for an
explanation.

We're standing at the base of Mount Hermon, at another spring of water
flowing out of the mountain. Above and to the left of the spring is a large cave,
which was, at one point in time, the spot where the water gushed out. When
Alexander the Great came through this area, he brought with him the Greek
language and culture. And this spot, with its flowing stream and lush vegetation,
seemed like the perfect place to worship the Greek god Pan, the god of shepherds, flocks, and nature. So the place became known as Panias—Pan's place.[1]

When the region was conquered by the Muslims in the seventh century,
they introduced a new language—Arabic. But Arabic lacks a "p" sound. The
closest sound they have is "b." As a result, the name *Panias* became *Banias*,
and that has remained its name until today.

But if all that's true, why was this place called Caesarea Philippi in the
Bible? That's where ancient politics come into play. After the death of Herod
the Great, the Romans placed Herod Philip, one of his sons, over the region

north of the Sea of Galilee and east of the Jordan River, including the region of Panias. He built a city here and dedicated it to Caesar. But since his father had already built the port city of Caesarea on the Mediterranean, Philip named his city Caesarea Philippi —"Philip's Caesarea." Philip could change the "official" name of the city, but he couldn't change the history of the region or the hearts of the people. They kept calling it Panias, and that name continued after the city built by Philip fell into disuse.

The niche where the shrine for the god Pan once stood

Yet during the time of Jesus, the area was officially called Caesarea Philippi. And the city was thoroughly pagan. A temple dedicated to Augustus Caesar stood directly in front of the cave, with the life-giving water from the cave seeming to flow out from the temple's base. Next to the temple of Augustus was the court of Pan and the nymphs, and beside that stood the temple to Zeus, the king of the gods.

JESUS' POP QUIZ

Jesus took His followers on a field trip to Caesarea Philippi—away from the pious masses of Galilee and Judea and into the very heart of this pagan stronghold. This was the perfect spot to quiz His followers on the key issues of His life and ministry. The visit is recorded in Matthew 16.

Jesus first asked His followers to explain who others thought He was. So He asked, "Who do people say that the Son of Man is?" (Matt. 16:13). Their response? "Some say John the Baptist, some say Elijah, and others say

Jeremiah or one of the other prophets" (v. 14). People recognized that Jesus was no ordinary man, and they were even willing to admit He was a prophet. And the three candidates suggested by the people are significant. John the Baptist was the most amazing and dramatic prophet raised up by God at the time of Jesus. And in the Old Testament, Elijah and Jeremiah were willing to stand alone for God in times of great distress and spiritual darkness.

The people acknowledged that Jesus was a prophet, but that was as far as they would go. Jesus then turned the spotlight on His own followers. "But who do you say I am?" (Matt. 16:15). Peter jumped in with the correct answer. "You are the Messiah, the Son of the living God" (v. 16). Peter understood that Jesus was more than just a prophet. He was the Messiah, God's Anointed One. If Jesus didn't match other people's perceptions of what the Messiah was to be, it's because their perceptions were flawed. Peter understood that Jesus *was* the promised Messiah.

Just as importantly, Peter declared that Jesus was the *Son of the living God*. This is a remarkable affirmation of both the power of God and the deity of Jesus. The God of Israel is the only *living* God; and Jesus, Israel's Messiah, is God's eternal Son. Jesus commended Peter for his spiritual understanding. "You are blessed, Simon son of John, because my Father in heaven has revealed this to you. You did not learn this from any human being" (Matt. 16:17). This is a great place to pause and think about Peter's confession because it has eternal ramifications. Do *you* believe Jesus was the promised Messiah of the Old Testament? More importantly, do you believe He was God's eternal Son who was sent to "save his people from their sins" (Matt. 1:21)? Your eternal destiny could ride on your answers to those questions.

MARK TWAIN AT CAESAREA PHILIPPI

Caesarea Philippi was the first biblical site visited by Mark Twain in what is now Israel. Before arriving at Banias, Twain spent an unpleasant day in Damascus sick in bed with a stomach virus. And he hadn't particularly enjoyed his time in Syria *before* getting ill. The illness just added to his sarcastic evaluation of Syria. "Syrian travel has its interesting features, like travel in any other part of the world, and yet to break your leg or have the cholera adds a welcome variety to it."[2] He also poked fun at his fellow travelers—from their outlandish clothing to their habit of chipping off souvenirs from the different monuments they visited. But after arriving at the ruins of Caesarea Philippi, at least for a brief moment, Twain ceased being a witty cynic and became very open and transparent.

> For a brief moment, Twain ceased being a witty cynic and became very open and transparent.

He began by recounting Jesus' question and Peter's response in Matthew 16. Then he explained why this troubled him. "I cannot comprehend yet that I am sitting where a god has stood, and looking upon the brook and the mountains which that god looked upon, and am surrounded by dusky men and women whose ancestors saw him, and even talked with him, face to face, and carelessly, just as they would have done with any other stranger. I cannot comprehend this; the gods of my understanding have always hidden in clouds and very far away."[3]

Flowers growing along the stream at Banias

Sadly, Mark Twain was never able to overcome his struggles and come to personal faith. As one biographer has said, Twain "wanted to believe, but he couldn't believe."[4] Twain's struggle is a sobering reminder that visiting the Holy Land—as wonderful an experience as it is—doesn't automatically resolve one's personal spiritual struggles. As the writer of Hebrews makes clear, "It is impossible to please God without faith. Anyone who wants to come to him must believe that God exists and that he rewards those who sincerely seek him" (Heb. 11:6).

THE POWER OF WATER

Our next stop is a mile downstream. While many Israeli families and school groups enjoy hiking along the stream to reach that spot, we're going to save time by taking the bus. Our destination is a beautiful waterfall. Now, don't expect something the size of Niagara Falls, or the height of Yosemite Falls. By American standards this waterfall is rather modest, but it's still worth visiting. It's a relatively short hike—about 180 steps—to descend to the viewing platform. Of course, it also requires a short hike —and those same 180 steps—to climb back out to the bus afterward.

The pathway to — and from — the waterfall

The hike isn't difficult, though one must be careful not to slip. I know this from painful experience. I was at the Banias waterfall with a busload of friends from my radio program. The hike down and back went off without a hitch. Before driving away, we counted to make sure everyone was on the bus. Unfortunately, not all were present. My cohost was missing! The producer and I left the ninety-and-nine in safety on the bus and ran back to find our compadre.

As I ran down the steps I spotted my cohost beside the stream taking pictures. Jon is an excellent photographer, and he had simply lost track of the time. I shouted to him to get his attention, but as I did I missed the next step

153

and started over the side of the bank. When people say time slows to a crawl in some moment of crisis, I know exactly what they mean. In slow motion I remember dropping toward a large rock jutting out of the ground at a sharp angle. I realized that if my right foot landed on that rock by itself, I would likely break my leg or my ankle. Somehow I managed to position my left foot so both landed on the rock at the same time. My momentum kept me going, and I careened off the rock and began rolling down the rest of the hill. Thankfully, there were no other rocks along the way. We made it back to the bus, and the only thing that hurt, besides my pride, were a few cuts and bruises on my arms and legs.

Visitors to the Banias waterfall hear the roar of the water before the waterfall ever comes into view. And while it's not massive in size, it is both beautiful and refreshing to those who take the time to hike down. But I believe it also has biblical significance. And so while you're standing by the falls, read Psalms 42 and 43.

These two psalms were intended to be read as a single composition with

The waterfall at Banias

three separate stanzas. Each stanza ends with the same refrain: "Why am I discouraged? Why is my heart so sad? I will put my hope in God! I will praise him again—my Savior and my God!" (Pss. 42:5, 11; 43:5).

In the first stanza (Ps. 42:1–5), the psalmist looked fondly to the past even as he lamented his present condition. He thirsted for God much as a deer thirsts for water in times of drought. Tearfully, he contrasted the present jeers of his captors ("Where is this God of yours?") to the past joy he had experienced when he journeyed to Jerusalem to worship the Lord.

In the second stanza (vv. 6–11), the psalmist rehearsed the pain and confusion he felt at being carried into exile from the land of Israel. The progression he gives is from "distant Mount Hermon, the source of the Jordan" to "the land of Mount Mizar" (on the slopes of Mount Hermon). While his desire was to travel *south* toward God's temple in Jerusalem, he was being carried *north* into captivity, away from the very land God had promised His people.

The psalmist pictured his turmoil, pain, confusion, and heartache as if their crushing weight were a roaring waterfall relentlessly pounding down on him. I like to think he had just walked near this waterfall just below the base of Mount Hermon. Tourists look at the falls and see great beauty, but to the psalmist the waters represented the weight of sorrow that seemed to be overwhelming him. In his pain he cried out to God, "Why have you forgotten me?" (v. 9).

The psalmist's answer to his own penetrating question is found in two parts. The first comes in a remarkable reminder of God's faithfulness. "But each day the LORD pours his unfailing love upon me, and through each night I sing his songs, praying to God who gives me life" (Ps. 42:8). This is the only time in these two psalms

> God's loyal love and words of comfort are active day and night, even when our circumstances might make it seem otherwise.

where the psalmist refers to God as "LORD" (using the Hebrew word *Yahweh* to refer to the covenant-keeping God). Though the writer might have felt abandoned and alone, God was still present . . . and still at work on behalf of

His people. God's loyal love and words of comfort are active day and night, even when our circumstances might make it seem otherwise.

The second answer to one of life's hardest questions is found in the last stanza of this three-stanza psalm (Ps. 43:1–5). The psalmist gained perspective and hope by going to God in prayer and by focusing on the future. His problems seemed overwhelming, but he needed to remember that God's power is greater than any possible difficulties he might face. As a result, he could ask God to rescue him and guide him through life's floodwaters. The psalmist ended with a sense of expectancy and hope. He knew that someday he would make his way back to Jerusalem to worship God. He didn't know how everything would work out, but he was convinced God would answer his heartfelt prayer. And this gave him renewed hope.

With the wonderful message of Psalms 42–43 in our hearts, let's work our way back up to the bus. Take your time . . . and watch your step. If you want, you can also go along the pathway down by the stream and take some photos of this amazingly refreshing spot. Just make sure to keep an eye on the time. I don't want to have to walk back down to find you!

The stream below the Banias waterfall

The view of Mount Hermon from atop the Golan Heights

The Golan Heights:
Near the Road to Damascus

The road from Banias to the Golan Heights is steep and narrow. I appreciate our driver's skill as he navigates the many twists and turns in the highway. Most bus drivers are highly skilled, but not all. Early on I had a driver who reminded me of Jehu, the man whom the King James Version rather picturesquely said "driveth furiously" (2 Kings 9:20). A more modern translation captured the driving skills of both Jehu and this bus driver in a clearer fashion—"he drives like a madman." After riding with that driver for just one trip, I told the tour company I *never* wanted him as my driver again. But I have seen him from time to time at different sites. His passengers look as if they've spent the day inside Jehu's chariot.

I mention Jehu and this driver because of one particular stretch of road heading up onto the Golan Heights. It's a narrow, two-lane road with a steep grade and a rather sharp drop-off on one side. I ask the group to look down into the canyon, and then I tell them the story about modern Jehu—comparing him to our kind and safe driver. On one trip I mentioned "Clouseau"—the name I had given to the other driver because of his resemblance to Inspector Clouseau from the Pink Panther movies. My driver shared that Clouseau had driven his bus off this very road during a storm, killing several tourists. His company kept him on as a driver and gave him a new bus! Through the rest of the tour our pilgrims go out of their way to thank our driver for his skill. Some are also watching to see if they can spot Clouseau seated behind the wheel of another bus.

As we reach the top of the Golan Heights, the landscape changes. The area becomes relatively flat, with the occasional hill providing a change in scenery. The hills are extinct volcanic peaks, and they have left behind dark, fertile soil. Because we're now almost three thousand feet above sea level, the temperature has dropped. In the summer this is a welcome change from the hot and muggy conditions around the Sea of Galilee. But in the winter it can be cold and rainy. A few times we've encountered sleet and even snow.

Off to our northwest we can see the summit of Mount Hermon rising up another six thousand feet. Depending on the time of year, snow can still cap the summit. We have been following the roadway a zealous Saul of Tarsus would have been traveling when he encountered Jesus on his way to Damascus.

Just ahead are two volcanic peaks standing side by side. The right peak is Har (the Hebrew word for a hill or mountain) Avital. Israel has a listening post on top to keep an eye on the situation in Syria. For security reasons I recommend you *not* take pictures of that site! Of course, that means everyone immediately wants to pull out their cameras and cellphones! It's a great illustration of the principle Paul shared in Romans 7:9: "When the commandment came, sin came to life, and I died" (NASB). So keep your sinful impulse in check and remember that if you are caught and told to surrender your photos, none of us will come to your defense. In fact, I suspect many of the group will pretend not to know you!

Our destination is the left volcanic peak—Har Bental. The hill is a deactivated army base now open to the public. And it provides us with a great view into Syria.

HAR BENTAL

On my first visit to Har Bental I was leading a group of pastors. The site had just been opened to the public, and there was nothing on top except the closed-up bunkers of the base. To locate the spot, we were using a photocopy of a Hebrew map sent by a friend. Thankfully, our ever-resourceful driver was willing to drive up the steep roadway to the top even though we weren't sure if there would be space to turn around. There was, and we discovered a view from the top that was spectacular.

Since that first trip, Har Bental has become a significant tourist destination. It has no direct biblical significance, though it is an excellent spot to talk about Mount Hermon and Paul's encounter with Jesus on the road to Damascus. And the site provides a wonderful spot to talk about more recent events in the Middle East, including the drama that unfolded all around it during the Yom Kippur War of 1973.

A signpost outside the main bunker helps visitors understand the strategic significance of the Golan Heights. Damascus is sixty kilometers away—a mere thirty-seven miles. Jerusalem is less than 150 miles, Baghdad only five hundred miles, and Tehran just nine hundred miles. The entire Golan Heights is only forty-three miles long and nine to twelve miles wide. But capturing and holding it has allowed Israel to achieve a greater sense of security and stability along their border with Syria.

The signpost and bunker on Har Bental

Looking through a gun turret into Syria

THE ART OF HAR BENTAL

Some of the most whimsical additions to Har Bental are the sculptures along the walkway. They are the creation of Dutch/Israeli sculptor Joop de Jong. The sculptures are all made of scrap metal recovered around the area.

"Heavy metal" motorcycle riders

A vicious "Rustasaurus"

JUST SOME BULLETS

At the end of each Israel trip, I help prepare travelers for what they'll encounter when they go through Israel's airport security. Israel takes security very seriously, and some aspects of the process can be intimidating if a traveler isn't prepared. One part of this involves going over the typical questions a traveler can expect to be asked by security personnel. And those questions take me back to an earlier trip to Israel . . . and to the Golan Heights.

We were on a student trip, but we seemed to be having trouble with one particular student. He wasn't lazy, or disrespectful, or malicious. He was just, well, oblivious. We stopped counting heads on the bus. If this student was on the bus, so was everyone else because he was *always* last. He had the maddening habit of getting distracted on the way to a site and then showing up to ask questions *after* we had given the explanation. I knew that if we were going to have any problems at the airport, *he* would be the cause. And that's when I came up with my plan.

In the old airport check-in area, groups were herded into lines formed by retractable belt stanchions. I asked our potentially troublesome student to "anchor the back of the line" for me. He was taller than most, and I told him that would enable me to see where our group ended. But it was a lie. I wanted him in the back of the line so everyone else could get through security before they reached him.

I felt pretty smug as I led the group back and forth through the check-in line. I should have remembered Proverbs 16:18: "Pride goes before destruction, and haughtiness before a fall." I looked up and realized the line they had directed me to ended at a wall, not at the security person. I was now at the *back* of the line, and security would start at the other end—with our problem student. I tried to maneuver my luggage trolley back to the other end, but security arrived first and took our special student aside for questioning.

"Were you ever apart from your group?"

"Yes." (He went to the bathroom all by himself.)

"Did you meet with anyone who is not part of the group?"

"Yes." (The bus driver and guide—when he sat with them for lunch.)

"Was your luggage ever outside your sight since you packed it?"

"Yes." (We physically carried our luggage to the bus and loaded it ourselves . . . but it was *underneath* the bus as we drove to the airport, so he couldn't actually *see* it.)

I could see our chances for a smooth, quick check-in going down in flames. And then the security person asked his final question: "Do you have any weapons or anything that can be used as a weapon?"

Time seemed to slow to a crawl as I heard his response: "Just some bullets!"

It took nearly three hours for security to do a detailed check of all our luggage. We made the plane, but just barely.

Years later, I was part of a doctoral oral exam for this student. I had been added late in the process and was the third reader for his dissertation. The first two readers asked all of the relevant questions. They finally turned to me to see if I had any questions I wanted to ask.

"Just one. Why did you have bullets?"

It turned out that the man's son had a bullet collection. And when we were on the Golan Heights he found some unexpended ammunition on the ground. He picked it up to take back to his son, but forgot to tell any of us. However, when asked by security, that's when he remembered.

And the moral of the story is that when you're in Israel, on the Golan Heights, don't pick up any bullets.

Cherry tree in blossom on the Golan Heights

Galilee to
the Dead Sea

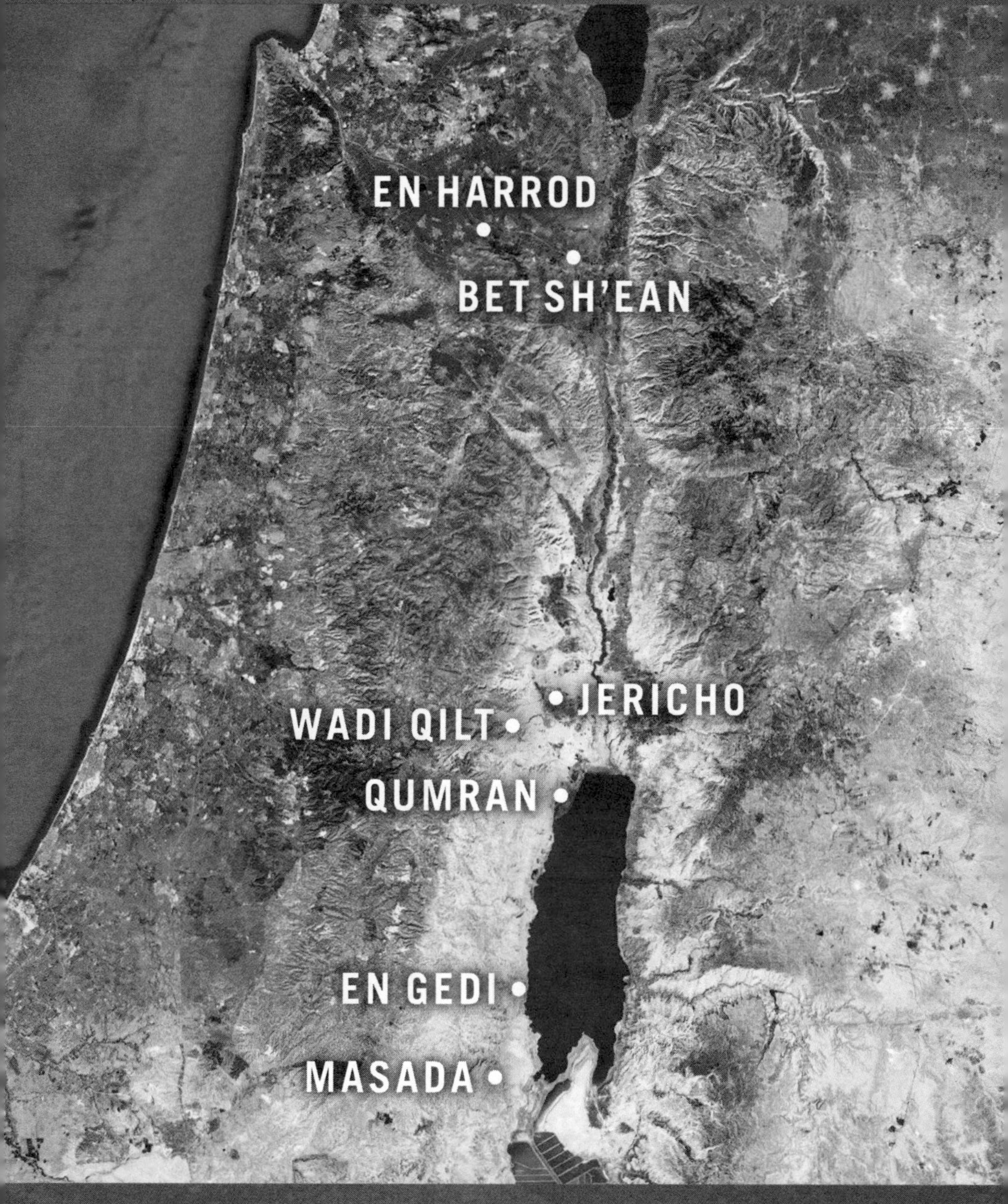
EN HARROD
BET SH'EAN
JERICHO
WADI QILT
QUMRAN
EN GEDI
MASADA

En Harod, Gideon's Spring, flowing out of Mount Gilboa

CHAPTER 19

Gideon's Spring:
Choosing the Three Hundred Men

En Harod—the Spring of Harod, sometimes called Gideon's Spring—is one of my wife's favorite spots in Israel. The fact that we have a grandson named Gideon might partially explain why she loves it, but the site itself is amazing. It provides still another of the many aha moments travelers experience on a tour. Some sites in Israel are disputed, but the location where Gideon chose his three hundred men is absolutely certain because the water still flows right from the base of Mount Gilboa. The mountain hasn't moved, and neither has the spring.

A REDUCTION IN SIZE

I vaguely remember as a child hearing the story of Gideon choosing his three hundred men. Most of the details were lost on me, but I knew he selected them by a stream—the Spring of Harod. In a confusing coincidence, the name in English looks similar to that of King Herod the Great, the ruler at the time of Jesus' birth. But the names aren't related, and the spring was there long before Herod arrived on the scene.

There's a sizeable stream near where I grew up called Fishing Creek. But in my mind it was too small to match the grandeur of the Bible, so I couldn't picture Gideon choosing his three hundred men there. Instead, I envisioned the story taking place near a body of water something like the Susquehanna River that flowed by my hometown. The river is a quarter-mile wide there, and

The stream flowing from the Spring of Harod

somehow this great story from the Bible seemed to demand that grand a stage.

And then I went to Israel and visited the Spring of Harod.

The spot has been beautified in recent years—colorful bougainvillea grows along the pathway; and large, flat boulders provide sturdy footing for those wanting to cross to the other side of the stream. But even that description might give a false impression to someone still trying to envision a wide stream, such as I had before visiting. The rocks might provide a sturdy pathway across the stream, but a good athlete could jump the stream without too much difficulty. It's only seven or eight feet wide!

Standing beside that small stream for the first time helped me see the story of Gideon with new eyes. While imagining a large *river*, I had missed the other details. The focus of the story isn't on the stream; it centers around a very real threat from an invading army—and the faith of a young man called by God to deliver His people. The Spring of Harod provides the perfect place to relive that story.

AN UNLIKELY HERO

Gideon was not voted "most likely to succeed" in his senior year at the local high school. In fact, he was Mr. Nobody. By his own admission, "My clan is the weakest in the whole tribe of Manasseh, and I am the least in my entire family!" (Judg. 6:15). Gideon had little faith in his ability, even though God saw him as a "mighty hero" (v. 12). It's obvious that one of them had a distorted view of reality.

As the story unfolds, the average reader might think God was the one who had it wrong. Gideon seems to be the consummate loser. Think about it. If God personally appeared to you, told you He had selected you to lead His people, then sent fire shooting up from a rock to consume the sacrifice you prepared, you might have at least a *little* confidence in your ability to do what He was requesting. But not Gideon.

Gideon needed additional proof, so he literally "put out the fleece"—twice. "If you are truly going to use me to rescue Israel as you promised, prove it to me in this way. I will put a wool fleece on the threshing floor tonight. If the fleece is wet with dew in the morning but the ground is dry, then I will know that you are going to help me rescue Israel as you promised" (Judg. 6:36–37).

The next day the fleece was full of water and the ground was dry. That

Looking across the Jezreel Valley from En Harod toward the Hill of Moreh

would be enough to convince most, but not Gideon. Maybe it was just a fluke. So Gideon asked for another sign. "This time let the fleece remain dry while the ground around it is wet with dew" (v. 39). And the next day Gideon got wet feet walking through the grass to reach a wool fleece that was bone dry.

It's at this point in the story where the Spring of Harod appears. The invading Midianites arrived in force from off the desert east of the Jordan River. These nomads rode in on their camels and camped on the slopes of the Hill of Moreh. Picture Gideon standing on Mount Gilboa, perhaps near the base of the mountain, looking across the valley at 135,000 Midianites camped just four miles away . . . and then turning to look at his relatively small army of 32,000. The odds were 4:1 against him.

That's when God said, "You have too many warriors with you" (Judg. 7:2). God instructed Gideon to announce that anyone who was afraid could leave, and 22,000 of his men accepted the offer. The odds against Gideon and his remaining soldiers were now over 13:1. And God's response? "There are still too many!" (v. 4). God then gave Gideon a way to select his final band. "Bring them down to the spring." Evidently Gideon wasn't camped in the valley along the stream. He and his men were up on Mount Gilboa. Camels don't do as well climbing hills, so Gideon and his men had taken up a defensive position. God ordered Gideon to take his remaining men down to the stream, which also happened to be a place where they were more vulnerable to attack.

People get confused over how Gideon selected those who were to remain with him. The verse says everyone who "laps the water with his tongue as a dog laps" was selected, while "everyone who kneels down to drink" was rejected. The key is the next phrase. The Bible says the three hundred men "lapped, putting their hand to their mouth" (Judg. 7:5–6 NASB).

Ever watch a dog drink water? It doesn't stick its nose *into* the water. Rather, it sticks its tongue in and pulls the water up into its mouth. The men selected by Gideon were the ones who cupped their hands in the water and pulled it up to their mouths. But why? Probably because as they crouched down, each man kept his sword in one hand while scooping the water from the spring with the other. These soldiers were either the most vigilant, or the most cautious. The soldiers who were rejected were the ones who got down on their hands and knees to drink, forcing them to lay down their weapons.

When the water break was over, Gideon had just three hundred men. But what could so few do against so many? There were 450 Midianites for every one Israelite. God then made one final offer to Gideon. "But if you are afraid to attack, go down to the camp with your servant Purah. Listen to what the Midianites are saying" (Judg. 7:10–11). Gideon decided to take God up on the offer, which strongly suggests he *was* still afraid. We might scoff at Gideon's lack of courage, but there's a little Gideon in all of us. We know that what God has said is true, but we still struggle to accept it in our hearts, and to act on it in our lives.

I find the next part of the story to be the most remarkable of all. Gideon—the man who struggled with fear in spite of God's constant assurance of victory—hears one of the Midianite invaders interpret the dream of another, and suddenly everything clicks into place. He "bowed in worship before the LORD" (v.15) and returned to lead his men to victory.

Pause and look at the spring. In many ways this little spring is a perfect symbol of Gideon. It looks insignificant, certainly not something we would describe as great or majestic. But God used this stream, and the man who stood along its banks, to demonstrate that He knows what's best . . . and that His power is sufficient. Gideon saw himself as little more than a frightened farmer, but God saw him as a valiant warrior. And then God patiently worked to help Gideon discover the courage he never knew he possessed.

As you gaze into the water of this spring, do you see Gideon's reflection, or your own?

As you gaze into the water of this spring, do you see Gideon's reflection, or your own? Like Gideon, do you struggle to believe God could ever use someone with your background, your doubts, your fears, your struggles? If so, look again at the Spring of Harod. God delights in selecting those who struggle to become His valiant warriors. Just ask Gideon.

THE OTHER EVENT AT THE SPRING OF HAROD

Guides will often point out a house sitting on a pathway just above the spring. The house, and nearby mausoleum, belong to Yehoshua and Olga Hankin. In spite of being quite poor, Yehoshua became convinced that his purpose in life was to redeem the land of Israel. Over the early decades of the twentieth century he managed to purchase almost 150,000 acres of land in the Jezreel Valley, land that eventually became part of the modern State of Israel. When he bought it, the land was a mixture of barren patches of dirt and rock and mosquito-infested swamp. But somehow Yehoshua saw it for what it would finally become—fertile agricultural land. He built the house so he could look out over the valley he helped purchase. Because of his vision and determination, Hankin is known today as the "Redeemer of the Land."

And yet, as wonderful as that beautiful story might be, it's not the first story that comes to my mind when our bus first arrives at En Harod. Years ago there was a large swimming pool at the site, along with restrooms and changing facilities. They're gone now, but I can still picture them—and the following event. Our bus stopped near the pool, and I jumped off to direct our group to the restrooms. The drive from the hotel at the Sea of Galilee had taken nearly an hour, and most were anxious to check out the facilities.

I stood with my back to the buildings and faced the group stepping off the bus. "Men to the left side of the building, women to the right!" Now, as I was saying that I had to extend my right hand for the men, and my left hand for the women. Giving directions in reverse takes some concentration, so I focused on what I was saying rather than looking back to make sure everyone was following my directions. What I failed to mention was that each side had *two* doors—one for the restrooms and the other for the changing area. The women selected the correct door, but several men did not.

The group of men who went into the changing facilities initially confused the shower stalls for walk-in urinals. It was still early in the trip, and they assumed this must be the way they were designed in Israel. They might have gotten away with their mistake, except one of the men reached up and pulled what he assumed was the flush handle dangling down.

The names of those individuals will remain unrecorded . . . but the story lives on in every trip.

Looking up the Cardo, ancient Bet She'an's main street, to the hill on which the original city once sat

CHAPTER 20

Bet She'an:

The Pompeii of Israel

History is punctuated with illustrations of seemingly insignificant human errors that resulted in catastrophic loss. The space shuttle *Challenger*—along with the seven astronauts on board—was lost because of the failure of a frozen O-ring seal during a cold weather launch. In 1999, the Mars Climate Orbiter crashed because the navigation team based their calculations on the metric system while the design team provided acceleration data based on the English system of inches, feet, and pounds. In fact, after nearly *every* major disaster—no matter what discipline—investigators uncover a *series* of seemingly small errors, mistakes, or miscalculations that ultimately led to the catastrophic failure. That reality will help us understand the spiritual significance of ancient Bet She'an.

As an archaeological site, Bet She'an is impressive. Yet few know much about the site itself, where it's found in the Bible, or why it's spiritually significant. In most English Bibles the town's name is spelled Beth-shan or Beth Shan, but a better transliteration would be Bet She'an, which means "house of rest." During the four-hundred-year period between the end of the Old Testament and the beginning of the New Testament, the city received a new name—Scythopolis, or city of the Scythians. The town was likely renamed after Scythian mercenary soldiers settled there during this time.

THE POMPEII OF ISRAEL

Today, Bet She'an is the Pompeii of Israel. Years of excavation have uncovered amazing remains of a large Roman/Byzantine city. At the time of Jesus, Scythopolis/Bet She'an was a thriving Gentile city, one of the cities of the Decapolis, a confederation of Hellenistic city-states. This town was the only city in the confederation located on the west side of the Jordan Valley.

A panoramic look at the theater of Bet She'an

The remains of the city's ancient theater hint at the grandeur Bet She'an once possessed. The theater originally had three tiers of seating that could hold up to 7,000 people, although only one tier has been restored. Behind the theater is the Cardo Maximus, a large colonnaded street extending north toward the city's acropolis. Flanking the street are remains of a large bathhouse along with the agora, or marketplace.

Look carefully at the acropolis. The hill is actually the location of the Old Testament city of Bet She'an. Picture that hill, ringed on top by a massive wall, and you can perhaps glimpse the importance this city played in Israel's history. The city straddled the main east-west road that stretched from the Mediterranean, through the Jezreel Valley, and across the Jordan River to the King's Highway. It watched over one of the few places where the Jordan River could be forded, and that made it a strategic location.

And yet, as strategic as Bet She'an was geographically—and as impressive as it still is archaeologically—the Bible connects the site with two catastrophic spiritual failures.

The colonnaded street and acropolis from the theater

THE CATASTROPHIC FAILURES AT BET SHE'AN

Bet She'an's first catastrophic failure is recorded in the book of Judges. Actually, it appears as nothing more than a brief historical footnote—a minor detail one could easily overlook. God had commanded Israel to inhabit the land, but the book of Judges records the tribe of Manasseh's incomplete obedience. "The tribe of Manasseh failed to drive out the people living in Beth-shan, Taanach, Dor, Ibleam, Megiddo, and all their surrounding settlements, because the Canaanites were determined to stay in that region" (Judg. 1:27).

Bet She'an was one in a series of fortified cities passed over by the tribe of Manasseh. These cities were well-defended and hard to overcome, and there was more than enough land in the rest of Manasseh's tribal allotment to meet the tribe's immediate needs. The leaders of Manasseh must have thought that allowing the Canaanites to remain in these few cities wouldn't be a major problem. Israel had captured *most* of the land. What harm could these few cities cause if they were cut off from the rest of the country?

Sadly, the rest of the book of Judges details the heartache caused by

Israel's failure to obey. As the angel of the Lord announced in Judges 2:3, the Canaanites left in the land would become thorns in the side of Israel, rising up to subjugate and enslave God's chosen people at various times throughout the period of the Judges. Israel experienced four hundred years of heartache because they didn't obey God when He told them to take *all* the land, including Bet She'an.

But if the hill of Bet She'an stands as a sad monument to failure during the period of the Judges, it's an even greater witness to the ruinous failure of Israel's first king. To study the life of King Saul is to discover the tragedy of a king who never lived up to his potential. Chosen by God, anointed by Samuel, empowered by the Holy Spirit, Saul started well. But a series of personal failures, some seemingly so insignificant that they were likely overlooked by most of his peers, led to his catastrophic downfall.

Saul's problems began, like the tribe of Manasseh before him, with incomplete obedience. In 1 Samuel 13, Saul was told to wait seven days for Samuel to arrive to offer a sacrifice. Saul waited six days and twenty-three hours—almost the whole time, but not quite. In 1 Samuel 15, Saul was commanded to destroy the Amalekites, and he wiped out *most* of them—but not quite all. These seem like minor variations, small flaws that would be within the tolerance of most quality control inspectors. But not if the inspector happens to be the God of the universe.

God described Saul's incomplete obedience as rebellion and arrogant insubordination (1 Sam. 15:23). Saul's inability to fully obey God cost him the kingdom. And it ultimately cost him the lives of his sons—and many of his soldiers. The book of 1 Samuel ends with a major battle between Israel and the Philistines. God was no longer with Saul, and his forces suffered a terrible defeat on Mount Gilboa along the edge of the Jezreel Valley. When the battle was over, the Philistines had split Israel in two. They controlled the Jezreel Valley all the way east to the Jordan River.

And as for Saul, "The next day, when the Philistines went out to strip the dead, they found the bodies of Saul and his three sons on Mount Gilboa. So they cut off Saul's head and stripped off his armor. Then they proclaimed the good news of Saul's death in their pagan temple and to the people throughout the land of Philistia. They placed his armor in the temple of the Ashtoreths, and they fastened his body to the wall of the city of Beth-shan" (1 Sam. 31:8–10).

The hilltop town of Bet She'an became the Philistines' trophy case. The headless torsos of Saul and his sons hung from the walls atop that hill, the stench of their rotting corpses fouling the air. Only too late did Saul learn the truth that God expects His followers to obey completely. The consequences for disobedience are too tragic to even consider as an option.

Another view of the hill on which the Old Testament city of Bet She'an once stood

I find it hard to take my eyes off that hill when I'm at Bet She'an. It stands as a solemn reminder that the consequences for disobedience are severe. We live in a world that makes excuses for failure and that seeks to minimize the consequences for mistakes. But God expects His followers to live by a higher standard.

181

THE COLLAPSE OF BET SHE'AN

Bet She'an, along with the entire Jordan Valley, rests on a geological fault line. It's part of the Great Rift that extends from Turkey down into Africa. And every few hundred years or so the region experiences a major earthquake. Bet She'an was a city in decline in AD 749 when just such a disaster struck.

Remains of stone columns and capitals toppled by an earthquake

In the early seventh century, the area of ancient Israel saw the arrival of several invaders. Persians conquered the land for a decade before being expelled by the Byzantines. But less than a decade later, Muslim armies swept in from Arabia and defeated the Byzantine forces, taking over the region. Bet She'an went into a period of decline. For the next hundred years the city limped along. But when the earthquake hit in 749, the city literally collapsed on itself. Massive stone capitals were toppled off columns, causing roofs to collapse. The columns then tumbled to the ground and broke, blocking streets. Roads buckled, and buildings gave way. The destruction was so complete that the survivors simply moved away rather than trying to rebuild. Over the centuries the site became covered by soil carried in by rain or blown in by the wind. The once-magnificent city was hidden, except for the ruins of the ancient theater and the hill on which the original city once stood.

THE ANCIENT TOILETS

Today, the remains of Bet She'an are coming back to life, thanks to the work of the archaeologists who have been excavating there for more than four decades. The theater was the first major structure restored, but it has been followed by the ancient gymnasium/bath complex, the amphitheater, and the Cardo Maximus and Decumanus Maximus—the two major road arteries of the ancient city.

And the public toilets are back as well!

This discovery fascinated me since I try to think about these ancient sites in practical terms. People like traveling with me because I focus on issues like the group's next bathroom break. We might not want to talk about it, but let's face it. Such issues are *very* important to someone traveling in an otherwise unknown area. And that also had to be true in the past. So I find myself asking at different sites, "What did people do to take care of such practical matters back then?" I've seen the public toilets in such ancient cities as Ephesus, Corinth, and Philippi. I've also seen private toilets in Ephesus and the City of David. The public toilets at Bet She'an are similar to those in Ephesus, and I like taking our group—or at least those interested in such things—on a short tour of these ancient loos.

Three details stand out when someone visits the ancient public toilets at Bet She'an. The first is the architect's attention to practical matters. The Romans built the toilets along three outside walls of the building. The area above the toilets was covered, offering protection to the patrons on a rainy day. But the building also had an open inner courtyard, which allowed fresh air inside.

The second detail that stands out is the plumbing. The Romans designed the structure so that running water would flow underneath the seats to carry

183

The ancient public toilets

away human waste. They also placed a small trough by the feet to carry running water that could be used for cleansing afterward—most likely using a long stick and attached sponge.

The third detail, and perhaps the most shocking to those from the West, is the sudden realization that the entire facility was unisex, and rather intimate—almost to the point of being "cheek-to-cheek." Evidently the Romans saw the toilets as a place of social interaction. Now, they also wore knee-length tunics or togas along with an outer cloak; so a degree of modesty was still observed. But private stalls didn't exist in these public restrooms.

I've seen many group photos taken in the ancient toilets of Bet She'an. I've also taken care not to pose for any myself!

Sign at the entrance to Old Testament Jericho

CHAPTER 21

Jericho:
From Rahab to Zacchaeus

I love Jericho, but probably for all the wrong reasons.

My favorite meal throughout the entire tour is at the Mount of Temptation restaurant just outside Old Testament Jericho. Those who've eaten in the main dining area might disagree. The restaurant has a nice buffet, but it hardly ranks as the average tourist's "favorite meal." Ah, but that's because the tourists don't eat with the bus driver and guide!

You see, there are two eating areas at the restaurant. The tourists are taken to the second floor, which has multiple buffet lines and a large eating area. Meanwhile, the guides and drivers go to a smaller eating area on the first floor. That's where Walid is in charge. Walid follows the Arab custom of showing great hospitality to guests. And by hospitality I'm referring to multiple courses of wonderful Arab cuisine. A large variety of salads with hummus, falafel, tahina, and fresh pita. But don't fill up on the salads, because they are followed by succulent lamb chops, kebabs, roast chicken, and mountains of French fries . . . all served with fresh-squeezed lemonade and your choice of soft drinks. And when you think it's all finally over, out comes the Arabic coffee and warm *kanafeh*. You can have my cup of coffee, but don't try to steal my kanafeh. Walid knows how much I love it, so he usually gives me a large piece.

The group upstairs doesn't really know what they're missing, which is probably a good thing. However, one time I was down below while our group was eating up above. The lower restaurant was located in a different area, with a small window near the ceiling that opened onto the seating area on the second floor. As I was enjoying Walid's sumptuous feast I glanced up to see one of our guests looking through the opening at our table and all the food. Jesus' parable of the rich man and Lazarus flashed through my mind as the guest gazed with longing eyes across the "great gulf fixed" to see the food I was enjoying in Abraham's—or Walid's—bosom!

The only problem with eating lunch at the Mount of Temptation restaurant is that it's over much too quickly, followed by a hike out onto the site of Old Testament Jericho in the heat of the day. And at first glance, Tell es-Sultan—Old Testament Jericho—hardly looks impressive. In fact, it looks more like several large piles of discarded dirt. Jericho plays such an oversized role in the story of Israel's entry into the land that travelers unconsciously expect to see ruins of a vast city. Most are underwhelmed when they first step onto the site of ancient Jericho.

The most impressive physical remain is a Neolithic tower uncovered by Kathleen Kenyon during her excavations in the 1950s. Looking down at the

Looking down at the Neolithic tower

tower reminds us that the site has been built up over the millennia. The buildings of each new era were constructed on top of previous layers of destruction. And most of the buildings, apart from this tower, were made of mud brick. Most of those bricks long ago dissolved back into mud, making it virtually impossible to envision the shape of whatever existed in the past.

It's not the physical ruins that give Jericho its significance. It was the city's strategic location that made it so important. And that's why we're first head-

Mount of Temptation from Old Testament Jericho

ing to an observation platform on top. While you catch your breath, turn to the west and look at the tall mountain. That's the traditional Mount of Temptation where Jesus was tempted in the wilderness. Was He tempted in that exact spot? Probably not. But just above that mountain is the start of the Judean Wilderness, and that *is* where Jesus was tempted. From the top of Jericho we have a panoramic view that extends from the Mount of Temptation north toward Gilgal, east across the Jordan Valley to the Plains of Moab, south toward the Dead Sea, and then southwest to the road leading past New Testament

Jericho to Jerusalem. And right next to where we are standing is the oasis of Jericho. It can still be called "the city of palms," as it was in Judges 3:13.

But Jericho wasn't important just because of its location. Its significance also came from the people who walked onto the pages of Bible history here. Now, if these individuals had lived where I grew up, they would all have been given nicknames. Some in my hometown were known for what they did for a living. Dick the Mailman delivered our mail. He went to our church, but as a kid I never knew his last name. He was just Dick the Mailman. Then there was Joe the Barber. That's the name he went by. He even had it inscribed on his tombstone! Others were given a nickname based on some physical characteristic. A close friend's mom was "Shorty." And still others had nicknames that defied understanding. For example, another friend's dad was simply called "Snipe." Nicknames aren't as common today, but they can help us connect with some of the unforgettable characters who lived in Jericho.

RAHAB THE HARLOT

The first person we need to meet is Rahab. But if you say her name, what comes to mind next? If you know the Bible, the next word out of your mouth is her occupation—prostitute, or harlot. Rahab is identified by name eight times in the Bible, and five of those times the word "prostitute" or "harlot" is attached. She's described in four different books of the Bible (Joshua, Matthew, Hebrews, and James) and the only one that *doesn't* add the word "harlot" is Matthew.

It's one thing to be known as Dick the Mailman or Joe the Barber. Those are honorable professions. But how would you like to go through life with everyone attaching the word "prostitute" to your name? To put it mildly, Rahab was a woman with baggage. Look at all the disadvantages she faced. She was a Canaanite, not an Israelite. She was a woman in a society that often viewed women more as possessions than people. And . . . she was a prostitute. She sold her body for the pleasure of others.

But circumstances don't determine destiny. One thing set Rahab apart.

And we see it in the words she spoke to the spies who came to her in Jericho.

> "I know the LORD has given you this land. . . . We are all afraid of you. Everyone
> in the land is living in terror. For we have heard how the LORD made a dry path
> for you through the Red Sea when you left Egypt. And we know what you did to
> Sihon and Og, the two Amorite kings east of the Jordan River, whose people you
> completely destroyed. No wonder our hearts have melted in fear! No one has the
> courage to fight after hearing such things. For the LORD your God is the supreme
> God of the heavens above and the earth below." (Josh. 2:9–11)

How did Rahab know this? She didn't have access to the five books of
Moses, the only part of the Bible written at that point, so how could she
know anything about the God of Israel? Likely, travelers passing through Jericho and stopping to use her services shared bits
of news and gossip about what was happening
in the region, including reports about a group of
people . . . and the God they served . . . and the
things that God had done. Rahab didn't know
much, but she believed—and acted on—the
truth she had heard. Rahab was willing to trust

> Rahab didn't know much,
> but she believed—and
> acted on—the truth she
> had heard.

her life, and the lives of her loved ones, to a promise made to her in the name
of the God of Israel—a God she had only heard about secondhand.

Rahab's faith saved her physically, but it did so much more. Because of
her willingness to risk her life to protect the two spies, this Canaanite harlot
was accepted among the Israelites in spite of her background. She ceased being just a mere object and became the beloved wife of Salmon. And Salmon
wasn't some bumpkin who couldn't get a respectable girl to be his wife. His dad
was Nahshon, who happened to be the leader of the tribe of Judah (Num. 2:3;
1 Chron. 2:10–11). In fact, Moses put Nahshon in charge of organizing the fighting men from the tribe of Judah (Num. 10:14). It's even possible that Salmon
was one of the two spies sent on that daring mission into Jericho by Joshua.

Rahab gave birth to an heir who would play a major role in Israel's transformation into a nation. His name was Boaz. And ultimately, through that son, Rahab became a link in the chain that led to both David and Jesus.

And yet, the story of Rahab still isn't finished. In the New Testament, the writers of both Hebrews and James point to Rahab as a shining example of faith. In fact, Rahab is one of only two women identified by name in the Hebrews 11 Hall of Faith. This woman who started out as a prostitute ended up as a mother in the lineage of kings. And the turning point came when she decided to trust God with her life. Rahab illustrates the truth that it doesn't matter where you're from, or what you've done. God is infinitely more concerned with who you are—and where you are going. Rahab is a reminder of what God can do with and through a person willing to put their faith in Him.

SHORTY THE TAX COLLECTOR

As we board the bus and drive through the oasis of Jericho, we still have two more stops to make. The next one is at a large tree with a whitewashed base. The tree is a sycamore fig tree, and it reminds us of the story of the "wee little man" from Jericho who "climbed up in a sycamore tree" to see Jesus. The man's name was Zacchaeus, and if he had lived in my hometown he would have been called Shorty.

The tree in front of us isn't the actual tree Zacchaeus climbed up, though some guides might try to convince you it is. The sycamore fig tree is very different from a typical American sycamore tree. The sycamore fig trees that grow in Israel are fairly tall and produce a small,

Sycamore fig tree in Jericho

fig-like fruit that grows on the trunk and branches. The tree also has lots of foliage that could hide anyone who wanted to see but not necessarily be seen. Someone like our tax collector named Shorty.

People today might complain about the IRS, but there's little comparison between Zacchaeus and someone working for the IRS today. Zacchaeus worked for Rome, the foreign occupying power. Tax collectors were usually wealthy individuals who purchased the right to collect the taxes. This authority allowed them to extort additional funds for themselves—the equivalent of legally sanctioned robbery. Zacchaeus was a wealthy man, but at least some of his wealth came by collaborating with the Romans against his own people.

Imagine Zacchaeus's surprise when, reaching the spot where he was perched, Jesus stopped, looked up, and said, "Zacchaeus! . . . Quick, come down! I must be a guest in your home today" (Luke 19:5). After this encounter, Zacchaeus might have remained a "wee little man" physically, but God transformed him into a spiritual giant among those living in Jericho.

BLIND BART

It's time to get back on the bus and drive to our final stop in Jericho—New Testament Jericho.

Jericho was the Palm Springs of Herod the Great's empire—a place of warmth, sunshine, and sweet fruit from the many date palm trees that grew there. But Herod had a problem. The original city had a large Jewish population, and Herod had a rather tense relationship with the subjects he governed. The location was superb . . . but the neighbors could be disagreeable. So Herod worked out an ingenious solution. He built a new city—Roman administrative Jericho.

> Jericho was the Palm Springs of Herod the Great's empire.

This new Jericho lacked the water supply of the original city, so Herod built an aqueduct to bring water from a spring in the Judean Wilderness several miles away. He built a palace for himself straddling the streambed at the edge of the mountains. His palace complex included a swimming pool, where Herod later murdered his own brother-in-law whom he saw as a threat to his rule. And just above the entire complex stood the fortress of Cypros, a well-defended refuge should Herod ever feel threatened by his nearby subjects.

Like Minneapolis and St. Paul, or Dallas and Fort Worth, the two cities of Jericho were separate, yet inextricably linked together. And knowing that fact

The swimming pool in New Testament "Roman" Jericho

helps the story of Jesus' encounter with Blind Bart make more sense. Matthew says the miracle happened as Jesus "left the town of Jericho" (Matt. 20:29), but Mark and Luke say the miracle happened as Jesus "reached Jericho" or "approached Jericho" (Mark 10:46; Luke 18:35). This apparent discrepancy is easily explained. Matthew wrote his account to a Jewish audience and explained to them that the miracle happened as Jesus was heading *out* of the Jewish area of Jericho. Mark and Luke wrote to Gentile audiences and described the miracle from the perspective of Jesus as He "approached" the Roman area of Jericho. A proper understanding of geography—and of each writer's specific purpose and audience—causes the alleged difficulties to vanish.

But back to the story of Blind Bart.

Bart's official name was Bartimaeus, which means the "son of Timaeus." The name seems to perfectly match his location. It's a mixture of the Aramaic word *bar*, which means "son," and the Greek word *timaios*, which means "honorable." He was a man with a mixed Jewish and Gentile name sitting along a road connecting cities with separate Jewish and Roman cultures. But where I grew up, he would have simply been called Blind Bart.

Though his full name meant "son of honor," Bart's life had fallen far short of the aspirations of his parents at birth. He had been reduced to the lowest status of society, "sitting by the road, begging" (Luke 18:35 NASB). Bart heard a large throng of people heading his way as they left Old Testament Jericho on their way toward New Testament Jericho and the road that went past it to Jerusalem. While most beggars would have used the opportunity to call out to everyone passing by, Bartimaeus focused with laser-like precision on one specific person in the crowd. "Jesus, Son of David, have mercy on me!" (Luke 18:38).

How did he know to focus on Jesus? Mark tells us that "Bartimaeus heard that Jesus of Nazareth" was about to pass by (Mark 10:47). And it's likely he had heard stories about Jesus' miracles, and perhaps His teaching. But Blind Bart's words—and his persistence—tell us he had a greater depth of insight about Jesus than most of those in the crowd. He recognized that Jesus was the "Son of David." This is more than just a genealogical reference to Jesus being from the tribe of Judah. He was acknowledging that Jesus was the Messiah. With 20/20 spiritual insight, Blind Bart shouted out, "Jesus, you are the Messiah!"

His second phrase captured the essence of what he wanted from his Messiah. "Have mercy on me!" It's almost certain that the word he shouted came from the Hebrew word *hesed*, a word that means "unmerited favor" or "loyal love." He was asking Jesus to extend His gracious help to someone who possessed nothing of value to justify it. Such mercy is based on the inherent goodness of the One giving the help, not the worthiness of the one receiving it.

The crowd rebuked Bart and told him to be quiet, but he cried out all the more. And that's when Jesus stopped and summoned him. "What do you want me to do for you?" Jesus asked. "My Rabbi . . . I want to see!" was his simple response. And Jesus then announced, "Go, for your faith has healed you" (Mark 10:51–52). Blind Bart was blind no more.

The Judean Wilderness in the spring

CHAPTER 22

The Judean Wilderness:
My Favorite Spot in All Israel!

Today, buses drive from Jericho to the Judean Wilderness on a modern highway. But years ago travelers had two options—both challenging. The first was the main road from the Dead Sea to Jerusalem. It was a two-lane road that wound its way through the hills and valleys of the wilderness. Long lines of cars and buses would creep up the road behind fully loaded trucks crawling along in low gear. The second road led from Herod's palace at New Testament Jericho to an overlook near Saint George's Monastery in the Wadi Qilt. This road was a narrow dirt affair, bulldozed into the hills along the edge of an increasingly steep canyon. Because the front wheels of the tour bus are positioned behind the driver, those sitting in the front felt as if the bus were driving over the edge of the cliff on every hairpin turn.

I loved traveling up this second road with the same driver I have used for over twenty-five years. He would wait until someone commented on how frightful the drive was for those afraid of heights. Then he would shout out, "If you are afraid, do what I do. Close your eyes!"

For many years the road was closed. Boulders were placed across it to block potential terrorists from trying to drive into Jerusalem. I missed the amazing views looking down into the canyon below, but I suspect those with a fear of heights were happy to travel on the modern highway instead. But whichever route you travel into the Judean Wilderness, the destination is worth it. The Judean Wilderness is my favorite place in Israel for several reasons. First, it hasn't really changed much over the centuries. Looking out at the desolate hills, one can imagine Abraham with his flocks, or the young shepherd David with his sheep, or Jesus being tempted by Satan to "tell these stones to become loaves of bread" (Matt. 4:3).

I also like the Judean Wilderness because it serves as a good visual illustration of the role the wilderness plays throughout the Bible. The wilderness was always a place of testing. But it was also the spot where God continually demonstrated that His grace was sufficient. Whether it was supplying manna to a hungry nation, or having David affirm "The LORD is my shepherd; I have all that I need" (Ps. 23:1), God showed His great power during those experiences in the wilderness.

HIKING THROUGH THE WILDERNESS

A third reason I like the Judean Wilderness is because on my very first trip to Israel I got to walk through it between Jerusalem and Jericho. We drove from Jerusalem to a spring called Ein Fawwar before beginning our eight-hour hike. The day divided into three segments: (a) walking along the valley floor, (b) walking on the lip of an aqueduct carrying water to Jericho, and (c) walking on a trail hundreds of feet above the canyon floor. It was a blistering hot day, and before we were halfway through the hike I had emptied both of my canteens. And then I got the Israeli version of Montezuma's revenge . . . in the middle of nowhere. As gruesome as that might sound, it gave me a visceral appreciation for Moses, David, Jesus, and everyone else in the Bible who spent time in the wilderness.

Let me take you on a journey through the Judean Wilderness. And I promise you won't get Montezuma's revenge on this hike! Our journey actually begins in the book of Ecclesiastes.

THE TWISTING HILLS OF THE JUDEAN WILDERNESS

In Ecclesiastes, an older but wiser King Solomon wrote about life in all its stark, unvarnished reality. In one particularly profound observation he wrote,

"What is crooked cannot be straightened" (Eccl. 1:15 NASB). Whether it's an unbent paper clip or the crumpled fender of a car, something that has become twisted and changed can't be completely restored to its original shape. You can get close, but it's never quite the same.

What's true of paper clips is also true of life. The innocence of youth fades and the harsh reality of life seems to harden, burn, and scar those exposed to its unrelenting pressures. Poor choices shape destiny and direction. The chasms and valleys of anger, depression, disappointment, and loneliness carve their way into a person's soul, leaving him or her marked for life. Or so it seems.

Group hiking through the Judean Wilderness

That's how the people of Judah must have felt twenty-five centuries ago. Their rejection of God, their pursuit of pleasure, and their callous disregard for the needs of others left deep marks on the nation. Eventually those selfish, sinful choices cost them everything in life that mattered. The nation of Babylon invaded Judah; captured, looted, then destroyed Jerusalem; and killed or carried into exile the people of the land.

Only when it was too late did the people see the awful consequences of their actions. Pain, anguish, suffering, loneliness, depression, and hopelessness cut into their very souls. They felt trapped with no hope of escape—their lives as scarred as the twisting valleys cutting through the Judean Wilderness.

And yet, God's very answer to Judah's feelings of discouragement lay just beyond the summit of the Mount of Olives in those same barren hills. This harsh land—marked by deep serpentine valleys, jagged cliffs, and high hills laced with knife-edged flint—held God's message of hope for His people in their time of desperate need.

> **This harsh land held God's message of hope for His people in their time of desperate need.**

Imagine the impact the words of Isaiah 40:4 had on those who were living in depression, seeing no hope. "Let every valley be lifted up, and every mountain and hill be made low; and let the uneven ground become a plain, and the rugged terrain a broad valley" (NASB).

"Let every valley be lifted up, and every mountain and hill be made low." (Isa. 40:4 NASB)

The God of impossibilities was about to use the Judean Wilderness as an object lesson for the people of Judah.

Isaiah pictured a day when God would turn desolation into delight . . . heartache into happiness . . . pain into pleasure. What seemed to be permanent was only temporary to an all-powerful God. Isaiah wasn't just speaking about these physical hills and valleys. The God who can reverse the ravages of nature is the God who can also heal the emotional scars in a human heart.

Isaiah boldly announced that when God comes to rescue His people, nothing can stand in His way. What appears to be an obstacle to us is not a problem for Him. God specializes in filling in *every* valley and tearing down *every* mountain, including those that seem so powerful or permanent we can't even begin to imagine how they can be overcome.

The prophet looked beyond Judah's temporary trouble and saw God's ultimate triumph. "Then the glory of the LORD will be revealed, and all people will see it together. The LORD has spoken" (Isa. 40:5). God had not abandoned His people. His coming deliverance was certain because God Himself was the one making the promise.

THE SHEPHERDESS AND PSALM 23

As I said earlier, one of my greatest adventures in Israel was an all-day hike through the Judean Wilderness. About an hour into that trip we rounded a bend in the gorge and came across a shepherdess tending a small flock of goats. She had positioned herself so she could keep a watchful eye on her flock as it grazed its way through the valley.

That young shepherdess reminded me of David watching over his flock in the same region three thousand years ago. Before his rise to prominence as Israel's king, before his victory over Goliath, before his appearance in King Saul's court as a musician . . . before all that, David's job was to watch over his father's flock in the Judean Wilderness. It was *here* that he became skillful in using a sling, and it was probably here where he honed his musical skills and composed songs that later found their way into the book of Psalms.

A shepherdess with her flock in the wilderness

We're not sure when David penned Psalm 23, but the first four verses come from his experience as a shepherd. You can almost hear the bleating of the flock in the background as David takes us into the rugged Judean Wilderness to share the lessons he learned about God during his time of solitude there.

"The LORD is my shepherd; I have all that I need" (Ps. 23:1). The word for shepherd comes from a root that means "to look upon" or "to watch over." A shepherd "watched over" the flock under his care. David began by affirming that God was the Shepherd watching over him. And with God as shepherd, the flock will have everything it needs to thrive.

I remember being confused when I memorized Psalm 23 as a child. "The LORD is my Shepherd; I shall not want." But why wouldn't I *want* God to be my shepherd, I thought. Later I learned that the word "want" in the King James Version of the Bible really meant "to be in need." The shepherd's role was to make sure the flock had sufficient grass and water. Since *God* is the One watching over me, I can trust Him to meet my needs.

David illustrated his statement with two word pictures that look back to his time watching over the flock. How does a shepherd provide for his sheep? First, "He lets me rest in green meadows" (Ps. 23:2), picturing the new grass that sprouts when the winter rains arrive. It's succulent, moisture-rich, and tender . . . the most beneficial food for the flock.

His second word picture comes from the springs of water that dot the wilderness. "He leads me beside peaceful streams" (Ps. 23:2). Such springs and streams aren't numerous in the wilderness, but the wise shepherd knew their location. We think of these as pools with little movement of the water, but that's not exactly what David says. It's not "peaceful streams" but "waters of rest." He's picturing waters that are calming and restful, where the flock can drink in quiet safety, unafraid of any wild animals that might be lurking nearby.

So what happens when the good shepherd leads his flock to hillsides covered in sprouts of tender grass and to restful springs of water? "He renews my strength" (Ps. 23:3). The flock is *nourished* and *refreshed*. The hungry are satisfied; and the thirsty revived.

David then adds, "He guides me along right paths, bringing honor to his name" (Ps. 23:3). God's ways are good, because God

A spring gushing from the rock in the wilderness

Himself is good. Though we might not understand all that happens in our lives, we can be confident that the specific path on which He takes us is the right one because it's God's name—that is, His reputation—that's at stake.

The good shepherd nourishes and sustains the flock under his care. But his role involves more than just providing for the *physical* needs of the flock. He's also expected to guard the flock from danger. "Even when I walk through the darkest valley, I will not be afraid, for you are close beside me" (Ps. 23:4). But what is the "darkest valley"?

There are two words in Hebrew to describe valleys—one pictures a broad, wide valley, the other, a steep, narrow valley. David here uses the word for a narrow valley, which perfectly describes the deep gorges that cut through the Judean Wilderness. The word for "darkest" occurs seventeen times in the Old Testament. Jeremiah used it to picture the Sinai desert as a land of "deep darkness" (Jer. 2:6 NASB), while in the book of Job it was used nine times to characterize the place of the dead.

David used the word to picture life's dangers. As night fell, dark shadows crept into the deep valleys of the Judean Wilderness. The darkness hid a multitude of dangers from the unwary flock. Wild animals left their dens to prowl for unsuspecting prey. Death itself seemed to lurk in the shadows. But when the flock was under the care of the Good Shepherd, it needn't be afraid. "Your rod and your staff protect and comfort me" (Ps. 23:4). The shepherd was standing guard with his club and his sturdy staff. These were the weapons he had ready in his hands to beat off any animal threatening the flock. His presence, and promised protection, provided "comfort" in what otherwise could be a time of anxiousness and concern.

SO WHAT IS A WADI?

During my hike through the Judean Wilderness we first walked along the valley floor, skirting huge boulders pushed into place by past floods. This part of the hike ended at a pool of chest-deep water flowing right out of the rock in an otherwise barren desert. It reminded me of the words of Isaiah 32:2 where God compared the Messiah's arrival to "streams of water in the desert."

That was my first opportunity to see a wadi "up close and personal." But you might be wondering to yourself, "What's a wadi?" Let's face it, that's not a word we use too often. A wadi is a seasonally dry riverbed. That is, it's a canyon that can fill with water during the rainy season but that turns dry for the rest of the year.

Several years later I visited Israel during an unusually rainy winter. We didn't walk the wadi on that occasion, but we did look down into the previously dry canyon to see a steady stream of flowing water. Those visiting for the first time might have thought it was a normal stream or river that flowed year-round, but I knew better. A few months later, that streambed would again be bone dry.

And that's why in the Bible wadis are metaphors for something undependable. In the winter, especially when the rains are plentiful, a wadi can give the appearance of an ever-flowing stream. But if you pass that way again in the hot, dry summer months, hoping to fill your water jugs at that so-called stream, forget it!

When Job was under satanic attack he searched for answers as to why he was suffering. His three friends came by to offer comfort, but they were about as helpful as a dry wadi in the middle of a blistering heat wave. In utter exasperation Job finally shouted to them, "My brothers, you have proved as unreliable as a seasonal brook that overflows its banks in the spring when it is swollen with ice and melting snow. But when the hot weather arrives, the water disappears. The brook vanishes in the heat" (Job 6:15–17).

A wadi is an unreliable stream that offers great promise when times are good . . . but that vanishes at the very time it's needed most. During Job's times of prosperity and success his friends always seemed to be around for the party. But when the wheels came off the wagon, these so-called men of wisdom turned out to be a bunch of wise guys who did little more than pour the salt of false accusations into Job's very open, painful wounds. When the going got tough for Job, these friends decided it was time to abandon their needy friend and join forces against him.

The prophet Jeremiah also had doubts about God's dependability. At one critical point in his life Jeremiah experienced a crisis of faith. He was so discouraged he cried out, "Why then does my suffering continue? Why is my wound so incurable? Your help seems as uncertain as a seasonal brook, like a spring that has gone dry" (Jer. 15:18). God, can I even trust You—or are You nothing more than a wadi that will let me down?

Thankfully, God came to Jeremiah in those dark days and showed how dependable He really was. Jeremiah's problems didn't vanish, but he discovered that God's grace was sufficient to meet his deepest needs. Just a few chapters later Jeremiah recorded the answer to his own question. He wrote, "O LORD, the hope of Israel, all who turn away from you will be disgraced. They will be buried in the dust of the earth, for they have abandoned the LORD, the fountain of living water" (Jer. 17:13). God is indeed the "fountain of living water," the absolutely dependable hope for all seeking help in times of trouble.

PREPARE FOR THE PEDDLERS

For many tourists, the Judean Wilderness is the spot where they first encounter peddlers. Once they reach Jerusalem they will be inundated with street vendors selling everything from *keffiyehs* (Arab head scarfs) to jewelry and "camel leather" belts. But that first encounter with these persistent salesmen can be unnerving, so as we drive up to our overlook I try to prepare the travelers with some tips that I call "bargaining baseball."

If a tourist makes eye contact, the peddler is on first base. This is hard for Americans because we're taught to look someone right in the eye. But if you're not interested in shopping, do everything possible not to make eye contact. Glance at the peddler's arm, or shoulder, but *don't* make direct eye contact.

If the peddler can get the merchandise into the tourist's hand, he has now reached second base. Most people on the bus are thinking, "That's easy! I just won't pick anything up." But these peddlers are *good*. With a flick of the wrist, the unsuspecting tourist is now wearing a *keffiyeh* or is sporting a "genuine silver" bracelet on his or her arm. The best defense is to look the peddler squarely in the shoulder and pull your arms back to your side while saying, "No, thank you!"

If the peddler can get the tourist bargaining, he has then reached third base. Some tourists foolishly think they can short-circuit the process by making a ridiculously low offer. "How much will you give for the *keffiyeh*?" "How about a dollar!" What they don't realize is that they have now started bargaining. And these peddlers are *masters* at bargaining.

Finally, if the peddler can get the tourist to agree to a price that the peddler is also willing to accept, then the expectation is that the tourist has agreed to purchase the item. The peddler has just crossed home plate.

That lengthy explanation reminds me of a trip I led that included the chaplain of Dallas Seminary. Chaplain Bill was a dear friend who is now in heaven. I had no sooner finished explaining bargaining baseball when the bus pulled up to the site. Bill bounded off, looked a peddler straight in the eye, and said, "How much for the sheepskin?" (This perfectly round "sheepskin" had obviously come from a polyester sheep!) The bargaining went something like this:

Bill: "Ten dollars?"

Peddler: [Stunned silence]

Bill: "Fifteen dollars!"

Peddler: [Stunned silence]

Bill: "Twenty dollars!"

Peddler: [Stunned silence]

Bill: "Twenty-five dollars!"

At that point, the peddler simply handed the "sheepskin" to Bill who began fishing in his wallet for the cash. For the rest of the trip, we hounded Bill about his bargaining skill in buying a genuine polyester "cheap skin."

Cave 4 at Qumran

CHAPTER 23

Qumran:

Discovering the Dead Sea Scrolls

If the Dead Sea Scrolls had not been discovered, no one would visit the ruins at Qumran. The archaeological remains at the site aren't really impressive. The most significant photo someone can take at the site is of Cave 4 where a number of manuscripts and fragments were discovered. The real significance of Qumran was in the thousands of scrolls and fragments found in twelve caves along the hills around the site. It's because of those discoveries that Qumran is on the must-see itinerary of most trips.

Some tour groups drive from Galilee down to the southern end of the Dead Sea to spend a night or two at one of the spa hotels located there. These groups stop off at Qumran on the way down or back. Other groups visit Qumran as part of a very long touring day from Jerusalem. Qumran is normally the last stop of the day, following visits to Masada, the Dead Sea, and En Gedi. It's the final bathroom break before the hour-long drive back to the hotel in Jerusalem.

I like having my groups spend two nights at the Dead Sea, but on many of my earlier trips our Dead Sea excursion began and ended in Jerusalem. On one particular trip in June, the weather was brutally hot. By the time we had visited Masada and En Gedi, and stopped off for a brief "float" in the Dead Sea, the group was hot, tired, and ready to head back to Jerusalem for a relaxing shower before dinner. As the bus approached Qumran, our Israeli guide sensed the group was wiped out physically and decided to make an executive decision. "It is late, and I know you are tired, so we will skip Qumran and continue on to our hotel in Jerusalem."

Most were in agreement, but *not* all. We had a seminary professor on the trip who had done his doctoral dissertation on the Essenes, the group who had inhabited Qumran and produced the Dead Sea Scrolls. I'm not sure where he found the energy, but that professor ran up the aisle of the bus. "We have to stop at Qumran!"

At his insistence our guide gave in, and the bus drove up the hill to the entrance. The guide led the weary group out onto the site until we were facing Cave 4. He decided to compress the story and give our group the *Reader's Digest* version. What happened next went something like this:

Guide: "Imagine a young shepherd boy throwing a rock into that cave and hearing a jar break."

Professor: "Er, this is Cave 4. That happened in Cave 1."

That's when the guide made a serious tactical error. "Well, perhaps you would like to share the story."

Today, there are canopies for shade over the viewing area for Cave 4, but back then there was no shade. As the sun beat down from above, our group was treated to a full lecture on the Essenes, the Dead Sea Scrolls, and Josephus.

JEREMIAH AND THE CRACKED MIKVEH

Today, the time I spend with our group looking over at Cave 4 is much shorter. My *brief* overview of Qumran is followed by this announcement: "Those who wish to stay out here to look around and take pictures are welcome to do so. The rest can follow me back into the air-conditioned building where there are restrooms, a cafeteria offering cold beverages and ice cream, and a gift shop." Almost everyone follows me back into the air-conditioning.

But we do need to make one brief stop along the way. And this stop will require us to use a little imagination. By now everyone on the trip understands the importance of water in this land. Unlike the civilizations that grew up along the Nile, Tigris, or Euphrates rivers, the people of Israel looked to the heavens for their water. In Deuteronomy 11:11 Moses described the promised land as "a land of hills and valleys [that] drinks water from the rain from heaven" (NASB). It's little wonder that water became a metaphor for life in the Bible. It was essential for life, but its availability was as unpredictable as the rain.

So how did someone in ancient Israel access the water that fell from heaven? (Hint: they didn't "turn on a faucet.") Most people living in Israel during Bible times had three basic water sources from which to choose.

The most dependable sources of water were the streams and springs. The water from these sources was cool, pure, and absolutely refreshing. And it was reliable. It came from the rain that fell on the land and filtered through the rock until it reached an impervious layer. Then it collected and traveled along the contours of the rock until it broke to the surface in a spring.

We've already visited a number of springs and streams on this journey. Some, like those at Dan and Caesarea Philippi, were quite large. Others, like the spring of Harod where Gideon chose his three hundred men, or the springs that appear in the Judean Wilderness, aren't as large or powerful. But they are almost as dramatic because they provided life-giving water in the most unexpected of places. Springs flow in both winter and summer. They're found at the foot of Mount Hermon, and in the wilderness to the south where they become vivid illustrations of the "streams" that will "water the waste-land" described in Isaiah 35:6.

Unfortunately, the number of springs and streams in Israel is relatively small. Most Israelites weren't fortunate enough to have such a dependable supply of water. So their second option was to dig a well to reach the water table. Well water was also cool and refreshing. But a sustained drought, or an earthquake, could change the water table, and a well could run dry.

Both Abraham and Isaac dug wells in the Negev. The town of Beer-sheba—which we'll soon visit—literally means "well of the seven," a reference in Genesis 21 to the seven ewe lambs Abraham paid to buy the well he had already dug. The well Jacob dug at Shechem was still in use 1,800 years later when Jesus met there with the Samaritan woman in John 4. In fact, that well is *still* around today, nearly 3,800 years after it was first dug. *That's* a dependable supply of water.

But to reach the water table throughout most of the hill country in Israel requires someone to dig through hundreds of feet of solid rock. And what's possible today with modern drilling equipment was beyond the ability of those in the past who had nothing more than a hammer, an iron chisel, and the strength of their own bare hands to do all the work. Cool, refreshing well water was not an option for most.

What about the rest of the people? Where did most people get their water?

Those who didn't live near a spring or well had to dig their own underground storage facilities—they carved out cisterns to trap and hold rainwater. A cistern is essentially a hole dug into the rock and then lined with plaster to enable it to retain water. This was the most common source of water for the people of Israel, but it was also the most *unreliable* source. If the winter rains weren't sufficient to fill the cistern, or if the cistern developed a crack in the plaster, the rainwater gathered during the winter could run out before the hot summer was over.

Cistern water was not only undependable; it was also the most polluted. The cistern was dug at a low spot in the ground so all the water would run toward the pit. But imagine the first rain after a hot, dry summer. The ground is covered in dust . . . and a few other surprises left by the occasional goat or bird that wandered through. As the hard, driving rain hits with a vengeance, torrents of water rush across the ground toward the entrance of the cistern, carrying everything else on the ground into the pit along with the water.

When Jeremiah was placed in a cistern in Jerusalem he sank into mud (Jer. 38:6). Every so often a homeowner would need to dig the muck out of his cistern to keep it from filling up. Cistern water was the least satisfying and most unreliable source of water, but it was also the most common.

And that brings us back to our final stop here at Qumran—the place where you need to use your imagination! This hole in front of us is a *mikveh*

The mikveh at Qumran with a crack in the plaster

used by the Essenes for ritual purity. You can still see remains of the plaster on the walls. And if you look carefully, you can even see a large crack in the plaster that was likely caused by an earthquake.

Imagine being in Qumran when that quake hit. After the shaking stopped, you walked by this covered *mikveh* only to hear the *glug, glug, glug* of water draining out of a newly formed crack in the plaster. For a time the entire site had to be abandoned because of the loss of water. Now pretend this *mikveh* is your cistern, and that you are living in the time of Jeremiah. Your very life depends on the water stored in this cistern—water that is leaking out of that large crack in the plaster. You're *now* ready to listen to Jeremiah's message.

The prophet stood before the people of Judah and proclaimed in Jeremiah 2:12–13, "'The heavens are shocked at such a thing and shrink back in horror and dismay,' says the LORD. 'For my people have done two evil things: They have abandoned me—the fountain of living water. And they have dug for themselves cracked cisterns that can hold no water at all!'"

God or idols. The choice is clear . . . and dramatic. God is the spring of living water. He's ever dependable, ever satisfying. To turn away from God and trust instead in idols is like walking away from a cool stream to depend instead on a cistern to meet your need. And not just any cistern, but one that is cracked and broken—a cistern that will prove to be unreliable to anyone foolish enough to trust in it. To turn from God and place your trust in anything else is utter insanity.

Now it's time for us to head into the air-conditioning to get something cold to drink. But as we do, imagine that cold drink you will soon be holding came from a crystal clear stream. Then imagine a glass next to it filled with brackish water from a cracked cistern—a cistern whose water level is already starting to drop. Given a choice, which source of water would *you* choose?

A close-up of the crack in the mikveh

Ibex at En Gedi

CHAPTER 24

En Gedi:

David's Encounter with Saul

Irst impressions can be deceiving. The highway through En Gedi winds along a torturous detour to avoid sinkholes dotting the landscape, and near the park entrance are the remains of a dead date palm grove. En Gedi doesn't come close to matching the description of her lover given by the bride-to-be in the Song of Solomon. "He is like a bouquet of sweet henna blossoms from the vineyards of En-gedi" (Song 1:14). The henna and grapes are nowhere to be seen.

But visitors need to look beyond these first impressions to discover the real beauty and significance of the site. The sinkholes are actually quite recent. A prolonged drought, coupled with the pumping of water for agriculture from the Sea of Galilee and Jordan River, has greatly reduced the amount of water flowing into the Dead Sea. In fact, the Dead Sea has been dropping nearly three feet every year for several decades. The retreating shoreline has left behind layers of salt, and the water that flows down off the hills into the Dead Sea during winter storms has dissolved these underground layers, causing thousands of sinkholes to form.

We have two stops to make at En Gedi. The first is at a Field School located on the bluff just above the entrance. Thankfully, the bus will drive us up. During our two stops we'll examine three snapshots from the Bible—three portraits of individuals whose willingness to follow God took them into the wilderness of En Gedi.

The Field School is a great place to view En Gedi. The deep ravine below is the Nahal David. It's one of two deep canyons that bracket the oasis of En Gedi. Midway up the canyon, where the two sides seem to join, is a patch of green with a tiny, vertical ribbon of white. That's the waterfall of En Gedi.

If you listen closely, you can hear the laughter and shouting from busloads of Israeli schoolchildren hiking up to the falls. It's a wonderful hike, and we'll journey that way shortly to focus on David's encounter with Saul. But we came to the Field School first because of all the schoolkids. They're actually helping chase all the ibex, the wild goats, out of the canyon up to where we are gathered. The name En Gedi means "spring of the wild goats," and this overlook at the Field School is one of the best places to catch a glimpse of these amazing animals.

View up the Nahal David toward the waterfall

If you look closely at the cliff face on the other side of the canyon, you might be able to spot a narrow pathway clinging to the side of the hill. That trail leads from the waterfall up to the top of the cliff. Every so often you will see a few people climbing up the path. And when you do, you'll appreciate how long and hard that climb is. It could take someone in good physical shape the better part of a morning to work their way back and forth up that trail to reach the top of the cliffs. That's a *serious* climb!

Now turn just to the left and look south along the Dead Sea. From this perch you can just make out the outline of Masada on the horizon, eleven miles away. The ground between En Gedi and Masada is extremely rough and rocky. Imagine walking for hours through that rough ground, under a brutally hot sun, with no place along the way to stop for a drink of water. It's easy to see the wilderness isn't a place for wimps! And it's also easy to see why En Gedi was so special—an oasis of water and trees in an otherwise barren region.

Now it's time to look at our three snapshots from En Gedi.

RUTH AND NAOMI

Standing at this overlook is a good place to review the story of Ruth. Most people know the basics of the story. Ruth was a Moabite who married one of Naomi's two sons when Naomi and her family fled to Moab during a time of famine. Sadly, Naomi's husband and her two sons died, leaving Naomi, Ruth, and Orpah as three grieving widows. Eventually, Naomi decided to return home to Bethlehem. Ruth and Orpah planned to follow her as obedient daughters-in-law, but Naomi released them from any remaining obligation. "Why should you go on with me?" (Ruth 1:11). Naomi had no other sons. There was nothing positive she could offer to them.

Orpah did turn back, giving Naomi a parting kiss, but Ruth refused to leave. Naomi again tried to talk Ruth into returning to her family, but Ruth responded with a powerful statement of commitment. "Wherever you go, I will go; wherever you live, I will live. Your people will be my people, and your God will be my God. Wherever you die, I will die, and there I will be buried. May the LORD punish me severely if I allow anything but death to separate us!" (Ruth 1:16–17). Those are beautiful words, and standing here at the Field School helps us gain even greater appreciation for what those words really meant.

How did Ruth and Naomi get from Moab to Bethlehem? They started on the east side of the Dead Sea, just to the east of Masada. Working their way down from the hills of Moab, they came to the Lisan, the tongue of land that sticks out into the Dead Sea from the east. If the water level of the Dead Sea was low, they could walk across to the western side on dry ground. But if the water level was higher, they would cross the Lisan and then float the remaining mile or so to the other side. After crossing, they had to walk the eleven miles from Masada up to En Gedi. The only drinking water available to them that entire time was the water they carried from Moab. And then came the hard part of the trip!

Take another look at those schoolkids down below and picture Naomi and Ruth walking along that same path. They would have stayed near the springs of water for as long as possible. But eventually they needed to begin the climb up the side of the cliff. Picture them clawing their way up that tiny pathway in the distance. How long would it have taken these two women to climb all the way to the top? Half a day? A whole day? But they're still not home. They now have an additional day's journey through the Judean Wilderness until they finally reach Bethlehem.

Most of us like to jump to the end of the story and skip over all the unpleasant parts. Ruth meets Boaz. They fall in love, get married, and have a child . . . who becomes the grandfather of King David. But when we do, we miss the toil, and sweat, and heat, and exhaustion, and pain that were the soil in which the seeds of Ruth's faithfulness were planted.

> Ruth's commitment to Naomi was a sacrificial promise that very quickly brought Ruth sore feet, aching knees, and parched lips.

Ruth's commitment to Naomi, which is matched by Boaz's later commitment to Ruth, isn't some glamorous, romantic, larger-than-life scene from a Hollywood movie. It was a sacrificial promise that very quickly brought Ruth sore feet, aching knees, and parched lips. She backed her promise with sweat, and thirst, and hard work. She had no idea how the story would end. When she made her pledge, all she could look forward to were years of hard work gleaning in the fields of strangers to support an aging mother-in-law, discrimination from a society that saw her as a foreigner, and eventually growing old alone. The mountain looming up in front of us was likely one of the first reminders of what her life would be like.

The book of Ruth begins with "in the days when the judges ruled" (Ruth 1:1) and ends with the birth of David. It takes the reader from a period of spiritual darkness to one of spiritual blessing . . . from a time of trouble to a time of hope. And in one sense that entire transition turned on the decisions of two people—Ruth and Boaz—who chose to walk a different path, a path that was more difficult and that required personal sacrifice. But it was also a path that put them in a place where God could use them to change the destiny of an entire nation.

We live in a day, much like the time of the judges, when everyone does what's right in their own eyes. Sadly, the world is paying the economic, moral, and spiritual consequences of those poor choices. But God is still looking for men and women willing to put the needs of others ahead of themselves.

From that snapshot of Ruth, we turn to view a photograph of Ruth's great-great-great-great-great-great-great-grandchild—King Jehoshaphat.

JEHOSHAPHAT AND THE SURPRISE ATTACK

This overlook is a wonderful spot to explore an otherwise obscure event in 2 Chronicles 20 from the life of King Jehoshaphat. He was ruling over the kingdom of Judah when men came running into Jerusalem from the wilderness with shocking news. "'A vast army from Edom is marching against you from beyond the Dead Sea. They are already at Hazazon-tamar.' (This was another name for En-gedi.)" (2 Chron. 20:2). The Edomites joined forces with the Moabites and Ammonites to launch a surprise attack against Judah. They had already crossed the tongue of land near the southern end of the Dead Sea and were organizing their combined armies at En Gedi—less than a two-day march from Jerusalem.

The king and people were in shock. They had little time to prepare any defenses. Trembling in fear, they cried out to God for help. "We are powerless against this mighty army that is about to attack us. We do not know what to do, but we are looking to you for help" (2 Chron. 20:12).

If you have ever faced problems that seemed absolutely overwhelming, you know how Jehoshaphat and the people of Jerusalem felt as they cried in desperation to God. At their moment of greatest need, God answered. His

Spirit came on Jahaziel, one of the men charged with leading singing in the temple. Jahaziel's words from God were simple and direct. "Do not be afraid! Don't be discouraged by this mighty army, for the battle is not yours, but God's. Tomorrow, march out against them . . . But you will not even need to fight. Take your positions; then stand still and watch the LORD's victory" (2 Chron. 20:15–17). The king and people bowed before the Lord with their faces to the ground in worship to thank God for His promised deliverance.

The next day, the army of Judah began its march from Jerusalem into the wilderness. And the order of the march was unlike any battle formation in history. Leading the army were singers appointed by Jehoshaphat "singing to the LORD and praising him for his holy splendor." Their words became the cadence by which the entire army marched. "Give thanks to the LORD; his faithful love endures forever!" (v. 21).

How did this amazing march to battle end? God had the coalition of invading armies turn on one another. By the time Jehoshaphat and his army reached the spot where they expected to encounter the enemy, the invaders were already vanquished. The Bible says it this way: "So when the army of Judah arrived at the lookout point in the wilderness, all they saw were dead bodies lying on the ground as far as they could see. Not a single one of the enemy had escaped" (v. 24).

Three days later, the people of Judah assembled in a valley along the route they had just traveled to praise God for His victory. They actually renamed that valley the Valley of Beracah, which means the "Valley of Blessing." There they gathered to praise God for His deliverance. But the compiler of Chronicles shares an important lesson on praise and thanksgiving that still rings true 2,800 years later. Before Judah thanked God for what He had done, they were first told to thank God for who He is. "Give thanks to the LORD; his faithful love endures forever" (2 Chron. 20:21). We can trust God to do great and wonderful things because He is a great and wonderful God.

Before examining our third portrait, we need to drive down to the park entrance and hike up to the waterfall.

DAVID AND SAUL

While standing at the Field School, the hike up the Nahal David to the waterfall looks relatively easy. But down below the ruggedness of the valley becomes clearer. The first part is easy enough, but the pathway is soon obscured by large boulders that have broken loose from the cliff face through earthquakes and erosion. These boulders have then been pushed down the valley in torrential flooding from the wilderness above. Taking advantage of steps carved into the rock, along with metal handrails and the occasional wooden bridge, tourists are able to work their way up the canyon, though not without some difficulty.

Along the route up the canyon there are several natural pools and smaller waterfalls. And most are filled with Israeli schoolchildren laughing and splashing in the water. But as inviting as those pools are, we keep pressing on toward the top of the trail—the spot where the two sides of the canyon seem to join together.

When we finally reach the top of the trail, the canyon seems to end in a rock wall with a ribbon of water cascading down. The waterfall pales in

One of the many pools and waterfalls in the oasis of En Gedi

223

comparison to Niagara Falls or Yosemite Falls, but out here in the wilderness this stream provides welcome relief from the desert heat. As the spray and mist evaporate, they cool the surrounding air—God's original air conditioning. The pool is only ankle deep, but the cool water feels good on hot, tired feet. For thousands of years, travelers journeying through En Gedi on their way through the wilderness must have thought the same thing as they took advantage of this amazing oasis.

And that's why King Saul thought he could finally capture young David right here.

As Saul returned from one of his frequent skirmishes with the Philistines, he received a welcome bit of good news. "David had gone into the wilderness of En-gedi" (1 Sam. 24:1). Saul knew David would have to be camped near the water, and he hoped that finding and trapping David in such a narrow canyon wouldn't be too difficult. "So Saul chose 3,000 elite troops from all Israel and went to search for David and his men near the rocks of the wild goats" (v. 2).

Why was Saul so obsessed with David? It was because David, even as a young man, was everything Saul could never be. David had courage. He boldly fought Goliath while Saul was as "terrified and deeply shaken" as everyone else (1 Sam. 17:11). David trusted in the Lord while Saul could never rise to that level of faith. David demonstrated faithfulness to Saul, but Saul was treacherous in his dealings with David. And all that made David a threat, at least in Saul's eyes. It was Howard Hendricks who wisely said, "Once the saying went out, 'Saul has slain his thousands, and David his tens of thousands,' David had his first critic."[1]

Handling critics isn't the same as handling criticism. Criticism can be constructive. But the goal of a critic is to destroy an individual, not to help him or her get better. And in 1 Samuel 24, David presents an excellent model on how to handle critics. When Saul accidentally entered the cave where David and his men were hiding, David's followers thought the ideal time to settle scores had come. "Today the LORD is telling you, 'I will certainly put your enemy into your power, to do with as you wish'" (1 Sam. 24:4). But David refused to retaliate. "The LORD forbid that I should do this to my lord the king. I shouldn't attack the LORD's anointed one" (v. 6).

Rather than taking matters into his own hands, David gave the situation over to the Lord. After revealing himself to Saul, David said to this one who was unjustly seeking his life, "May the LORD judge between us. Perhaps the LORD will punish you for what you are trying to do to me, but I will never harm you" (1 Sam. 24:12). David recognized God's sov-

The largest of the waterfalls at En Gedi

ereign control over the situation. God was in charge, so David didn't need to take matters into his own hands.

But there's at least one final nugget of truth in this passage when it comes to handling critics. Be wise, not stupid! When dealing with critics, don't retaliate, and recognize that God is in control. But at the same time, be wise enough to know that critics seldom change—so don't let down your guard. This truth shows up in the very last verse of 1 Samuel 24, though you really need to be standing at En Gedi to appreciate it. "So David promised this to Saul with an oath. Then Saul went home, but David and his men went back to their stronghold" (v. 22). David agreed not to kill Saul's family, and Saul agreed not to pursue David. David had every intention of keeping his part of the agreement, but he also recognized Saul was very *unlikely* to do the same.

As Saul led his soldiers home, first through the wilderness to the west and then north toward his capital of Gibeah, David led his men south along the shore of the Dead Sea toward the "stronghold." That word in Hebrew is *met-sudah*—Masada! David went eleven miles to the south and climbed a barren mesa known even in his day as the "stronghold" to watch and make sure Saul and his men didn't try to double back and catch him unawares.

A SUCCESSFUL VISIT TO EN GEDI

A successful visit to En Gedi is any visit that allows our pilgrims to see ibex. And most trips are successful. There's nothing like seeing these graceful animals climbing a nearly vertical cliff to cement in one's mind the meaning of En Gedi—Spring of the Wild Goats.

On one occasion, we had two buses of travelers together at the Field School. We hadn't yet seen any ibex, and I was just a little concerned. Our group settled in for a devotional time as my friend opened his Bible to talk about Saul's encounter with David. He was leaning against a large rock with his back to the building, while the group was standing along the railing or seated at picnic tables facing him.

Just after he began speaking, an ibex noiselessly appeared from the embankment to our right and began to walk across the lawn between the speaker and the building. And then another ibex appeared. And another. And another. An entire herd of ibex silently paraded across the lawn while my friend kept talking about the encounter between Saul and David at the Spring of the Wild Goats. I'm not sure how many people remember exactly what he said, but they got some incredible photos of those ibex.

Looking up at Masada from the east

CHAPTER 25

Masada:

Herod's Doomsday Fortress

To say Masada is impressive is an understatement. But one needs to get close to this rock mesa to really appreciate its massive size. Masada was the desert doomsday fortress built by Herod the Great. His seemingly impenetrable palace towered 1,200 feet above the Dead Sea with sheer cliffs on every side. And if the cliffs didn't offer enough protection, Herod ringed his citadel with walls and stored up weapons and water sufficient, he thought, to repel all attacks.

Masada was Herod's security blanket, his refuge of last resort should his greatest fears ever come to pass. And he had a lot to fear! Josephus, the ancient Jewish historian, described Herod's obsession with Masada this way. "Herod thus prepared this fortress on his own account, as a refuge against two kinds of danger: the one for fear of the multitude of the Jews, lest they should depose him and restore their former kings to the government; the other danger was greater and more terrible, which arose from Cleopatra, queen of Egypt, who did not conceal her intentions, but spoke often to Antony, an[d] desired him to cut off Herod, and entreated him to bestow the kingdom of Judea upon her."[1]

An uprising on the part of his subjects. Threats from Cleopatra, coupled with her influence in Rome. Herod must have slept lightly because he did indeed face grave dangers. Little wonder he was obsessed with making Masada the most secure palace in all the Middle East.

Herod put his trust in Masada. It became his hope for protection; his insurance policy for survival should he ever lose his grip on power. He didn't give the site its name, but in Hebrew the name Masada, *metsudah*, means "fortress" or "stronghold." And the name certainly matched his confidence in the location. It was the strongest, most defensible, most secure location in all the land.

APPROACHES TO MASADA

Josephus described two ways to reach the summit of Masada. A pathway from the west was the shortest and most direct route. On the east side, a much longer pathway led up from the bottom. Josephus referred to it as the snake path because of its continual winding back and forth as it snaked

its way up to the top. But today there's another approach to Masada, and it's the one taken by most travelers—a cable car that whisks visitors to the top in just three minutes!

Some tourists do struggle with the cable car because of a fear of heights. The best advice for those afraid of heights is to stand in the middle of the car with eyes closed. We

The modern cable car to the top of Masada with the snake path beneath

haven't yet lost a single passenger, though for a number of panicky pilgrims the three-minute ride seemed more like three hours.

The cable car doesn't actually travel all the way to the top of Masada. Visitors need to walk up a wood-and-metal bridge anchored into the mountain before actually reaching the summit. And for those afraid of heights: walk on the *inside* of the bridge and admire the rock face just to your right. The view of the Dead Sea and wilderness 1,200 feet below might not be to your liking. But once you reach the top, the sheer size of the mesa will take away any fear of heights.

LUXURY IN THE DESERT

Herod spared no expense to both fortify and beautify Masada. He had workmen carve out massive cisterns and then filled them with water that rushed down the desert canyons in the winter. In spite of the cliffs on all sides, Herod still ringed

Walking up the bridge from the cable car into Masada

the entire site with a wall. He built a Roman bathhouse complete with *frigidarium*, *tepidarium*, and *caldarium*. And he had storehouses constructed to hold vast quantities of both food and weapons.

Herod actually built two palaces on the site. One, on the southwest side, was for official visitors and guests. But Herod chose a more dramatic spot for his own palace, the stepped cliff face on the north side of the mesa. Here,

Herod had his architects construct a three-tiered palace that seems to hang off the side of the mountain. The view from this perch was magnificent, and the location was ideal to catch even the slightest breeze.

We have no written records of Herod visiting the

Remains of the storehouses on Masada

palace after it was constructed, but it's hard to imagine him not traveling to this desert retreat to admire the view, enjoy the luxurious accommodations, and revel in what he thought was the ultimate in personal security.

Sadly, Herod was tragically wrong.

The three-tiered northern palace at Masada

THE DOOMSDAY FORTRESS THAT FELL

Less than eighty years after Herod died, his doomsday fortress was put to the test. And its final Jewish defenders discovered that any stronghold built with human hands could eventually be overcome. Masada fell to the Roman army in AD 73 after a several-month siege, ending the first Jewish revolt against Rome. Masada was the last fortress in the land to fall to the Romans . . . but it *did* fall.

The Romans, with their military precision, set up camps all around the base of Masada. They constructed a siege wall around the entire site to keep anyone from escaping, and they placed guard posts at regular intervals. Then they began constructing a siege ramp on which they could hoist a battering ram to smash through the walls. Rome built the ramp using Jewish slave labor. And when everything was set, they brought their siege tower up the ramp.

The Jewish defenders knew where the Romans would attack and built an earth-and-wood wall behind Herod's stone wall. The Romans responded by shooting flaming arrows at the wood, setting it ablaze. The flames almost set the siege engine ablaze until the wind shifted, driving the flames against the wall, destroying it. It was late in the day, so the Romans returned to camp to prepare for their final assault the next day. But according to Josephus, that night the 960 defenders committed suicide. Men killed their own wives and children. Then ten were chosen by lot to kill all the men. Then those ten chose lots to determine the one who would kill the remaining nine. Finally, that last individual took his own life. But if everyone was dead, how do we know what happened? Josephus reports that two women and five children hid during the mass suicide. They reported to the Romans what took place that final night.[2]

Remains of the Roman siege ramp used to breach the walls of Masada

"MASADA" BEFORE MASADA

Herod made Masada into his doomsday fortress, while Rome's attack—and the mass suicide of its Jewish defenders—helped make the site famous. Yet Herod wasn't the first to notice the strategic advantage of Masada. As we learned in our time at En Gedi, David walked across the summit of this mesa a thousand years before Herod. And the name given to this rocky plateau—*metsudah*, the stronghold—preceded even David.

In 1 Samuel 22 we catch a glimpse of young David as a fugitive from King Saul. He's a man on the run, pursued by a jealous king bent on killing anyone he saw as a potential rival to the throne. After hiding in a cave at Adullam in Judah's western foothills, David and his band of followers went to Bethlehem to rescue his parents from potential harm and to carry them safely to Moab, on the eastern side of the Dead Sea. Why Moab? Perhaps because it was the home country of David's great-grandmother Ruth, the Moabitess. David hoped his family would be safe in the care of distant relatives and outside the clutches of King Saul.

As he crossed back over the Dead Sea, returning from Moab, David looked for a hideout in the Judean desert. He sought a place where he could be safe from attack, perhaps even a location with a remarkable view in all directions that would not allow Saul to sneak up on him undetected. So where did he go? First Samuel 22:4 says David went to the "stronghold." The mesa was already known as *metsudah*—Masada—even in David's day.

From a human perspective, Masada seemed like the perfect hideout. But it's not where God wanted David to stay. The prophet Gad received a message from God to tell David, "Leave the stronghold and return to the land of Judah" (1 Sam. 22:5). David obeyed God and climbed down from Masada. But just a few chapters later he was back.

David's encounter with Saul at En Gedi happened eleven miles to the north of Masada. After the encounter, Saul and his army went northwest toward Saul's capital at Gibeah. But as Saul turned and marched north, David and his men headed south—back to the "stronghold" (1 Sam. 24:22)—to make sure Saul didn't try to double back and catch them off guard. From the northern edge of Masada David would have had an excellent view all the way north to En Gedi.

At first glance we might not be surprised that both David and Herod discovered the strategic advantage of a location like Masada. Both men faced military threats during their lives, and both came to appreciate the importance of a strong defensive position. But that's where the similarities end.

Herod trusted in his military might . . . in fortresses like Masada. He didn't live long enough to learn that even this fortress would fail.

Unlike Herod, David trusted in God for protection. How do we know this? David wrote Psalm 18 to commemorate God's promised protection "on the day the Lord rescued him from all his enemies and from Saul." David begins with a summary statement of God's great protection. "The Lord is my rock, my fortress, and my savior; my God is my rock, in whom I find protection. He is my shield, the power that saves me, and my place of safety" (v. 2). And guess what word David uses for "fortress"? You're right. It's *metsudah*, Masada.

In Psalm 31 David makes a similar statement. He doesn't provide the specific background for the psalm, but it was evidently written during a time of great difficulty when even David's friends abandoned him. He pleaded with God to be a "rock of protection, a fortress where I will be safe" (v. 2). Then one verse later David declared with confidence, "You are my rock and my fortress." And the word he uses for "fortress" in both verses is *metsudah*. David didn't depend on a physical fortress when he faced times of trouble. His *metsudah*, his real fortress, was the living God.

Just like David and Herod, we also face times of trouble. And when those difficult times come, where do we ultimately turn for help? Herod looked at a mesa and saw a physical fortress that seemed safe, almost impregnable. But history ultimately proved him wrong. David spent time on the same mesa but came to a different conclusion. He ultimately found his protection not in *metsudah*, but in the Rock of Ages, the living fortress of God Almighty. And so can we!

THE SYNAGOGUE

One of the unexpected discoveries on Masada was a synagogue. It was *not* built by King Herod. Rather, the religious zealots who captured and held Masada converted one of the rooms in the outer wall into a synagogue. That historical tidbit is interesting, but it's the air-conditioned room in the back of the synagogue that I find most fascinating. On many days, visitors to the synagogue can peer through a window to see a modern scribe at work copying a Torah scroll. Watching him meticulously scratch out Hebrew letters on parchment, just as scribes have done throughout history, is worth watching. And the scribe will often write a visitor's name in Hebrew on a piece of paper. Just be sure to ask nicely!

Scribe copying a Torah scroll

Sunrise over the Dead Sea

CHAPTER 26

The Dead Sea:
You Can't Sink, But You Can Drown!

WHAT'S IN A NAME?

Two thousand years ago, the Roman historian Pliny the Elder described the Dead Sea in his book *Natural History*. But from what he wrote, it seems he was less than enamored by this unusual body of water. He called it Asphaltites, a name also used by the Jewish historian Josephus. Pliny said this was its name because it "produced nothing besides bitumen," which is a tarry substance that can still float to the surface on occasion. Pliny added that the lake had been "cursed by nature," and he called it the "Pestilential Lake."[1] Lake Pestilence! Somehow, I don't think Israel's Tourism Board will be hiring Pliny to write advertising copy for any brochures.

Pliny did add one other interesting detail. He said there was a report that nothing could sink in the lake. "No body of any creature doth it receive: Bulls and camels float upon it."[2] I've never seen a camel try to float in the Dead Sea, but I *can* say with confidence that it's impossible for any *person* to sink in the Dead Sea. They can drown, but they can't sink.

To Pliny and Josephus, this large body of water was Lake Asphaltites, though today we know it as the Dead Sea. Yet it surprises many pilgrims to learn it's *never* called the "Dead Sea" in the Hebrew Bible. Instead, in Hebrew it's referred to using four other names. Nine times in the Pentateuch and the book of Joshua it's called the "Salt Sea," emphasizing its dense mineral content. Five times it's called the "Sea of the Arabah," referring to its location in the Rift Valley. Three times it's called the "Eastern Sea," focusing on its location on the eastern boundary of the land of Israel. And on two occasions it's called simply "the Sea," though both passages also refer to it either as the Salt Sea or Eastern Sea within the same context.

Mark Twain also had mixed feelings about the Dead Sea. His initial description conjures up an image of desolation and barrenness similar to that of Pliny. "There is no pleasant thing or living creature upon it or about its borders to cheer the eyes. It is a scorching, arid, repulsive solitude. A silence broods over the scene that is depressing to the spirits. It makes one think of funerals and death."[3]

The desolation described by Twain is still present, but the place also has a stark beauty. I'm always fascinated by the salt-covered rocks along the shore, glistening white in the sun. Walking along the water's edge, it's hard to imagine we're actually at the lowest point of land on the surface of the earth . . . nearly 1,400 feet *below* sea level. For most of the year, the sea is bathwater warm, and the heavy concentration of salt gives it the silky texture of oil when rubbed in one's fingers.

Salt forming on rocks along the shore

But for all its beauty the Dead Sea is still devoid of life—at least for now.

BUY YOUR FISHING LICENSE!

Imagine the surprise of the Jewish captives in Babylon when the prophet Ezekiel tried to sell them fishing licenses for the Dead Sea. Well, he didn't actually try to *sell* them licenses, but he did describe a day when fishing would be a common occurrence along its shore.

Ezekiel was a captive in Babylon during the time when the nation of Judah fell to King Nebuchadnezzar. In the first twenty-four chapters of his book, Ezekiel wrote to his fellow exiles in captivity telling them that Jerusalem was going to be destroyed—something they felt could never happen. Once the final siege began, Ezekiel turned his prophetic voice away from Judah and announced God would also judge the surrounding nations. But beginning in chapter 33, just as the first captives from Jerusalem arrived in Babylon to announce the city's destruction, Ezekiel began predicting the restoration of the nation and city.

Ezekiel 33–48 describes the ultimate return of the people to the land. God promised to regather His people, enter into a new covenant relationship with them, forgive them of their sins, rebuild His temple, and dwell among His people forever. The message seemed almost impossible to believe for his audience. The nation had been destroyed. The people were in exile, the king had been ripped from the throne, and the temple was a pile of rubble. How could the nation ever live again? But Ezekiel went beyond simply predicting the return of Judah. He also announced that the northern kingdom of Israel, the other ten tribes who had gone into captivity almost 150 years before, would also return to the land and be reunited with Judah as a single kingdom—something that hadn't been true since the death of King Solomon, nearly 350 years earlier.

What do Ezekiel's amazing prophecies have to do with the Dead Sea or buying a fishing license? The answer is found in Ezekiel 47.

Having announced God's miraculous physical and spiritual regathering of His people, Ezekiel said the Dead Sea would serve as an object lesson of God's incredible promise. Along with the prophets Joel and Zechariah, Ezekiel said that when God restored His people to the land, living (or running) water would flow from the rebuilt temple. The stream would flow east "down into the Arabah," which is the Jordan Valley, and "into the sea" (Ezek. 47:8 NASB). The sea, of course, is the Dead Sea.

Ezekiel then predicted the amazing transformation that will take place.

When the water empties into the Dead Sea, the water there will become fresh.

"There will be swarms of living things wherever the water of this river flows. Fish will abound in the Dead Sea, for its waters will become fresh. Life will flourish wherever this water flows. Fishermen will stand along the shores of the Dead Sea. All the way from En-gedi to En-eglaim, the shores will be covered with nets drying in the sun. Fish of every kind will fill the Dead Sea, just as they fill the Mediterranean." (Ezek. 47:9–10)

Ezekiel announced that when God restores His people physically and spiritually to the land, even the Dead Sea will come alive!

> A great lesson to take away from the Dead Sea is the reality that God specializes in doing the impossible.

We recently visited En Gedi, one of the two specific locations mentioned by Ezekiel in this passage. But where is En-eglaim? The name means "the spring of two calves." This is the only time it's mentioned in the Bible, so we can't be absolutely sure of its location. But our best guess is that it refers to one of the springs at the northwestern edge of the Dead Sea, near Qumran. The distance between En Gedi and Qumran is twenty miles. Someday the best twenty miles of shoreline for fishing in all Israel will be along the northwestern shore of the Dead Sea.

A great lesson to take away from the Dead Sea is the reality that God specializes in doing the impossible. Israel has a future because God made a promise. And although there were times when that future seemed impossible, God's promise never wavered. Israel's presence in the land today is a prelude to what God has promised for the future. In that day, fishermen *will* crowd along the shore of a "dead" sea that will be teeming with fish. And the God who can transform Israel and the Dead Sea is the same God who can transform your life as you trust in Him.

FLOATING IN THE DEAD SEA

Mark Twain and his companions spent an hour floating in the Dead Sea. The guidebook they had brought with them warned against going into the Dead Sea. "All our reading had taught us to expect that the first plunge into the Dead Sea would be attended with distressing results—our bodies would feel as if they were suddenly pierced by millions of red-hot needles; the dreadful smarting would continue for hours; we might even look to be blistered from head to foot, and suffer miserably for several days." Twain debunked that description with one magnificently terse sentence. "We were disappointed"—referring to the book, not to his experience in the Dead Sea. He described his time in the water as a "funny bath."[4]

Going for a "swim" in the Dead Sea is still something every visitor should try at least once. The best way to enter the Dead Sea is simply to wade out until the water is mid-thigh deep. Then extend your arms out from your side, bend your knees, and pretend you are sitting down in a recliner. Your legs will pop out in front, and you will be floating! Two words of caution, though.

Floating in the Dead Sea

First, don't splash. You don't want to get any of the water in your mouth or eyes. Second, be careful when standing up. The water is so dense—and you're so buoyant—that it's actually possible to turn upside down—with your legs dangling in the air while your head is under the water. As I said before: you can't sink . . . but you *can* drown.

When we arrive at the Dead Sea, I explain one final time what to do—and not do—in the water. Don't wear any jewelry. Don't dive in. Don't splash. And if you get any water in your eyes, don't rub them. (Your wet hands will only rub in more salt.) Thankfully, the beaches along the Dead Sea today have freshwater showers near the shore, should someone need to rinse salt from their hands and eyes.

On one particular trip I had just finished giving that explanation when a busload of tourists pulled up to the public beach where we had stopped. One young man jumped off the bus and began running toward the water. With a shout of "Yahoo!" he plunged headfirst into the water. As he bobbed to the surface he suddenly realized his eyes were on fire, so he began rubbing them vigorously as he screamed to his fellow passengers for help. Someone mercifully waded into the water to lead him back to shore. It was the best object lesson for our group on what *not* to do.

SODOM AND GOMORRAH

The southern third of the Dead Sea should have evaporated years ago. The area is relatively shallow, and the only thing keeping it from drying up completely is the canal that brings in water from the northern two-thirds of the sea. The water is brought in for two reasons—tourism and minerals. A cluster of spa hotels at a place called Ein Bokek caters to tourists from around the world who come to the Dead Sea to float in its waters, bathe in sulphur pools, and relax in the hot sun.

A few miles south of Ein Bokek, a commercial operation extracts minerals like bromide, magnesium, and potash from the Dead Sea. The entire southern third of the Dead Sea is lined with evaporative ponds to extract these minerals. As the mineral-dense water collects in these ponds and evaporates under the sun, it leaves behind a thick, chemical slurry that is extracted, dried, and then shipped around the world.

Most tourists enjoy their time at Ein Bokek, but few realize the area where they have been floating was once the location of Sodom, Gomorrah, and the other cities of the plain described in the book of Genesis. In Genesis 14:3, Moses identified the kings of Sodom, Gomorrah, Admah, Zeboiim, and Zoar who "joined forces in Siddim Valley (that is, the valley of the Dead Sea)." Five cities dotted this region that is now covered by water.

Looking out over the sea, it's hard to imagine it was once a fertile and lush land. Perhaps that's why Moses added a descriptive note when he explained why Lot chose the region around the Dead Sea to live. "Lot took a long look at the fertile plains of the Jordan Valley in the direction of Zoar. The whole area was well watered everywhere, like the garden of the LORD or the beautiful land of Egypt. (This was before the LORD destroyed Sodom and Gomorrah.)" (Gen. 13:10).

*Looking across the southern part of the Dead Sea
toward the location of Zoar*

This area, which had once been lush and well-watered, was destroyed by God when He judged Sodom and Gomorrah. "Then the LORD rained down fire and burning sulfur from the sky on Sodom and Gomorrah. He utterly destroyed them, along with the other cities and villages of the plain, wiping out all the people and every bit of vegetation" (Gen. 19:24–25). Lot, his daughters, and one of the five cities in the region were not destroyed. The city of Zoar was spared because it was near enough for Lot and his daughters to run to (vv. 20–23). Zoar was located on the eastern side of the Dead Sea, tucked in near the bottom of the mountains of Moab. It survived, but the rest of the valley was completely destroyed. And then, for good measure, God had the land subside to allow the water from the Dead Sea to flow in and cover any remains.

Gazing across at the mountains mirrored in the water, it's hard to realize this was once considered choice real estate—a garden spot in the land. But perhaps the desolation itself is a good metaphor for the impact sin can have on a person's life. No matter how promising an individual's potential might be, choices have consequences. Starting well isn't the same as ending well. Those are the dark lessons we don't always want to hear, but really need to hear. And those lessons shout loudly at us as we gaze at the desolation here at the Dead Sea.

Going Up to Jerusalem

AIJALON

SOREK

ELAH

GUVRIN

LACHISH

JERUSALEM

BETHLEHEM

HERODIUM

ARAD

BEERSHEBA

The Iron Age citadel at ancient Arad

CHAPTER 27

Arad:

An Obscure Site with Great Significance

Arad doesn't make the must-visit list for many tours, and that's a shame. True, the city is only mentioned four times in the Bible. Three of those are in connection with Israel's defeat of the king of Arad just after the death of Aaron (Num. 21:1; 33:40; Josh. 12:14). And the fourth uses Arad as a geographical marker to pinpoint the location where the descendants of Moses's father-in-law settled (Judg. 1:16). But the lack of biblical references doesn't diminish the site's importance. Arad might be an obscure site, but it offers three significant biblical lessons.

VISITING THE CITADEL

Take your time climbing up the stairs to the citadel . . . and watch out for lizards! I don't want anyone being surprised by one darting out from under the steps. Have your cameras ready as well. You just might see a fox climb over the ancient walls.

Arad is another of the *aha!* sites on a trip to Israel. It illustrates the importance of controlling the roadways through the biblical Negev. It also illustrates two major stories from the Old Testament and one key truth from the New Testament.

Arad dominated the eastern end of a region the Bible calls the Negev. On modern maps the Negev stretches all the way down to the city of Eilat at the very southern tip of Israel. But in Old Testament times the Negev referred to a relatively narrow region of land that marked the boundary between the hill country of Judah to the north and the wilderness to the south. It was the preferred campgrounds of the patriarchs Abraham, Isaac, and Jacob.

The Negev is an area of marginal rainfall. In normal years it can receive enough rain to grow wheat. One season, "When Isaac planted his crops . . . he harvested a hundred times more grain than he planted, for the LORD blessed him" (Gen. 26:12). And yet, when his father Abraham arrived in the Negev "a severe famine struck the land of Canaan, forcing Abram to go down to Egypt" (Gen. 12:10).

As you stand on the site, look first to the north. See that flock of sheep in the distance? It's a reminder that today this region is home to the Bedouin —a group that lives much like the patriarchs did so long ago. Just beyond that flock you can see the hill country of Judah starting to rise up. Travel a short distance into those hills and you will come to the location of the biblical towns of Carmel and Maon. You might not remember them in the Bible, but they're part of the first lesson we can learn while visiting Arad.

THE WISE, THE FOOLISH, AND THE NAÏVE

The book of Proverbs talks about three different kinds of people. Some are wise, some are foolish, and some are naïve. All three are on display in 1 Samuel 25, and the view here from Arad helps bring each one into sharp focus. The chapter begins by announcing the death of Samuel the prophet. With Samuel gone, young, naïve David feels very vulnerable to threats from a jealous King Saul. His impulse is to flee. "And David set out and went down to the wilderness of Paran" (v. 1 NASB).

If the hill country of Judah begins just to our north, the wilderness of Paran begins just to our south. If you turn and look south, you can see the ground rising in elevation. That's where the wilderness begins. The Negev is actually this shallow depression between the hill country of Judah and the wilderness of Paran. By heading to this wilderness, David was putting as much distance between himself and Saul as possible.

The scene in 1 Samuel 25 shifts, and we need to again turn and look back to the north . . . to the start of the hill country of Judah. Just a few miles up into those hills were the Old Testament towns of Carmel and Maon. And that's where we're introduced to the second character in our drama. "There was a wealthy man from Maon who owned property near the town of Carmel. He had 3,000 sheep and 1,000 goats, and it was sheep-shearing time. This man's name was Nabal" (1 Sam. 25:2–3). Nabal's name means "fool." This is the same word found in Psalm 14:1: "Only *fools* say in their hearts, 'There is no God.'"

It seems almost inconceivable that Nabal's parents named him "fool" at birth. More likely, this was a nickname given to him by his parents or others as he grew up, probably because of his foolish actions. As Abigail sadly admits later to David, "He is a fool, just as his name suggests" (1 Sam. 25:25). It's likely people didn't call him that to his face because of his wealth and influence. But mention "Fool" and everyone knew whom you were talking about.

The writer then quickly adds the third character to the story—Abigail. She was "a sensible and beautiful woman" (1 Sam. 25:3). Abigail becomes the hero of the chapter. Her wisdom and her discernment save her entire household from a rash decision by David. But I'm getting ahead of the story.

David was hiding out in the wilderness of Paran, but he had sent his men to help protect Nabal's flocks. Unfortunately, when David sent some of those men back to see if Nabal would reward their service by providing him with supplies, Nabal rudely sent them away. David ordered four hundred of his men to follow him as he set out vowing to kill Nabal and his family. When Abigail discovered what had happened, she sent a supply convoy to David and started out on her own donkey to intercept him.

Here's where your perch atop Arad will help the story come into focus. Listen carefully to 1 Samuel 25:20. "And it happened as she was riding on her donkey and coming down by the hidden part of the mountain, that behold, David and his men were coming down toward her; so she met them" (NASB). Notice anything odd? How could both Abigail and David meet if they are both "coming down"? If two people meet on a hillside, coming from opposite directions, you would expect one to be coming *down* while the other is coming *up*. Yet the writer uses the same word, "coming down," to describe both. How is this possible?

Look north at the hill country of Judah. If Abigail was heading toward the wilderness of Paran to meet David, she would first head *down* into the Negev. Now turn toward the wilderness of Paran to the south. If David is traveling from there to reach Nabal, he would first head *down* into the Negev. So if both are heading *down*, then they must have met here in the Negev basin, somewhere near where we're now standing.

Abigail apologized for the actions of her wicked husband and presented her gifts to David. David recognized the wisdom in her advice, which kept him from following through on a foolish vow. "Thank God for your good sense! Bless you for keeping me from murder and from carrying out vengeance with my own hands" (1 Sam. 25:33).

A wise, discerning woman kept a young, naïve man from fulfilling a very unwise vow. And of course, the rest is history. Nabal the fool died, and the wise woman became the wife of the young man. Perhaps the theme of the entire story should be Proverbs 19:20. "Get all the advice and instruction you can, so you will be wise the rest of your life." It's likely that Nabal never bothered to listen to Abigail. Thankfully, David did.

IDOLATRY IN THE KINGDOM OF JUDAH

The second lesson from Arad comes from the excavations here at the site. Standing on this viewing platform, you can see that the citadel was relatively small. This was more like a military outpost than a town. Its primary role was to guard the trade route leading through the Negev and to watch over the roadway into the hill country of Judah. Space inside this fortress would have been at a premium, and yet a significant amount of that space was devoted to just one building. And that building is right below us, here at the northwest corner of the site.

The temple of Arad

Just inside the entrance to the building is an open courtyard with a stone altar. The altar was made of fieldstones, just as God had commanded. Beyond the altar is a doorway leading to an inner chamber, and at the far end of that chamber are stairs leading up to a smaller room with two incense altars at the entrance. In the small room is a flat stone resting against the back wall.

The altar of sacrifice and incense altars let us know this structure was a temple. And it seems to be patterned after the tabernacle in the wilderness, or perhaps even after Solomon's Temple in Jerusalem. But some things are amiss. Why are there two incense altars rather than just one? And what is the purpose for the flat stone in what should be the holy of holies? Even more importantly, what's a temple doing here in the first place?

In Deuteronomy 12, God announced that sacrifices were only to be offered at the location He would select. "Be careful not to sacrifice your burnt offerings just anywhere you like. You may do so only at the place the LORD will choose within one of your tribal territories. There you must offer your burnt offerings and do everything I command you" (vv. 13–14). The place ultimately chosen by God was Jerusalem. So why was this temple built at Arad? Most likely it was for the convenience of those who lived here. Rather than traveling all the way to Jerusalem, they decided it was easier to build their own worship center here.

It's possible the people living here weren't even worshiping the true God of Israel. Certainly, they had deliberately chosen to disobey His command to worship only in Jerusalem. And by placing a flat stone in the holy of holies, the spot where the shekinah glory of God was to dwell above the ark of the covenant, they were replacing the one God of Israel with an image that could represent whatever god the people wanted. Sadly, Arad wasn't the only town in Judah where such practices were taking place.

Through Jeremiah the prophet, God described the idolatrous practices happening throughout the land. "Don't you see what they are doing throughout the towns of Judah and in the streets of Jerusalem? No wonder I am so angry! Watch how the children gather wood and the fathers build sacrificial fires. See how the women knead dough and make cakes to offer to the Queen of Heaven. And they pour out liquid offerings to their other idol gods!" (Jer. 7:17–18). Later Jeremiah writes, "Look now, people of Judah; you have as many gods as you have towns. You have as many altars of shame—altars for burning incense to your god Baal—as there are streets in Jerusalem" (Jer. 11:13). The temple uncovered at Arad is an actual example of the kind of idolatry rampant in Judah.

This temple is a reminder that we also need to examine our hearts to make sure we're aligning our lives by God's standards rather than trying to bend His commands to fit our preferences.

THE MAN FROM KERIOT

We've already talked about Carmel and Maon, but there's another town even closer to where we're standing. It was located just a little way up the road heading into the hill country of Judah. It's likely you don't ever recall hearing of the town before, but I don't think you'll ever forget it after your time here.

The town is mentioned only one time in the Old Testament, and in that one passage it's actually given two names.

After conquering Canaan, Joshua divided the land among the tribes of Israel. The first tribe to receive its allotment in the land was the tribe of Judah. Caleb was given the city of Hebron in Joshua 14, and then the boundaries for the tribe of Judah were laid out in the first half of chapter 15. Finally, Joshua identified the different towns within their tribal allotment.

This list of towns, which begins in Joshua 15:21, is a grocery list of places we can't pronounce and which we struggle to find on a map. And as a result, most people simply skip over them. The fourteenth town on the list is "Kerioth-hezron (that is, Hazor)" (v. 25). Let's look at that name in a little more detail.

The word "Kerioth" in English would actually be pronounced *Keriot* in Hebrew. It's the plural form of the word *keriat*, which is related to a Hebrew word for village. The second word *Hezron* means "enclosure." The town was given the additional name *Hazor*. But don't confuse this town with the city of Hazor we visited earlier. That city was north of the Sea of Galilee while this one is in the far south of Judah. Think of it in this way. We also have multiple towns in our country that share the same name—like twenty-four towns or cities named Springfield, fifteen named Danville, and at least three named Peoria. The word *Hazor* also means "enclosure." Perhaps the town began as two villages that later joined together, or possibly the town had a double wall around it.

Keriot-hezron was just one of several towns in Judah. It wasn't the largest or the most strategic, but it was still one of the first towns singled out within the area allotted to the most powerful tribe in Israel. The town certainly had nothing about it that would cause you to be ashamed if you lived there. In fact, the Bible tells us about a rather promising man named Judah who came from the town of Keriot.

Judah stood out from his peers. Most of the crowd he ran around with came from Galilee. They were country bumpkins who spoke with a quirky accent that gave them away. Judah, on the other hand, came from Keriot, a mere

257

thirty-six miles from Jerusalem. He spoke with a *proper* accent.

Judah also seemed to have been respected, even trusted, by the other members of the group. When they needed someone to keep the books and handle all the finances, Judah was the go-to guy. This man from Keriot had a natural bearing, the marks of leadership that caused others to trust him.

By now you might have put the pieces of this puzzle together. In Hebrew, the phrase "man of Keriot" would be pronounced *ish Keriot*, since the word for "man" in Hebrew is *ish*. And as names got transliterated from Hebrew into the Greek in the New Testament, Judah morphed into the name Judas. You see, Judas Iscariot, the man who betrayed Jesus, was really *Judah ish Keriot*—Judah the man from Keriot. He was born and raised just over that hill in the distance.

This is when Paul Harvey used to say, "And now you know . . . the rest of the story." But there's more to *this* story. I'm referring to its application to us today. What difference should our understanding about Judas's background make in our lives? First, it should remind us never to judge a book by its cover. Which man would become the greater follower of Jesus? The refined disciple from Keriot in the territory of Judah, or the rough, smelly fisherman from Galilee named Simon bar Jonah? Judas had the pedigree, but Peter ultimately had the character, courage, and faith. The lesson for us is to take care never to judge others by their appearance or their accent, but by their character and their deeds.

That leads to a second truth. What's important in your life is not where you're from, but where you're going. You didn't choose your parents, or your economic or social background, or your childhood. That was all beyond your control. But you can choose where you're going today and tomorrow. Judas was responsible for the choices he made. And though he started with great advantages, Judas Iscariot—Judah the man from Keriot—ended life as a failure. The consequences of his poor choices should be a flashing warning light to all of us.

Arad is definitely an obscure site, one many Israeli guides prefer not to visit. As one blurted out, "What am I supposed to say here? I haven't visited this place since guide school!" But Arad is a gem, a real diamond in the rough for those who want to understand the Bible. From David and Abigail, to Jeremiah and the idolatry of Judah, to Judas Iscariot, this one spot helps bring the message of the Bible into greater focus. It's also a wonderful spot to occasionally be surprised by a fox or by a shepherd with his flock of sheep. And depending on the time of year, it's also a wonderful spot to see a black iris . . . or perhaps even a ripening pomegranate!

A fox scampering through a field at Arad

Black iris growing at Arad

Pomegranate ripening on a tree

The well outside the entrance to ancient Beersheba

CHAPTER 28

Beersheba:
From Dan to Beersheba

Beersheba was the southernmost major city of ancient Israel. It was the temporary home to the patriarchs Abraham, Isaac, and Jacob. Elijah the prophet also visited the city ever so briefly as he fled from wicked Queen Jezebel. A number of other men and women from the Bible walked its dusty streets. And yet, while many of the sites in Israel are often packed with pilgrims and tourists, this historical treasure *isn't* one of them. Apart from the occasional tour bus, Beersheba's parking lot sits empty. That's great for those who do visit because they have the site to themselves. But it's sad that so few tourists come here.

FROM DAN TO BEERSHEBA

Before we begin our visit, we first need to understand two idiomatic expressions from the Bible. Every society has its own cultural idioms—expressions that convey more than just what's suggested by the words. You can be "fit as a fiddle" and still have the "cat get your tongue" when you realize "all that glitters is not gold." We understand those expressions even if we've never taken violin lessons, owned a cat, or gone panning for gold. But to someone from another culture, idioms like that can be incomprehensible if they're not explained.

The Bible also uses idiomatic expressions. For example, when the Bible says "from Dan to Beersheba," it's similar to someone in the US saying "from

New York to L.A.," meaning from one end of the country to the other. Dan was the last major city as one left Israel going north, and Beersheba was the last major city as one left going south. So the expression "from Dan to Beersheba" referred to the whole country, from north to south and, by extension, to everything in between.

Another idiomatic expression found in the Bible was to sit "under your vine and under your fig tree." Grape vines were usually grown close to the ground, but there were times when they were also grown on trellises, usually at a person's home, to provide shade during the hot summer months. In the same way, fig trees were planted near homes with their branches trimmed high so someone could sit underneath in the shade provided by the dense leaves. The expression pictures a place of rest and relaxation, but it also has the idea of safety and security. After all, it could take years for the vines and the fig trees to grow large enough to provide that shade. If you were able to sit under *your* vine or fig tree, it meant things were going well enough for you to relax a bit because you've been experiencing a time of peace and prosperity.

All well and good, but why should someone talk about such biblical idioms here in Beersheba? Looking around, we don't see *any* vines or fig trees nearby. In fact, the land looks somewhat barren. Pausing here outside the entrance to the city, near the well that once provided water for the caravans traveling through the area, we wonder to ourselves: What can vines and fig trees possibly have to do with Beersheba? The answer is found in the description of Solomon's reign over Israel in 1 Kings 4.

The compiler of 1 Kings provides a long list of King Solomon's accomplishments, and most of the focus is on territorial control, provisions for the royal court, and personal achievements. But tucked away in the chapter is a one-verse description of the impact Solomon's reign had on the average citizen of the kingdom. "During the lifetime of Solomon, all of Judah and Israel lived in peace and safety. And from Dan in the north to Beersheba in the south, each family had its own home and garden" (1 Kings 4:25). The last phrase is literally "each under his own vine and fig tree."

From Dan to Beersheba. Solomon's reign had an impact on the entire country. We're now standing in Beersheba. It was only a short time ago that we visited Dan. And the contrast between the two places is remarkable. Dan to Beersheba is not only an idiomatic expression describing the whole country, from north to south, it's also a picture of contrast from a place of abundance to a place that's more on the margin . . . from a location with an amazing source of flowing water to a place that needed to dig wells and hew out cisterns to capture water that flowed through the wadis in the winter.

From a human perspective, the two sites did share one common problem—they were both vulnerable. Dan blocked the way of every major power that tried to invade the land of Israel from the north—Syria, Assyria, and Babylonia. The first town to feel their hammer blows was Dan. At the opposite end of the country stood Beersheba, staring at Egypt's threats from the south. Solomon inherited the land conquered by David, and his reign brought peace. That's why all Israel, from Dan to Beersheba, lived in safety.

But the verse speaks to more than just physical safety. Sitting under one's vine and fig tree also spoke of prosperity and peace. The land was productive and the nation was able to reap the benefits of being able to focus more on plowshares and pruning hooks than on swords and spears. Sadly, the peace didn't last. Solomon's foolish actions led to a division of the kingdom following his death. And the kings that followed, with few exceptions, never lived up to the spiritual stature of David and Solomon. Now, as we gaze out at the land around Beersheba, the vines and fig trees are absent. That time of universal peace and prosperity remains as elusive today as it was following the death of Solomon.

But we don't need to begin our tour of Beersheba feeling discouraged, because God has said His program isn't done. In fact, God promised that a time is coming that will far surpass the time of peace in Solomon's day. The prophet Micah described it as a day when "everyone will live in peace and prosperity, enjoying their own grapevines and fig trees, for there will be nothing to fear" (Micah 4:4). And the prophet Zechariah described it as a time when each one living in the land "will invite your neighbor to sit with you peacefully under your own grapevine and fig tree" (Zech. 3:10).

When will that time of peace, prosperity, and security finally come to this war-scarred world? In the verses immediately before his promise of vines and fig trees in chapter 4, Micah announced the coming of "the last days" (v. 1) when God will establish His kingdom and when "the Lord's teaching will go out from Zion; his word will go out from Jerusalem" (v. 2). In Zechariah 3, the prophet said this day will come when God will "remove the sins of this land in a single day" (Zech. 3:9). Later in his book, Zechariah explained that enigmatic message by describing a day when God will pour out a spirit of grace on the inhabitants of Jerusalem and they will "look on me whom they have pierced and mourn for him as for an only son" (Zech. 12:10). That's when God promises to open "a fountain . . . for the dynasty of David and for the people of Jerusalem, a fountain to cleanse them from all their sins and impurity" (Zech. 13:1). The vines and fig trees are awaiting the return of Jesus!

Solomon, the son of David, brought a time of temporary peace, prosperity, and security to the land. But the ultimate Son of David—the one to whom both Micah and Zechariah were pointing—will return as the Prince of Peace to fulfill *all* the promises to Israel made in the Old Testament. Just think, a day is coming when you will be able to return here to Beersheba and see a lush, green land covered with vines and fig trees. And when that happens, don't be surprised if one of the locals calls out and asks you to pull up a chair and take a seat. When you do, make sure you tell them how much things have changed since your last visit.

A TAMARISK TREE

Before we walk up onto the site, I want to give you a chance to use the restrooms. We've been on the road for a while, so it's definitely time for a bathroom break. But while we're waiting for everyone to use the facilities, look back at the large tree we just walked past. It's a tamarisk tree. This one is thirty or forty feet tall. If you look closely, you'll notice it doesn't have leaves.

It has needles—something like those on a pine tree. And those needles have a bit of a whitish coating in places. That's actually salt, which is excreted by the needles. In fact, the tree is sometimes called a "salt cedar." At night, any moisture in the air is attracted to the salt and forms tiny droplets on the needles. Then when the sun comes up, the water evaporates. That evaporation cools the air around and under the tree. In essence, the tamarisk tree is God's natural "swamp cooler."

Standing here in the shade is the perfect place to talk about the tamarisk tree—and the events of Genesis 21. Abraham was living in this region and having problems with some of the locals. As we could see as

Tamarisk tree at modern entrance to Beersheba

we drove here, this region, which the Bible calls the Negev, is rather dry. It would normally receive between ten and fifteen inches of rain a year. That was enough to provide good grazing for sheep and goats, and it was also enough to grow wheat and barley. But the amount of rain varied from year to year, so water was *always* an issue.

That's why Abraham was struggling with the other inhabitants of the region in Genesis 21. Abraham dug a well, but servants of a regional leader named Abimelech seized the well. A dispute over water rights, in a region where water was in short supply, could have turned into a destructive range war between Abraham and his adversaries. But Abraham defused the situation by going directly to Abimelech to resolve the conflict. Abraham made an agreement, buying outright the well he had originally dug. This enabled him to establish, beyond any doubt, his ownership. The range war was settled, and Abimelech and his commander returned home, leaving Abraham with free access to the water so essential to his very life.

Genesis 21 and Beersheba are an excellent place to learn some Hebrew words. The word for "well" is *beer*. And the Hebrew word for "seven" is *sheva*. In an interesting twist, the word for taking an oath, or making a solemn promise, is *shava*. So, Beersheba (*beer sheva*) means "well of the seven," though it also sounds very much like "well of the oath." This helps explain the details of the agreement made between Abraham and Abimelech. Abraham said, "Please accept these seven lambs to show your agreement that I dug this well." Moses then adds, "Then he named the place Beersheba (which means 'well of the oath'), because that was where they had sworn the oath" (Gen. 21:30–31).

At the very end of Genesis 21, Moses adds a rather strange postscript to the whole episode. "Then Abraham planted a tamarisk tree at Beersheba, and there he worshiped the LORD, the Eternal God" (v. 33). What do a treaty, a tamarisk tree, and a unique title for God have in common? This is a question that has puzzled people for centuries.

Some look for answers in other ancient Near Eastern cultures. The tamarisk tree did have religious significance in some cultures, and sacred groves of trees were often part of pagan worship. But those ideas seem totally foreign to this passage. Abraham planted a single tree, not a sacred grove. And after planting that tree, he called on the name of the "Eternal God." In Hebrew that's *Yahweh el ôlam*, the covenant-keeping God Yahweh who is God of all eternity. It's the *opposite* of the pagan worship of Abraham's day, which built multiple shrines to a pantheon of gods and goddesses. Abraham was worshiping the one true God who has existed forever.

But if Abraham wasn't following some pagan custom, then what was he doing? Why did he plant this tamarisk tree? I see two reasons. First, the tree was a symbol of Abraham's ownership of the land. God had promised him the land, and Abraham had just made an agreement with a regional leader who recognized Abraham's right to be in that land and to control the resources there. Abraham wasn't a stranger passing through, someone with no rights. He was the recognized owner of the well, and the tree was a landmark that said to everyone, "This well is the property of Abraham."

But the tree was more than just a property marker. It was also intended as a reminder to Abraham, and his descendants, of God's faithfulness. A tamarisk tree takes decades to grow. Israel's National Parks Authority transplanted one next to the well outside the gate of ancient Beersheba. After twenty years, the tree was removed because it had barely begun to grow. When Abraham planted his tree he was making a statement, both to himself and to his descendants. It was God, the covenant-keeping God of all eternity, who had promised Abraham the land. And Abraham wanted everyone to know he believed God's promise. The tree he planted was a reminder.

Abraham was already over a hundred years old when he planted that tree. Now, since he lived to be 175, he got to watch the tree take root and grow. Perhaps toward the end of his life he even spent time sitting under God's evergreen swamp cooler, thinking about the faithfulness of the covenant-keeping God of all eternity—a faithfulness God had promised to extend to generations yet unborn. Abraham planted a tree that would outlive him, just as the promises given to him by God would remain long after he was gone.

It's time to leave the shade of this tamarisk tree and head up on the site, but what lesson can we carry from here on *our* journey of faith? A key lesson is a proper understanding of hope. Hope is not some uncertain, wish-upon-a-star kind of desire. In the Bible, hope is a confident expectation that God will do what He's promised. It's an expectation that is so certain in its outcome that we can act on it today. Abraham could "root himself to the land" through that tree because God had given him a promise. It wasn't the covenant with Abimelech that gave Abraham hope; it was the covenant made to him by

Yahweh el ôlam, the covenant-keeping God of all eternity. It was *His* promise that allowed Abraham to settle down and plant a tree for coming generations.

WALKING AROUND BEERSHEBA

Our journey through Beersheba begins at the city gate. The well just outside the gate is not the well dug by Abraham. Very likely his well was down closer to the riverbed. Since he had to dig down to reach the water table, common sense suggests he started digging at the bottom of the hill rather than the top! We can make a second observation about this well. It was *not* the water supply for the city because it's located *outside* the city's walls. All an enemy would need to do to capture the city would be to deny the inhabitants access to the water.

So what was the purpose for this well? It was used to provide water to those living nearby who were tending flocks and herds. They could bring their animals up to the well to draw water for them. The well would also be used to provide water for travelers and caravans passing through the area. In exchange for paying tolls, caravans could travel through the region and secure water for

The storehouses just inside the city gate

their animals. It's also possible that they would trade some of their goods for food or other supplies needed on their journey. The local governor of the district converted grain paid in taxes by local inhabitants into silver, gold, spices, and other merchandise that could be sent to Jerusalem for the royal treasury.

The storehouses discovered just inside the gate complex help confirm the importance of trade for Beersheba. These elongated buildings would have stored wheat, barley, and other goods paid in taxes by residents of the region. Those commodities would then be used to support the regional governor and any soldiers under his control. They could also be sold to the caravans passing through.

When archaeologists excavated the storehouses, they discovered another surprise. In the fieldstone-and-mud brick walls of the building, they uncovered pieces of dressed limestone. Eventually, they realized the pieces had originally been part of a stone altar. Much like Arad, the people at Beersheba had set up their own worship center to keep from making the long journey to Jerusalem. Their altar was made of cut stone, which God had expressly prohibited. "If you use stones to build my altar, use only natural, uncut stones. Do not shape the stones with a tool, for that would make the altar unfit for holy use" (Ex. 20:25). This altar was likely torn down and buried in the storehouse walls during the religious reforms of either King Hezekiah or King Josiah.

The horned altar discovered at Beersheba, on display at the Israel Museum in Jerusalem

One of the most remarkable discoveries at Beersheba is also one of the most recent. If the well outside the city gate wasn't the main water supply, then how did the people inside the city get water? The mystery was solved in the past few decades when archaeologists discovered a massive system designed to bring water into the city. The city's inhabitants dug a shaft more than sixty feet down into the bedrock on which the city sits. They then carved cisterns into the bedrock that could hold nearly 185,000 gallons of water, and they dug a channel to divert water from the nearby Hebron stream to fill the cisterns. Visitors to Beersheba today can walk through the entire water system as they leave the city.

Entrance to the water system at Beersheba

THE BATTLE THAT CHANGED THE MODERN MIDDLE EAST

Beersheba played a strategic role in the Bible, but it's also responsible—from a human perspective—for the shape of the modern Middle East. During World War I, southern Palestine witnessed a struggle between England and the armies of Germany and the Ottoman Empire. England controlled the Suez Canal and Egypt, while Germany and the Ottomans controlled Palestine and the Arabian Peninsula.

German and Turkish forces were entrenched in Gaza, blocking any British move forward. In the spring of 1917, the British tried twice to take Gaza, but they were defeated both times. A new commander, General Edmund Allenby, was sent to assume control over Britain's Egyptian Expeditionary Force. On October 31, Allenby's forces, led by the Australian and New Zealand Army Corps (ANZAC), surprised the German and Turkish forces by circling to the east to attack Beersheba. In what was perhaps the last great cavalry charge in history, the ANZAC forces, using their bayonets as swords, overran the defending forces and captured the town of Beersheba. By November 7 Gaza fell, and on December 11 Allenby's forces liberated Jerusalem.

The battle of Beersheba on October 31, 1917, was the event that opened Palestine to British control. But something else was happening in London on that same day—the British cabinet met in London to discuss the future of Palestine. The Cabinet made a decision enshrined in a letter issued two days later by British Foreign Secretary, Lord Arthur James Balfour. That letter said, in part, "His Majesty's Government views with favor the establishment in Palestine of a national home for the Jewish people . . . "[1]

Though separated by nearly 2,500 miles, the military victory at Beersheba and the decision to push for a national home for the Jewish people took place on the same day. Coincidence? Or yet another illustration of God's guiding hand in history? Walking through Beersheba, I'm convinced the juxtaposition of those events is no accident. They are another reminder that *Yahweh el ôlam*, the covenant-keeping God of all eternity, is also the God in *control* of all history.

The entrance ramp and gate at Lachish

CHAPTER 29

Lachish:
Israel's Archaeological Gem

THE VALLEYS OF THE SHEPHELAH

Our journey to Jerusalem takes us through a new part of the land. In Hebrew it's called the *Shephelah*. In most English Bibles it's translated as low hills, foothills, or western foothills. The Shephelah is a very distinct region situated between the mountainous hill country of Judah and the Philistine plain on the Mediterranean coast. It was the front door into the hill country. Towns were built on the low hills while the valleys were used for travel and growing crops.

Five main valleys run through the Shephelah, taking travelers from the coast into the hill country. The towns guarding these valleys became places of conflict between the Israelites in the hills and the different nations that tried to come up the valleys into those hills. From the Philistines through the Egyptians, Assyrians, and Babylonians, the towns in the Shephelah saw more than their share of conflict.

Our drive through this region is a good place to help you master some key Bible facts about geography and history. Over the years, I've developed a relatively simple way to help people remember these valleys. I need to start by asking you a question: When you drive toward the coast, what type of bird will you see? If you answered, "A seagull," you're correct. Now, you just need to learn to spell like an Israeli—since the Hebrew language is mostly consonants with virtually no vowels. So let's spell "a seagull" as follows: A-S-E-G-L—"a segl." If you can remember "ASEGL," you will be able to remember the five key valleys that cut through the Shephelah. From north to south they are Aijalon, Sorek, Elah, Guvrin, and Lachish.

Now we need to populate each valley with someone from the Bible. We'll put Joshua in the Aijalon Valley. This is the valley where Joshua chased the Canaanites after rescuing the inhabitants of Gibeon. As the Israelites pursued the Canaanites, Joshua shouted out, "Let the sun stand still over Gibeon, and the moon over the valley of Aijalon" (Josh. 10:12). When we reach the Valley of Aijalon, remember Joshua. The roadway that began in the Aijalon Valley was the main road up to Jerusalem.

The "S" stands for the Sorek Valley. We could populate this valley with a number of individuals, but we'll choose Samson. He was born near the eastern edge of the Sorek Valley, and the Philistine woman he first married was from Timnah at the other end of the valley. Later, "Samson fell in love with a woman named Delilah, who lived in the valley of Sorek" (Judg. 16:4). Samson's "eye problems" were finally solved by the Philistines when they "gouged out his eyes" (v. 21).

The "E" points to the Elah Valley. This valley features the clash of two warriors who come from opposite directions. Just to the west of the valley was the Philistine city of Gath and its champion Goliath. And at the eastern end of the valley was a road that led up into the hill country to the city of Bethlehem, the hometown of David. The Elah Valley is where David fought Goliath.

The "G" in "ASEGL" stands for the Guvrin Valley. This valley controlled a roadway that led up to the city of Hebron. The individual we'll connect with this valley is the prophet Micah. His hometown was Moresheth Gath right on the edge of the valley, and many of the towns he identifies in Micah 1 were located around this valley.

The final letter in our "fowl illustration" is "L," which is for the Lachish Valley. The city of Lachish was the second largest city in the kingdom of Judah. Only Jerusalem was larger. And military strategists knew that to capture Jerusalem they had to first take this city. That's why the two individuals in the Lachish Valley are King Sennacherib of Assyria and King Nebuchadnezzar of

Babylon. Both kings captured and destroyed the city of Lachish.

We're approaching these valleys from the south, so the first one we will visit is the Lachish Valley. And now that our geography and history lesson is over, it's time to start exploring. So, grab your camera and follow me off the bus.

THE HIDDEN GEM

If I were asked to select the most amazing sites in Israel *not* seen by most tourists, Lachish would be on that list. Those who have never been to Israel might not even recall seeing the name in the Bible. That's because people often skim over the names of unfamiliar places and people when they read. But even those who've been to Israel aren't likely to have visited the site. So why does it rank so high on my list of amazing places?

One reason Lachish is so significant is because it anchored the southern part of the Shephelah and guarded a major roadway up to the city of Hebron. A second reason for its significance is the role it played in Bible history. Lachish was one of the five cities in the coalition that attacked Gibeon at the

Looking up the Lachish valley toward the hill country of Judah

time of Joshua (Josh. 10:3–4). Later, King Amaziah of Judah was assassinated in Lachish (2 Kings 14:19). And the city was attacked and destroyed by both King Sennacherib of Assyria and King Nebuchadnezzar of Babylon. Both understood the strategic importance of Lachish for the defense of Judah. Seizing Lachish was so significant that Sennacherib decorated a room in his palace at Nineveh with a series of reliefs showing its capture.

Lachish also has great archaeological potential. It's been excavated several times, but much remains to be uncovered. The city must have had a secure water supply, but it hasn't yet been discovered. One area that has been excavated is the massive gate complex guarding the entrance into the city. Standing at the foot of the hill and looking up at the foundations of the gate, it's clear why Sennacherib boasted about capturing this city.

A little over a century after the city fell to Sennacherib, the Babylonians set up camp outside Lachish. King Nebuchadnezzar had ordered his army to Judah for the third time, and on this campaign he intended to finally destroy the nation that had once again dared to rebel against him. His operation against Judah was long and ferocious. Nebuchadnezzar began by moving his army through the land, systematically eliminating one city after another. Toward the end, only three major cities remained. Jeremiah described it this way. "At this time the Babylonian army was besieging Jerusalem, Lachish, and Azekah—the only fortified cities of Judah not yet captured" (Jer. 34:7).

Lachish, Azekah, and Jerusalem. Every other major town was gone. Captured. Destroyed. And now Nebuchadnezzar could concentrate his forces on these three remaining fortress cities. But in what order did they fall? The answer was discovered inside the gate of Lachish. So follow me up the ramp to that gate.

THE GATE AT LACHISH

When archaeologists excavated the plaza between the outer and inner gates of Lachish, they came across several pieces of broken pottery with words written on them. In an era when papyrus or parchment wasn't widely available, the quickest way to pen a note was to write it on a piece of broken pottery. The pottery fragments discovered in this gate were written to the commanding officer at Lachish by one of the remaining army units out in the field. They were military reports, intended to keep the commander informed.

Imagine standing here in the gate with the commander of the forces at Lachish. It's the middle of the night, and the soldiers on duty have just used a rope to pull an exhausted soldier over the wall. He's out of breath, partly from running for several miles, and partly out of fear. He just snaked his way through the Babylonian lines with a message from the field commander.

As you listen intently, the city scribe reads the faint writing on the broken piece of pottery, squinting as he tries to make out the letters in the light of a flickering oil lamp. "May Yahweh cause my lord to hear, this very day, tidings of good! And now according to everything which my lord hath written, so hath thy servant done. I have written on the door according to all that my lord hath written to me . . . And let (my lord) know that we are watching for the signals of Lachish, according to all the indications which my lord hath given, for we cannot see Azekah."[1]

We cannot see Azekah! The evening signal fires were a means of communication. The cities could signal to each other, and they could also use such beacons to communicate with the army in the field. The distance between Lachish and Azekah was eleven miles—eleven miles of strategic territory that guarded the roadways from the coast into the hill country of Judah. But now the lights of Azekah, one of the two remaining cities anchoring this region, had gone out. The message was clear. Azekah had fallen.

Azekah. Then Lachish. Finally Jerusalem. Like dominoes, each fell in order—the last of the cities standing against Babylon. And the letters found in the gate of Lachish help us reconstruct the order of their fall.

The broken pieces of pottery discovered in the city gate are a sobering reminder for our own day. In Jeremiah 34–39, the prophet recorded the final collapse of the kingdom of Judah, including the city of Lachish. But much earlier in his ministry, at a time when such things couldn't even be imagined,

Jeremiah issued a warning to those who thought they could disregard God with impunity. "A horrible and shocking thing has happened in this land—the prophets give false prophecies, and the priests rule with an iron hand. Worse yet, my people like it that way! But what will you do when the end comes?" (Jer. 5:30–31). These broken pieces of pottery remind us that there is a price to pay for ignoring, disregarding, and disobeying God. We can choose our actions, but we can't choose the consequences.

Just ask the people of Jeremiah's day who lived in Lachish.

Part of the relief from Sennacherib's palace in Nineveh, now on display in the British Museum, showing the fall of Lachish

Inside the Bell Caves at Guvrin

CHAPTER 30

Guvrin

The "G" valley in our journey through the Shephelah is the Guvrin Valley. That's the name of the valley today, although it's not the name found in the Bible. The biblical name of the valley is less clear. The compiler of 2 Chronicles described a battle between the armies of Asa king of Judah and Zerah the Cushite that took place "in the Valley of Zephathah at Mareshah" (2 Chron. 14:10 NASB). That could be the biblical name of this valley, although the Septuagint translates the word as the direction "north" (from the Hebrew word *tzaphōn*) rather than as a proper name. The passage does make one thing clear—the ancient city of Mareshah sat near this valley. Several other cities did as well, including Moresheth Gath, the hometown of Micah the prophet (Micah 1:1, 14).

The flattop hill of Mareshah stands out from a distance and helps mark the location of the Guvrin Valley. Today, Israel's National Park service provides a number of opportunities for families and groups to explore the region. Visitors can take part in an archaeological "dig for a day" in the underground basements of houses that were abandoned by the Edomites. They can climb through a series of interconnected passages, or explore painted Sidonian burial caves. There are also a number of hiking trails. But if you go hiking, make sure you stay on the trail. I'll explain why shortly. During our time at Guvrin, we'll be stopping at two sites within the National Park. The first is known as the Bell Caves.

THE BELL CAVES

The Bell Caves are a series of underground caverns quarried during the Byzantine and Islamic periods. As a result, you might not expect to find any biblical significance in them, but I believe these caves can teach us an important lesson from the Bible. So follow me up the pathway and into the first set of caves.

The cool shade is a welcome relief from the hot afternoon sun. And their size is impressive. From inside it's easy to see how the caves were formed. Those doing the quarrying first punched their way through a hard rocky crust to reach the soft chalk just underneath. Then they began removing the chalk—one bucketload at a time—creating a bell-shaped pit in the process. Once they reached the bottom of the chalky layer, they moved a short distance away and began the process again. Eventually hundreds of these interconnecting caves were formed. That's also why you need to stay on the pathway when walking through Guvrin. We don't want you to accidentally step into a hidden opening and find yourself at the bottom of a pit!

Some believe the chalk was quarried for building material. That's technically correct, though it gives a false impression. Those working here were not quarrying out stones to be used in construction. The chalk was too soft for stone blocks. (Imagine building a house with stones the consistency of the chalk once used on classroom blackboards.) The design of the caves is also wrong for quarrying stone blocks. The caves are round, not square, and the small opening at the top would have made the removal of large stone blocks very difficult. So what did they do with this chalk?

The chalk from these caves was converted into lime to be used to plaster walls and make cisterns waterproof. Think of it as the original "drywall" slapped onto the stone walls of a building to keep out moisture. It also helped beautify the walls, though it added nothing to their strength or durability. Rub your hand along the wall in this cave and feel the smooth softness of the chalk. It looks clean and white, and it would certainly help hide the cracks and gaps in the limestone walls. But it could also hide weaknesses and imperfections—warning signs that the wall was about to collapse.

Ezekiel the prophet used the imagery of chalky plaster smeared on a stone wall to illustrate the utter worthlessness of the messages of Judah's false prophets. They were leading the people astray by predicting peace even as the nation's doom drew ever closer. He compared their deceptive messages to a thin coating of plaster concealing a poorly constructed wall.

> "This will happen because these evil prophets deceive my people by saying, 'All is peaceful' when there is no peace at all! It's as if the people have built a flimsy wall, and these prophets are trying to reinforce it by covering it with whitewash! Tell these whitewashers that their wall will soon fall down. A heavy rainstorm will undermine it; great hailstones and mighty winds will knock it down. And when the wall falls, the people will cry out, 'What happened to your whitewash?'" (Ezek. 13:10–12)

Ezekiel's message is appropriate for us as well. Beware of those promising peace and prosperity while ignoring the "building code" of God's Word. Jesus used similar imagery in the Sermon on the Mount. He pictured a wise man who built his house on the rock and a foolish man who built his house on sand (Matt. 7:24–27). Sadly, even a poorly constructed house on sand can look good, if enough plaster is applied to the walls. But when the storms come, only the house built on the rock-solid foundation of God's Word will stand.

Beware of those promising peace and prosperity while ignoring the "building code" of God's Word.

A "GETHSEMANE"

A short hike brings us to our second stop at Guvrin. A modern metal stairway takes us below ground to an olive oil press that was in use before the time of Jesus. This ancient factory was carved into the soft chalk. You're now standing at "gethsemane"—but one spelled with a lowercase "g." Let me explain.

The name "Gethsemane" is actually a combination of two Hebrew words—*gath*, which is the word for a press, and *shemen*, which is the word for

Ancient olive oil press at Guvrin

olive oil. When Jesus went with His disciples to Gethsemane, He was literally going to the olive oil press. We're standing in an olive oil press, so in Hebrew this is *gath shemen* . . . or gethsemane. But it's not *the* Gethsemane where Jesus was betrayed. We'll visit that Gethsemane when we walk down the Mount of Olives in Jerusalem!

This site is a great place to illustrate how an ancient olive oil press functioned. Olives were harvested at the very end of summer, just as the rainy season was about to begin. As a result, presses were often placed in some type of enclosure, like a building or a cave. This underground facility was protected from the elements. There is also a large area behind us where olives could be stored. The olives were first crushed by rolling a millstone over them. This "mush" was then gathered in round wicker baskets and stacked in the three rectangular openings in front of us with open archways on top.

Long wooden poles were inserted through those openings and into niches in the back wall, with the poles resting on the baskets of olives. One such pole has been placed here to illustrate how this worked. The stone weights underneath the pole were then fastened to the pole, one at a time. The weight of the stone caused the pole to press down on the baskets of mush, allowing the oil to drip down into a collection trough just below. As each additional stone was fastened to the pole, the pressure forced more oil out of the crushed olives.

By being in a covered area, the olive oil press could continue working even after the fall rains had begun. During the rest of the year, the facility could serve as a convenient shelter or gathering point. That's likely why Jesus and His disciples used the olive oil press (Gethsemane) for shelter numerous times during their visits to Jerusalem. On the night of His betrayal Luke says Jesus "came out and went, as was His habit, to the Mount of Olives" and, with His disciples, arrived at "the *place*" (Luke 22:39–40 NASB). The group, minus Judas, came to the cave with its olive oil press. No doubt the disciples assumed this was where they would bed down for the evening, as they had in the past.

Gethsemane—the one in Jerusalem—is a cave. But that cave has been turned into a chapel, which makes it more difficult to envision what it might have looked like when Jesus and His disciples were there. That's what makes this "gethsemane" at Guvrin so helpful. Remember this olive oil press when we arrive in Jerusalem.

ALWAYS HAVE YOUR CAMERA READY!

One key principle in traveling through Israel is to always have your camera or smartphone ready. You never know when the perfect picture will suddenly appear beside of the road. We were driving past Mareshah when I saw a flock of sheep grazing on the hillside. The winter rain had produced an abundance of grass, and the sheep were happily munching away on plants that were taller than they were. Biblical illustrations can appear when you least expect them.

As I looked at that flock of sheep, they reminded me of a word picture from the pen of King David. His portrait of God's care in Psalm 23 comes from David's own time watching over his flock. How does a good shepherd provide for his sheep? "He lets me rest in green meadows" (v. 2). And as we discovered earlier, the word we translate "green" actually refers to new grass, the kind that sprouts when the winter rains arrive. It's the kind of grass in which these sheep were grazing.

A flock of sheep might be relatively easy to spot, but not every "Kodak moment" is so readily apparent. Sometimes you need quick reflexes and a

Sheep grazing on the hillside of Mareshah

good grasp of biblical imagery. Once at Guvrin, we spotted a solitary locust in the Bell Caves. He was sitting on the ground, enjoying the shade. The cool, damp floor had slowed him down, and we were able to catch him.

This locust looks almost identical to a large grasshopper we might see at home. There doesn't appear to be anything fearful about this tiny creature. In fact, he was little more than a snack for John the Baptist. But in a mysterious process still not fully understood, there are times when these solitary locusts mass together into a swarm. And while a single locust is an easy prey, a locust swarm can have tens of millions of locusts, making them an unstoppable army.

The prophet Joel described the devastation caused by successive invasions of locusts. "What

A locust spotted at Guvrin

286

the gnawing locust has left, the swarming locust has eaten; and what the swarming locust has left, the creeping locust has eaten; and what the creeping locust has left, the stripping locust has eaten" (Joel 1:4 NASB). Locusts could destroy fields of grain and strip the bark off trees, wiping out all plant life in their path. Those who managed to live through a locust swarm understood the picture of destruction painted by Joel.

Proverbs 30:27 also focuses on locusts to teach an important life lesson. "Locusts—they have no king, but they march in formation." They might seem leaderless, but they know how to wisely work together to defeat anything in their path. What did the writer of Proverbs have in mind when he identified the locust as one of four small animals that has much to teach us about wisdom? Perhaps his lesson for us is this: If the insignificant locust can do so much by cooperating and working together, what might we be able to accomplish if we cooperate and work together with others?

It's time to let our locust fly away so we can say that no insects were harmed in the taking of our photographs! But seeing this locust does give us something to ponder as we head to the bus for our drive to the next valley.

A panoramic view of the Elah Valley from atop Socoh

CHAPTER 31

The Elah Valley:
David and Goliath

Before we take the entire group to our stop in the Elah Valley, I want you to come with me on a private excursion. Lace up your hiking books because we need to do some climbing. I wish we could take the whole group on this hike, but if we did I feel certain our next stop would be the emergency room at Hadassah Hospital! We're going to hike to the top of the hill where the ancient town of Socoh once sat. The hike might be a little treacherous, but the view is worth it.

HIKING UP SOCOH

From down below, hiking to the top of Socoh doesn't look that difficult. But the rock is uneven, the soil is loose, and much of the shrubbery is covered

The hill of Socoh

with sharp thorns. So why are we climbing to the summit of Socoh? Once we reach the top the view is fantastic. Think of the destination as our own personal "sky box seats" to witness the epic battle between David and Goliath.

View down the Elah Valley from Socoh, with Azekah in the distance

From the summit of Socoh we can look down the Elah Valley toward the land of the Philistines. The tallest hill in the distance is where the Israelite city of Azekah was located. We talked about Azekah when we were at Lachish. The Elah Valley curves down and around Azekah before opening up onto the Philistine Plain.

We're standing on Socoh, and we see Azekah in the distance, but what is so special about these two sites? Here's how the two sites fit into the account of David and Goliath: "Now the Philistines gathered their armies for battle; and they were gathered at Socoh which belongs to Judah, and they camped between Socoh and Azekah, in Ephes-dammim" (1 Sam. 17:1 NASB). We are standing at the vanguard of the Philistine army, the front lines of their battle formation. Behind us, the different Philistine divisions stretched along this side of the valley from here all the way to Azekah in the distance.

As the Philistine juggernaut assembled and prepared to roll up the valley, word must have reached King Saul at his capital in Gibeah. Saul sent word to the towns along the anticipated Philistine route of conquest to send volunteers. His goal was to cobble together a force from the towns under threat to help him counter the Philistine attack. "Saul countered by gathering his Israelite troops near the valley of Elah. So the Philistines and Israelites faced each other on opposite hills, with the valley between them" (1 Sam. 17:2–3).

If the front lines of the Philistine army extended up to Socoh, then one would expect the Israelite forces to be on the other side of the valley, seeking to block the Philistine advance into the hill country of Judah. And that's exactly what took place.

The hill opposite Socoh in the Elah Valley

Look at the small hill just across the valley from where we're now standing. Just behind the hill are the mountains of Judah. And the road beside that small hill follows a ridge up into the hills, coming out near the town of Bethlehem. No wonder David's father Jesse sent his three oldest sons to follow Saul to war (1 Sam. 17:13). If the Philistines weren't stopped, Bethlehem itself was threatened.

Okay, it's time for us to *carefully* make our way down off this hill and join the rest of the group. We're taking them over near the base of that small hill just across the valley. From here you can see just how strategic that area is, but our group doesn't yet have that perspective. So watch me try to convince them that I'm not crazy for taking them to a most *unlikely* tourist spot.

AUTHENTICITY IN THE ELAH VALLEY

Sorry for making all of you wait here on the bus while I took a short detour. Hopefully you enjoyed the air conditioning. But now we're all going on a short hike. And as we do, I want you to remember one key word—authenticity. Keep that word in mind because you will think I've lost my mind as you follow me off the bus, over a guardrail, and along a path overgrown with weeds and bushes.

Okay, we're here. This is perhaps the most "unusual" stop we've made on our trip. Not scenic, but definitely different. We're here because plus or minus a few hundred yards, I believe we're standing at the *exact* spot where one of the most amazing battles in Bible history took place. But first, let me set the stage.

Sharing the story of David and Goliath in the Elah Valley

Look back at the bus. See that hill right behind it, on the other side of the road? That's Socoh, the hill I just climbed. Now look down the valley. See the taller mountain way out in the distance? It's about three miles away, and it's where the ancient city of Azekah was located. Just on the other side of that mountain is the Philistine Plain. If we had x-ray vision and could see through the mountain, we would see the Philistine city of Gath. It's just ten miles from where we are right now.

Next, look here, right behind me. See this ditch? It's actually the brook that ran through this rather narrow valley. It's dried up right now, but you can tell a small stream once ran through here. The old road through this valley crossed the stream right where we're standing. It then curved past the small hill on the other side, before climbing a ridge up into the hill country. Follow that road and you'll eventually arrive at Bethlehem, about fifteen miles away.

All these details are important, and here's why. The writer of 1 Samuel 17 starts his account by describing the preparations for a major battle between Israel and the Philistines. The Philistines were pushing their way into the foothills of Israel. If they weren't stopped, the heartland of the country itself could be threatened. And all the places I just pointed out are identified by name in 1 Samuel 17. Socoh was the front lines of the Philistine army. From Socoh all the way back to Azekah in the distance, the far side of the valley was carpeted with Philistine tents. Ephes-dammim means "boundary of blood" and suggests this location had seen its share of conflict in the struggle between these two nations.

The chapter then provides Israel's response to the Philistine aggression as Saul and the men of Israel gathered to block the Philistine advance. It specifically says the Philistines stood on the mountain on one side while Israel stood on the mountain on the other side, with the valley between them. If the Philistines were on Socoh, right behind you, then the Israelites were on the hill just behind me, and we're standing in the valley between the two. Israel had its back to the wall. If the Philistines broke through here, Bethlehem and the other towns in the hill country were threatened.

We know what happened next. Goliath came out to challenge Israel to a duel among champions. The tallest warrior from the army of the Philistines daring Israel to send out its best warrior to fight. All eyes turned to look at Saul, who stood a head taller than everyone else in the army of Israel. But, "when Saul and the Israelites heard this, they were terrified and deeply shaken" (1 Sam. 17:11). Who could stand against Goliath?

The answer arrived with David, a young shepherd from Bethlehem. Sent by his father to check on his brothers, David heard Goliath's boast. But David wasn't impressed. "What will a man get for killing this Philistine and ending his defiance of Israel? Who is this pagan Philistine anyway, that he is allowed to defy the armies of the living God?" (1 Sam. 17:26).

In desperation Saul selected this shepherd to stand against Goliath. Saul offered his own royal armor, but David politely refused. He felt more comfortable choosing the weapons he'd skillfully mastered while watching over his father's flock. "He picked up five smooth stones from a stream and put them into his shepherd's bag. Then, armed only with his shepherd's staff and sling, he started across the valley to fight the Philistine" (1 Sam. 17:40).

Stop and think about those words. If David was coming from the camp of Israel on the hill behind me, and heading toward Socoh to fight Goliath, where would he have stopped to pick up those five smooth stones? We're standing right next to the stream, on a direct line between the two hills. Remember what I said before? Plus or minus a few hundred yards, *this* is where the battle took place. But let's get back to the story.

Goliath was incredulous. He looked down on David with contempt and sneered. "'Am I a dog,' he roared at David, 'that you come at me with a stick?'" (1 Sam. 17:43). He cursed David, and threatened to tear him to pieces and feed him to the buzzards. And that's when we hear David's great confession. Listen carefully to his words.

"You come to me with sword, spear, and javelin, but I come to you in the name of the LORD of Heaven's Armies—the God of the armies of Israel, whom you have defied. Today the LORD will conquer you, and I will kill you and cut off your head. And then I will give the dead bodies of your men to the birds and wild animals, and the whole world will know that there is a God in Israel! And everyone assembled here will know that the LORD rescues his people, but not with sword and spear. This is the LORD's battle, and he will give you to us!" (1 Sam. 17:45–47)

David was not blind. He clearly saw Goliath's size . . . and his weapons. But David viewed Goliath not from a human perspective, but from God's perspective. Goliath was bigger than David, but he was no match for the God who was the *ultimate* commander in chief of Israel's army. If I had to choose one word to describe David's attitude, it would be *confidence*. He knew the God he served, and he was confident in God's ability to deliver because he had already seen God deliver him "from the claws of the lion and the bear" (1 Sam. 17:37). This wasn't a contest between David and Goliath, it was a contest between God and Goliath. David knew *he* was on the winning side.

What giants are you facing? What is it that has you quaking in your boots, dreading the confrontation? Whatever it is, remind yourself of this. Your "giants" might indeed be bigger, stronger, and more powerful than you. But they're no match for the God you serve. Remember, the battle is the Lord's—and He's the one who will deliver!

HUMOR IN THE ELAH VALLEY

I never have to worry about sharing this particular site with other groups. Don't get me wrong, other Christian tours do visit the Elah Valley, but almost none come to this spot. Most Israeli guides take their groups to the other end of the valley, close to Azekah. It's easier for buses to stop there, and access to the brook is also easier. But—and this is what I stress to the hardy souls who climb over the guardrail with me—those other groups are visiting the *wrong* spot. The front lines of the Philistines were at Socoh, not Azekah. I want to lead a tour that stresses *authenticity*. Thankfully, the group who climbed over the guardrail are now as excited about this spot as I am.

It's time to head back to the bus, but most of the group want to first gather five smooth stones from the brook to take home as souvenirs. I wonder how often Israeli security personnel at the airport have watched bags of rocks going through the x-ray machines. I can imagine the conversation in Hebrew between the person monitoring the machine and the supervisor.

Screener: "Shmulik, I've got something suspicious here. It looks like a bag of rocks."

Supervisor: "Don't worry about that. It's just a bunch of Christians who've been to the Elah Valley!"

Some tourists are very particular about finding just the right size and shape rocks. The stones used by David were round, and slightly smaller than a fist. But I've seen people come up from the brook with tiny pebbles that would have bounced off Goliath like a swarm of gnats. Others head back to the bus with rocks so large they would have snapped the leather straps on David's sling. And still others take so long to find just the right rocks that, had they been searching in David's time, Goliath would have killed them before they ever made it out of the brook.

I must admit that I brought home a stone from my first trip to the Elah Valley. I'm convinced I actually have one of the five original stones. David used one. I picked up one. So that leaves three more for our pilgrims to find!

Searching for five smooth stones in the Elah brook

For years I've been conducting a one-man campaign to get a restaurant built right next to this spot in the Elah Valley. I have all the details worked out. All that's needed is an investor . . . and some cooperation from Israel's Ministry of Tourism. Imagine a restaurant with a rooftop viewing area where groups could retell the story without having to climb over a guard-rail. Next to the restaurant, we would place a nine-foot model of Goliath. For a small fee, anyone wanting to try his or her hand at using a sling could try to slay the giant. (I've also learned from experience that this part of the operation would need to be fenced in. I have a friend who experimented with a sling here. He twirled and then released the sling's strap allowing the rock to shoot out. Unfortunately, the rock went in the *wrong* direction.)

This restaurant could be the official home of the "Goliath burger." It would feature clean restrooms, something needed in the Shephelah. It would also have a souvenir shop to match any in the land. Tourists could purchase rocks from the Elah brook, slings, official "Samuel anointing oil," and even camel-crossing signs like those along the highways. Sadly, I have my doubts this will open any time soon. But someday, if you spot a restaurant near So-coh, just remember I thought of it first.

Every group enjoys the Elah Valley, but in some ways student groups have more fun at the site. Perhaps it's because of their youthful ability to climb over guardrails. Or maybe it's because of their fertile imaginations. On one occasion I had a student group reenact the clash between David and Goliath—minus the sword, spear, and sling. It was still a memorable battle.

Students reenacting the battle between David and Goliath

Looking down the Sorek Valley from Beth Shemesh

CHAPTER 32

The Sorek Valley:

A Valley with Eye Problems

The Sorek Valley is easy to miss. The highway climbs over part of the hill on which the Old Testament city of Beth Shemesh once sat. Off to the right is the modern town of Beth Shemesh, and it's easy for travelers to become so distracted by the McDonald's and Aroma Café signs at the mall that they fail to notice the valley stretching out to the left. But we need to stop at the Old Testament site of Beth Shemesh because it's the perfect viewing platform for a number of Old Testament events connected with the Sorek Valley.

Beth Shemesh was in the tribal allotment of Judah (Josh. 15:10), and the Sorek Valley was the boundary between Judah and the tribe of Dan. The town of Beth Shemesh itself was one of the towns allotted to the Levites (Josh. 21:16). The name means "house of the sun," or perhaps "temple of the sun." The city received that name from the Canaanites in honor of the sun goddess they worshiped. But standing here on the site, our focus is on geography, not Canaanite religion.

Gazing down the valley to the west, it almost looks as if the valley ends at a low ridge on the horizon. In reality, the valley bends to the right just before that ridge and then continues out to the Philistine Plain. At the end of the valley was a Philistine town named Timnah, which plays a role in the life of Samson. Just on the other side of that ridge was the Philistine city of Ekron, the northernmost of the five major cities that made up the Philistine pentapolis—Gaza, Ashkelon, Ashdod, Gath, and Ekron (Josh. 13:3; 1 Sam. 6:17).

Immediately to our north is a hill, and near the eastern end of that hill were two Israelite towns. They were part of the tribal allotment of Dan that extended down the valley all the way to the Mediterranean. Those two towns—Zorah and Eshtaol—were the hometowns of Samson. "And the Spirit of the LORD began to stir him while he lived in Mahaneh-dan, which is located between the towns of Zorah and Eshtaol" (Judg. 13:25).

The valley looks very fertile and productive today, but it struggled with "eye problems" in the past.

THE SOREK VALLEY'S "EYE PROBLEMS"

Eye problems are not a laughing matter. A number of people in the Bible experienced eye problems. Jacob was able to trick his father because Isaac "was old and turning blind" (Gen. 27:1). Eli the high priest went blind near the end of his life. His "eyes were fixed and he could not see" (1 Sam. 4:15 NASB). Imagine living in a rugged land like Israel and having poor vision, or not being able to see at all, or developing cataracts or some other eye disease that causes your vision to decline with age.

But as difficult as physical blindness might be, spiritual blindness is even worse. Spiritual blindness is a total disregard for the spiritual realities of life—an utter cluelessness about God and His control of the universe. The consequences of spiritual blindness are even more devastating than physical blindness. And it seems that on at least three occasions the inhabitants of the Sorek Valley struggled with spiritual myopia.

THE NEARSIGHTEDNESS OF THE DANITES

The eye problems in the Sorek Valley showed up quite early in Israel's history. Judges 18 describes an event that took place soon after Israel entered the promised land. The account begins by describing a problem facing the tribe of Dan. "In those days the tribe of the Danites was seeking an inheritance for themselves to live in, for until that day an inheritance had not been allotted to them as a possession among the tribes of Israel" (Judg. 18:1 NASB).

A casual reader might feel pity for the poor tribe of Dan who had evidently been passed over by God when He was assigning land to the different tribes. But a more careful reading of the Bible reveals that this wasn't the case at all.

Joshua 19:40–48 shows that the tribe had *already* been allotted land by God. In fact, they possessed at least two of the towns named in that allotment—Zorah and Eshtaol (Judg. 18:2). The problem was that most of their inheritance was situated in land occupied by either the Amorites or the Philistines. And as Judges 1:34 makes clear, these local powers "forced them back into the hill country and would not let them come down into the plains."

Rather than fight to take and hold the land promised to them by God, the Danites went looking for an easier inheritance. And they thought they had found it in the far north of the country. When the five spies reported back to the rest of the tribe, they said, "Come on, let's attack them! We have seen the land, and it is very good. . . . When you get there, you will find the people living carefree lives. God has given us a spacious and fertile land, lacking in nothing!" (Judg. 18:9–10). *We have seen the land!* There is the beginning of the Danites' eye problems.

Remember back to our time at Dan? It *was* a beautiful, well-watered area. Unfortunately, every major power that attacked Israel from the north reached Dan first. By looking for something more appealing than the land given to them by God, the tribe avoided their immediate problem, only to encounter greater difficulties later.

SAMSON'S EYE PROBLEMS

The eye problems in the Sorek Valley continued with the remnant from the tribe of Dan who stayed here. The problems are highlighted during the extended account of Samson. He was a man deliberately raised up by God to "begin to rescue Israel from the Philistines" (Judg. 13:5). Unfortunately, Samson soon developed eye problems. Instead of delivering Israel from the Philistines, Samson saw something in Philistia that attracted his attention. "One day when Samson was in Timnah, one of the Philistine women caught his eye. . . . Samson told his father, 'Get her for me! She looks good to me'" (Judg. 14:1, 3). In Hebrew Samson literally says, "She is smooth in my eyes."

Samson's "eye problems" continued to lead him astray until he finally gave away the secret of his strength to Delilah, who then cut off his hair. That's when God used the Philistines to solve Samson's eye problems. They "captured him and gouged out his eyes" (Judg. 16:21). Then they took him to Gaza to work as a slave grinding grain. Samson's hair grew back, and he managed one last act of superhuman strength to topple the Philistine temple on those who were gathered. But the sad epitaph of this man chosen by God to deliver Israel highlights the shortcomings caused by his eye problems. "So he killed more people when he died than he had during his entire lifetime" (Judg. 16:30).

But the eye problems of the Sorek Valley aren't over. They surface again in 1 Samuel 5–6.

PEEKING INTO THE ARK

As 1 Samuel 5 ends, the Philistines were preparing to send the ark of the covenant back to Israel. They had captured the ark when Israel foolishly brought it into battle, trying to force God to fight for them. Israel lost, the priests carrying the ark were killed, and the Philistines hauled the ark away as a trophy of war.

But the Philistines soon wondered whether they had captured Israel's God, or if He had captured them. Every city where the ark was sent experienced divine judgment, which included a severe plague. When the ark finally arrived in Ekron, just to our west, the people cried out in fear, "They are bringing the Ark of the God of Israel here to kill us, too!" (1 Sam. 5:10). It seems the Philistines had more fear and respect for God than Israel did!

The Philistines worked out a plan to send the ark back to Israel. They still weren't sure the plagues were caused by God. Perhaps it had all just been an amazing coincidence. So they put the ark on a cart to be pulled by two cows who had just given birth and who, under normal circumstances, wouldn't want to leave their newborn calves. If the cows stood in place, the Philistines could assume the plagues that arrived in their land at the same time as the ark were nothing more than an unfortunate accident. But if the cows took the ark back to the Israelites, then the Philistines would know the plagues had come from the God of Israel.

The cows walked down the road directly toward Beth Shemesh! After seven months with the Philistines, the ark was finally back in Israel. The people of Beth Shemesh were overjoyed to see the ark, and they celebrated by breaking apart the cart to use as fuel while sacrificing the cows as burnt offerings to God.

So far, so good. But now the spiritual blindness of these inhabitants of the Sorek Valley shows up. And the consequences are catastrophic.

First Samuel 6 says God struck down some of the inhabitants of Beth Shemesh "because they looked into the Ark of the LORD" (1 Sam. 6:19). There are two possible problems with this account. One is textual, and the other is ethical. The textual problem centers on the number of people killed. Some accounts have 50,070, while others simply have seventy. The smaller number makes more sense based on the size of the town, so the larger number was likely caused by a scribal error. But either number represents a serious judgment from God on the people.

The larger concern would seem to be an ethical one. Why would God kill people simply for looking into the ark? After all, we reason, maybe they were just checking to make sure everything was still inside and that nothing had been stolen. Maybe they were just curious. Maybe they didn't know better. At first glance, it seems like a severe judgment on God's part against people who had just given thanks to Him for the ark's return. But in this case, first impressions are deceiving.

The key to understanding the spiritual blindness of the people of Beth Shemesh is to remember who lived in the town. While the region around Beth Shemesh had been given to the tribes of Dan and Judah, Joshua 21:13–16 said the town of Beth Shemesh itself was given as an inheritance to "the descendants of Aaron the priest." More specifically, it was given to the Kohath branch of the Levites. The men who peeked into the box were Levites who should have known better.

God had given the Kohathites specific directions about how to handle the articles of furniture in the tabernacle since they were the ones assigned to carry it through the wilderness. In Numbers 4:15, God warned them against touching the furnishings. "They must not touch the sacred objects, or they will die." The Kohathites knew God's command, but they chose to disobey. And sadly, they discovered God meant what He said.

Rather than repenting of their disobedience, these spiritually blind Levites made an even more foolish choice. In 1 Samuel 6:21, they "sent messengers to the people at Kiriath-jearim and told them, 'The Philistines have returned the Ark of the LORD. Come here and get it!'"

So where's Kiriath-jearim, and why was this a foolish thing to do? Kiriath-jearim was one of four Canaanite towns, including Gibeon, that had tricked Joshua into making peace with them. As a result, these four Gentile towns agreed to be "the woodcutters and water carriers for the community of Israel and for the altar of the LORD—wherever the LORD would choose to build it" (Josh. 9:27).

Think about this. The Levites, who were responsible for taking care of the articles of furniture in the tabernacle, handed over the ark of the covenant to Gentile servants for safekeeping. And they asked these Gentiles to carry the ark home, even though God had specifically commanded the Levites to carry it. Because of their spiritual blindness, the ark stayed among the Gentiles for another twenty years.

So how is *your* spiritual eyesight today? Do you have 20/20 vision when it comes to following God's Word, or are you starting to develop spiritual myopia? Look carefully at what happened to those who lived in the Sorek Valley to understand the importance of maintaining spiritual acuity when it comes to obeying God.

LEAPING LIZARDS!

While we've been standing here at Beth Shemesh, one of the ever-present lizards that live throughout Israel has climbed out onto one of the nearby rocks to sun himself. Some of you may have already seen other lizards on this trip . . . at Megiddo, in Caesarea Philippi, on Masada, and even scurrying along the steps leading up to Arad. But this lizard is almost preening for the group, puffing out its chest as if to say, "Welcome to my castle! I'm the master of all I survey!"

Then, as if tiring of our company, it scurries down the other side of the stone and disappears from view.

A lizard sunning itself on a stone at Beth Shemesh

The sudden appearance of that crazy lizard here in the ruins of Beth Shemesh reminds me of Proverbs 30:28. "Lizards—they are easy to catch, but they are found even in kings' palaces." Certainly, a lizard like the one we just saw is small, insignificant, and even despised as a nuisance. But it's also present nearly everywhere in Israel. I've seen them darting among the rocks in ancient ruins—and running across the patios of very nice hotels. Before the invention of glass windows, thermal seal doors, and pest control companies, lizards were the ever-present guests in virtually every home in Israel.

Have you ever wondered what lesson the writer of Proverb 30:28 wanted us to learn by watching this lizard skitter across the stones of Beth Shemesh? I think he focused on the lizard to teach us the wisdom of *perseverance*. Lizards might seem worthless and defenseless. After all, the writer notes that someone with quick enough reflexes can catch one in his hands. But the humble lizard had, as we might say today, learned how to "live like a king." Through his perseverance he had made his way into the king's palace—which is more than the average Israelite of that day could say.

It's time to finish taking your pictures and head back to the bus. We have one more valley to visit before we arrive in Jerusalem!

Looking down at the Aijalon Valley

CHAPTER 33

The Aijalon Valley:
The Front Door to Jerusalem

The Aijalon Valley is the last of our five valleys in the Shephelah. It's also the main valley that connected Jerusalem to the coast and the International Highway. Today, two main roads lead up to Jerusalem from the Aijalon Valley along two different branches of the valley. We're going to visit both.

During Bible times the most important route to Jerusalem went through the valley and then climbed a ridge at the northeastern end. Controlling this ridge were the towns of Lower Beth Horon and Upper Beth Horon. The road then continued past the city of Gibeon before turning south to Jerusalem. This is the road Joshua and the Israelites followed when they chased the Canaanites from Gibeon. "Then the Israelites chased the enemy along the road to Beth-horon" (Josh. 10:10). It was while traveling down this road into the Aijalon Valley that Joshua cried out, "Let the sun stand still over Gibeon, and the moon over the valley of Aijalon" (v. 12).

King Solomon later recognized the importance of protecting this approach to his capital, so he took considerable care to guard the route against attack. He fortified the city of Gezer (1 Kings 9:15) in the valley itself, and he "fortified the towns of Upper Beth-horon and Lower Beth-horon, rebuilding their walls and installing barred gates" (2 Chron. 8:5).

Let's travel along this route to see some of the sites.

EMMAUS

You might remember the account of Jesus walking with the two disciples on the road to Emmaus (Luke 24:13–35). It's a fascinating story, but it also has some major complications. How far was Emmaus from Jerusalem? And where specifically was this Emmaus located? We need to answer the first question before we can address the second.

A spring-fed pool at the site of ancient Emmaus

Most translations say the town was "seven miles from Jerusalem," but there is a textual issue. Depending on which Greek manuscript is used, the distance was either sixty stadia (seven miles) or 160 stadia (eighteen miles). I personally favor the longer distance. It's supported by the *Codex Sinaiticus*, one of the very early Greek manuscripts. And the longer distance also has good historical support. Eusebius, the early church historian and bishop of

Caesarea, reported that Emmaus "is now Nicopolis, a famous city of Palestine."[1] Nicopolis was located about eighteen miles from Jerusalem on the edge of the Aijalon Valley and seems to be the best candidate for Emmaus.

Traveling from Jerusalem to Emmaus in Jesus' day would not have been a simple journey. The two disciples needed to walk north from Jerusalem several miles before turning west to follow the same road taken by Joshua when he rescued the Gibeonites. They would have reached the Aijalon Valley and Emmaus after a five-hour walk.

As the two disciples walked along and discussed the bewildering events that had just transpired in Jerusalem, they were joined by a third person they didn't recognize. "What are you discussing so intently as you walk along?" he asked (Luke 24:17). They turned to address this stranger. "You must be the only person in Jerusalem who hasn't heard about all the things that have happened there the last few days" (v. 18).

The stranger pressed them for details, so they told him about Jesus of Nazareth. "He was a prophet who did powerful miracles, and he was a mighty teacher in the eyes of God and all the people. But our leading priests and other religious leaders handed him over to be condemned to death, and they crucified him. We had hoped he was the Messiah who had come to rescue Israel" (vv. 19–21). Their hoped-for Messiah had died. But the situation had taken an unexpected twist that very morning, the third day since His death. "Then some women from our group of his followers were at his tomb early this morning, and they came back with an amazing report. They said his body was missing, and they had seen angels who told them Jesus is alive! Some of our men ran out to see, and sure enough, his body was gone, just as the women had said" (vv. 22–24).

The response of the stranger must have startled them. "You foolish people! You find it so hard to believe all that the prophets wrote in the Scriptures. Wasn't it clearly predicted that the Messiah would have to suffer all these things before entering his glory?" (vv. 25–26). It's as if this stranger not only knew what had taken place, He knew *why* it had happened. He rebuked the two disciples for not recognizing that the recent events had been predicted in the Old Testament. "Then Jesus took them through the writings of Moses and all the prophets, explaining from all the Scriptures the things concerning himself" (v. 27). Imagine a five-hour Bible study with Jesus!

Eventually, the three reached Emmaus. The disciples urged the stranger to stay because "it is getting late" (v. 29). Literally they said it was "toward evening." According to ancient cultural tradition, the "evening" began after twelve noon, the point when the sun had reached its apex and begun to descend. If they left Jerusalem early that morning, it was likely early afternoon when they invited Jesus into their house for a meal. Jesus "took the bread and blessed it. Then he broke it and gave it to them" (v. 30). And at that point their eyes were opened, and they realized the stranger was Jesus Himself! Then He vanished.

> The greatest Bible study ever taught happened on a rocky road between Jerusalem and Emmaus.

And as the sun continued its descent toward the Mediterranean in the west, these two disciples rushed back toward Jerusalem, a return hike of eighteen miles. Their excitement kept them moving, but it was still another five-hour walk back to the house where the disciples were all gathered.

The greatest Bible study ever taught happened on a rocky road between Jerusalem and Emmaus. There were no multi-page handouts. No visual aids. No study guides. No group discussion. Just Jesus explaining how He fulfilled all the Old Testament predictions of the coming Messiah. Emmaus is a great place to remind ourselves that the goal of any Bible study is to focus on Jesus.

NABI SAMWIL

Our drive up the Beth Horon ridge route from Emmaus is uneventful. Our next stop is Nabi Samwil, which is Arabic for "the prophet Samuel." We're visiting a building that is venerated as Samuel's tomb by Jews, Muslims, and Christians. There's just one slight problem. Samuel *isn't* buried here.

According to 1 Samuel 25:1, "Samuel died, and all Israel gathered for his funeral. They buried him at his house in Ramah." Ramah is three miles *east* of Nabi Samwil.

The building perched atop Nabi Samwil

So why is this spot named for Samuel? I'm glad you asked! You see, seventy-five pages of my doctoral dissertation focused on the identification of this site. I'm convinced we're now standing at biblical Mizpah. Samuel began his public ministry by gathering all Israel to Mizpah (1 Sam. 7:5–6), and Samuel publicly turned over leadership of the nation to King Saul at Mizpah (1 Sam. 10:17–25). It was also one of the stops on Samuel's yearly circuit of cities he visited to judge Israel (1 Sam. 7:15–17), making Samuel the world's first "circuit judge." Since Mizpah bookends Samuel's public ministry as judge, it's easy to understand how his name came to be associated with this site.

We're not really going to spend time exploring the building. Instead, as we walk in the door, turn left and follow me up a long flight of stairs to the roof. As the highest spot in the area, we're going to use Nabi Samwil for a viewing platform. From this one spot you can see from Jerusalem in the south to Bethel in the north, with the towns of Ramah and Gibeah on the ridge in between. Below us is the town of Gibeon, which we'll visit next. On my very first study tour to Israel, the instructor made a statement that has stuck with me all these years. He said that 50 percent of all the action narratives in the Old Testament took place within viewing distance of this one spot. And he was right!

Those who know the geography of the Old Testament have always understood the significance of this site. Norman MacLeod, a favorite chaplain of Queen Victoria, visited Israel in 1864. Two years later, he published a detailed account of his journey. On his way to Jerusalem he stopped to view the surrounding landscape from Nabi Samwil.

> I did not look for beauty, and therefore was not surprised at its absence; but I did look for the battle scenes—for the Marathon and Thermopylae—of the world's civilisation, and for the earthly stage on which real men of flesh and blood, but full of the spirit of the living God, played out their grand parts . . . and I found it no other than I looked for, to my ceaseless joy and thanksgiving. . . . I left the top of Neby Samwil [sic] with devoutest thanksgiving, feeling that, if I saw no more, but were obliged to return next day to Europe, my journey would have been well repaid.[2]

In spite of its relatively small size, the area around Nabi Samwil played an amazingly significant role in Bible history. From Joshua during the time of the conquest, to Samuel, Saul, and David at the start of the monarchy, to Jeremiah at the time of Jerusalem's fall to Babylon, this tiny piece of real estate witnessed some of the most remarkable events in Bible history.

But visiting Nabi Samwil can also be hazardous to your health!

On one trip to Nabi Samwil, we arrived to find a group of Italian nuns already on the roof. The area is quite large, so I asked our group to follow me up the stairs. Unfortunately, we did have one woman in our group who wasn't in the best physical condition. She went last, and she paused several times to catch her breath. The rest of the group made it to the roof without difficulty, but when the nuns saw our group coming onto the roof they decided it was time for them to leave.

I was waiting at the top of the steps for our last traveler, and I realized that if the nuns started down, our wayward lamb would *never* make it to the top. So using hand gestures I asked the nuns to wait—while shouting down the steps to encourage our final pilgrim to keep climbing. The nuns began nudging me to get me to move out of the way. To block them, I turned my back toward them and spread out my arms.

That's when several of them tried to shove me down the stairs!

The stairway to the roof at Nabi Samwil

My thumbs jammed against the stone entrance, and the group of diminutive but persistent nuns pounded on my back to get me to move. I held my position until our last tourist made her way onto the rooftop. The nuns stomped their way down the stairs, and I spent the rest of the day nursing my bruised thumbs.

From the top of Nabi Samwil one can look down on a round hill rising up from the relatively flat area allotted to the tribe of Benjamin. This is the town of Gibeon. It is currently off limits to tourists because of the political

The round hill of Gibeon from Nabi Samwil

situation, but I've had the opportunity to visit several times. On one occasion, a group of students made a deal with a shopkeeper in the Old City of Jerusalem to rent a bus and visit sites closed to most tourists. Shaban took us to several biblical sites, including Gibeon.

One of the most amazing sites at Gibeon is the water system. Though it's called a "pool" in the Bible, it's actually a round shaft and stairway carved into the bedrock. At the bottom of the shaft was a tunnel leading to the city's water source. This pool is mentioned twice in the Bible, both times in connection with warfare. It first appears as the scene of a gruesome battle between David's men and the men of Saul's son, Ish-Bosheth.

According to 2 Samuel 2:13, these two groups of warriors met "at the pool of Gibeon. The two groups sat down there, facing each other from opposite sides of the pool." Each side chose twelve warriors, and all twenty-four died in hand-to-hand combat. The account ends by saying, "So this place at Gibeon has been known ever since as the Field of Swords" (v. 16).

The second time the pool of Gibeon appears in the Bible is after the fall of Jerusalem to the Babylonians. Gedaliah was appointed governor over

The pool of Gibeon

the surviving remnant, and the center of administration was moved to Miz-pah—Nabi Samwil. A renegade named Ishmael, and ten henchmen, came to the administrative center and killed Gedaliah and the Babylonian guards left behind to maintain order. Ishmael captured a number of hostages, including Jeremiah, and left Mizpah, heading east toward Ammon.

Word of what happened reached those still in the region, and they hurried after Ishmael to rescue the captives. "They caught up with him at the large pool near Gibeon" (Jer. 41:12). Evidently, Ishmael had stopped to stock up on water and other provisions before heading through the Judean Wilderness toward Jericho and then on to Ammon. The hostages—including Jeremiah—were rescued, but Ishmael escaped.

THE "LAST KING" OF ISRAEL

It's time to retrace our steps. We need to drive back down into the Aijalon Valley and then take the other road into Jerusalem. Though the other route was a secondary roadway in Bible times, today it's the main road from Tel Aviv and the airport to Jerusalem. It begins in a narrow finger of the Aijalon Valley and climbs up toward the ancient biblical site of Kiriath-jearim. That's one of the towns that joined with Gibeon to trick Joshua, and it's also the place to which the people of Beth Shemesh sent the ark.

This tiny slice of the Aijalon Valley ends near Kiriath-jearim. In the past, the road would have curved back to rejoin the other route near Gibeon. But today—thanks to earthmovers and dynamite—the modern road to Jerusalem continues through the upper reaches of the Sorek Valley. We'll continue along this road to Jerusalem, but we first need to make a quick stop for a bathroom break.

As you can tell from our journey through the Shephelah, bathrooms are a precious commodity. But the situation has been getting better. During my very first trip to Israel, bathroom breaks in the Shephelah sounded like this: "It's time for a rest stop. Men to the left; women to the right." Let's just say that Israel has come a long way in the last four decades.

This final stop takes most visitors to Israel by surprise. (Unless, of course, you are reading this book *before* you visit.) I assume a day will come when this stop will go the way of other sites in Israel—buildings and monuments that eventually collapse into decay and ruin. But hopefully that won't happen for many more years, because it is worth the investment in time.

We've talked about many kings and rulers during this trip. Some had hearts that followed after God; many others did not. But most left some physical mark on the land—something that said to those who followed "I ruled as king." And our final stop of the day is no exception. This spot is dedicated to the "last king" of Israel. No, it's not King Zedekiah. And it's not Jesus.

This king is Elvis!

The Elvis Inn is a gas station that has become a shrine to Elvis Presley.

Every square inch of the interior features pictures and posters of Elvis. Elvis music is playing constantly. You can buy Elvis wine or purchase a cup of coffee in your own souvenir Elvis mug. Pick up an Elvis-in-Israel postcard, or buy an Elvis T-shirt for your children or grandchildren. And be sure to get your picture taken with one of the Elvis statues—there are some inside and outside.

One time we stopped with a group of students on our way to the airport to fly home. I decided to have my picture taken beside the Elvis statue outside. Unfortunately, I wasn't paying attention, and I hit my head on one of the bronze tuning frets on his

Statue of Elvis at the Elvis Inn

guitar. I cut myself and went to the airport holding paper towels on my head to try to stop the bleeding.

As the bus pulled onto the highway, I told the students that I hoped they had enjoyed this final stop on their tour. And from the back of the bus came the voice of a student doing his best Elvis impression:

"Thank you very much!"

The Herodium with Herod's pool in the foreground

CHAPTER 34

The Herodium:
Herod's Funeral Monument

Before we explore Jerusalem we have two final stops to make outside the city. The first is the Herodium, a volcano-shaped fortress between Bethlehem and the Judean Wilderness. Herod the Great built many magnificent palaces throughout his kingdom, but this is the only one he named after himself. We'll talk about why shortly. In the meantime, get ready for a hike to the top. Take your time. I'll wait until everyone has reached the summit before I begin the explanation.

THE VIEW FROM THE HERODIUM

As I said at the bottom of the hill, this fortress was built by Herod the Great. Herod not only chose to name this spot after himself, he also decided that this is where he wanted to be buried. Archaeologists discovered the remains of his mausoleum on the side of the hill. Now that you've reached the top, pause to look out over the horizon. To the northwest you can just make out three towers that stand as sentinels on the Mount of Olives east of Jerusalem. The city is on the other side of those towers. Immediately to the west of us is Bethlehem. It's a large town now, but it would have been a relatively small village during Bible times. To our south we can see Tekoa, the hometown of Amos the prophet. But perhaps the most spectacular view from here is toward the east. On a clear day we can actually see across the Judean Wilderness to the Dead Sea and the mountains of modern-day Jordan on the other side.

During Old Testament times those hills were in the country of Moab.

The pool we passed below is clearly visible from up here. There wasn't a natural water source in this area, so Herod built a five-mile-long aqueduct just to bring in water from springs south of Bethlehem. Between the water brought to the pool and the occasional winter rains, the cisterns carved into the mountain were kept full.

Josephus provided an excellent description of this palace, which has now been confirmed by excavations. He wrote that Herod "built round towers all about the top of it, and filled up the remaining space with most costly palaces round about, insomuch, that not only the sight of the inner apartments was splendid, but great wealth was laid out on the outward walls, and partitions, and roofs also. Besides this, he brought a mighty quantity of water from a great distance, and at vast charges, and raised an ascent to it of two hundred steps of the whitest marble."[1]

The remains of Herod's palace inside the Herodium

The remains are impressive, but we still need to ask one key question. Why did Herod choose to name *this* palace after himself? Why not his palace in Jerusalem, or Jericho, or Samaria, or Masada, or Machaerus? What made this place so special?

Thankfully, Josephus has the answer.

Shortly after becoming king, young Herod was forced to flee for his life from Jerusalem, with the Parthians and some of his own countrymen in hot pursuit. They wanted to kill him before he could escape to Rome and get help to regain his throne. Herod raced toward Masada before heading to Idumea on a roundabout journey to reach Rome. But he was nearly captured and killed before he could even reach the Dead Sea.

Looking down at the pool from the top of the Herodium

Herod and his family had traveled sixty furlongs (just over seven miles) from Jerusalem when the cart carrying Herod's mother overturned. Josephus explained what happened next. "Yet was he once almost going to kill himself, upon the overthrow of a wagon, and the danger his mother was then in of being killed: and this on two accounts; because of his great concern for her: and because he was afraid lest, by this delay, the enemy should overtake him in the pursuit."[2]

As the enemy forces closed in, Herod drew his sword and was about to commit suicide, when those with him called on him to stop. Putting it in today's language, they said something like, "You can't kill yourself. We're depending on you. You're our king, so act like it!" Almost as if flipping a switch, Herod instantly changed. The forlorn fugitive who was so downcast that he was about to take his own life became a ferocious warrior.

> For by that time he was gotten sixty furlongs out of the city, and was upon the road, they fell upon him, and fought hand to hand with him, whom he also put to flight, and overcame, not like one that was in distress, and in necessity, but like one that was excellently prepared for war, and had what he wanted in great plenty. And in this very place where he now overcame the Jews, it was, that he some time afterward built a most excellent palace, and a city round about it, and called it *Herodium*.[3]

Herod named this palace after himself because this was the place he changed from a despondent fugitive to a determined fighter. And that's why he chose to be buried here as well.

THE KING BY MIGHT OR THE KING BY RIGHT

The Herodium is the perfect location to compare two "kings of the Jews"— Herod the Great and Jesus. And what better way to do this than to explore Matthew 2, the only passage in the New Testament where Herod the Great is mentioned.

Matthew picks up the narrative of Jesus' birth following the events described in Luke 2. At this point, Mary and Joseph were still in Bethlehem, though now living in a house. Herod was still king, though the end of his despotic reign was drawing closer. The birth of this "rival king" had escaped his notice until a caravan of wise men rode into Jerusalem from the east.

We're not told exactly where these wise men were from. Some have suggested Babylon, while others believe they came from Persia—modern-day Iran. However, it's also possible they were *sheikhs*, Arab princes of the desert who came to find the Messiah. And this possibility isn't as far-fetched as it might first seem.

In Isaiah 60, the section of the book looking forward to God's promised kingdom, the prophet writes, "Arise, Jerusalem! Let your light shine for all to see. For the glory of the LORD rises to shine on you . . . They will bring you the wealth of many lands. Vast caravans of camels will converge on you, the camels of Midian and Ephah. The people of Sheba will bring gold and

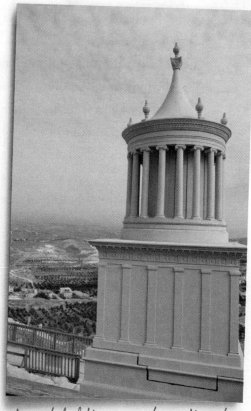

A model of the mausoleum Herod constructed on the hillside

frankincense and will come worshiping the LORD" (Isa. 60:1–6).

A light will shine, and men will come on camels from kingdoms in the Arabian Peninsula bearing gold and frankincense. Could Matthew be reminding his readers of this prophecy about Arab princes who will come to celebrate the arrival of the Jewish Messiah? I think it's quite probable! Herod had great wealth that he had gained through tyranny and extortion, but the king by right received gold, frankincense, and myrrh in an act of voluntary worship by the wise men (Matt. 2:10–11).

Let's return to the contrast between the king by might and the king by right. Herod might be the one sitting on the throne in Jerusalem, but the wise men came to see "the newborn king of the Jews" (Matt. 2:2). Herod had the power of Rome to back up his rule, but Jesus fulfilled God's prophecy showing He was the legitimate king. "And you, O Bethlehem in the land of Judah, are not least among the ruling cities of Judah, for a ruler will come from you who will be the shepherd for my people Israel" (v. 6, quoting Micah 5:2).

Herod, the king by might, "sent soldiers to kill all the boys in and around Bethlehem" (Matt. 2:16) to eliminate this potential rival to his throne, but God delivered His promised Messiah. "An angel of the Lord appeared to Joseph in a dream. 'Get up! Flee to Egypt with the child and his mother,' the angel said. 'Stay there until I tell you to return, because Herod is going to search for the child to kill him'" (v. 13).

The top of the Herodium is an excellent place to retell the story of Matthew 2. The three towers on the Mount of Olives help us identify the location of Jerusalem. The magi arrived there having come through the Judean Wilderness from Jericho. When the religious leaders mentioned the birth of the Messiah in Bethlehem, perhaps Herod instinctively glanced in that direction. He knew *exactly* where this small village was located because he passed nearby every time he visited the Herodium.

The wise men were warned in a dream the very night of their arrival and "returned to their own country by another route" (Matt. 2:12). The most likely route home would have taken them past the Herodium, through the Judean Wilderness, and past Masada. This allowed them to avoid Jerusalem, but they wouldn't have felt safe until they had passed the last of Herod's well-guarded fortresses. Mary and Joseph likely traveled south on the Way of the Patriarchs, from Bethlehem to Hebron, before turning toward the Mediterranean and the coastal road to Egypt. They must also have left the same evening as the wise men.

Herod would have expected the wise men to return the next day. After all, it was only a one- or two-hour journey from Jerusalem to Bethlehem. Allowing a few hours to check on all the newborn children in the area, they might have needed to spend the night there. But surely they would return the next morning. From the Herodium we can almost imagine the dust being kicked up by Herod's riders as they galloped toward Bethlehem "to kill all the boys in and around Bethlehem who were two years old and under, based on the wise men's report of the star's first appearance" (Matt. 2:16).

How did the soldiers know the age of the children since kids weren't issued birth certificates? And why did Herod select the age of two as a cutoff age? Was Jesus really two years old at the time? Children begin making "baby sounds" somewhere between twelve and eighteen months. By the age of two they are beginning to speak simple sentences. Jesus might only have been a few weeks or months old when the wise men arrived. Herod knew the baby was likely a small child based on the time of the star's appearance. But just to be thorough—and Herod was always an overachiever when it came to eliminating possible threats—Herod ordered the soldiers to kill any male child unable to speak. And though the Messiah was to be born in Bethlehem, Herod also ordered the soldiers to kill all the boys "in *and around* Bethlehem" (Matt. 2:16). The passage tells us far more about Herod's viciousness than it does about the actual age of Jesus.

LET'S GO EXPLORING

We have some time, so let's explore Herod's palace. The entire inside of this hill was a single palace reserved for Herod. He had other buildings constructed down below for anyone else invited to spend time here. But the well-guarded upper palace was *his* domain. It had a triclinium, a banquet hall with a table that allowed guests to recline along three sides. It had a very private, but very proper, Roman bath featuring a frigidarium (cold bath), a tepidarium (warm bath), and a caldarium (steam bath). The palace also featured an open courtyard along with private bedrooms.

Once you're done looking through the palace, we're going to head underground. Herod's workmen dug into the rock to carve out cisterns to hold all the water needed for the palace. In later history, Jewish rebels who captured this fortress also carved out tunnels to hide from the Romans. There's much to explore on our way out, so come along.

Next to the exit from the cisterns is a small theater carved into the hillside that was used for the entertainment of Herod's guests. The theater included a "luxury box" complete with painted frescoes. Just beyond the theater are the remains of Herod's mausoleum. An elaborate sarcophagus, thought to be Herod's, was found smashed into small pieces, probably by Jewish rebels during the revolt against Rome. The sarcophagus has been reconstructed and is on display at the Israel Museum.

Once you've taken all your photos, follow me back to the bus for the short drive to Bethlehem.

One of several cisterns dug into the bedrock underneath the Herodium

Stained-glass window at the Church of the Nativity

CHAPTER 35

Bethlehem:
O Little Town of Bethlehem?

Bethlehem. Along with Jerusalem and Nazareth, it is a key stop for most pilgrims to the Holy Land. That's especially true during the Christmas season. Most years, tourists pack Manger Square, the Church of the Nativity, and the stores lining the streets of this historic town. But disruptions—including wars and regional unrest—have periodically reduced the flow of pilgrims to a trickle, bringing financial hardship to a town dependent on tourist dollars for its livelihood.

There was a time when Bethlehem was little more than a postage-stamp-size hamlet that didn't even show up on the road maps of the day. In fact, when Israel first entered the land under Joshua, Bethlehem wasn't even important enough to be listed as a town among the clans of Judah. It's true! Joshua 15 describes the land allotted to the tribe of Judah, clan by clan. He identifies the boundaries of Judah's territory, and then he lists the key towns and villages within that area. In verses 48–60, Joshua lists thirty-eight towns in the hill country of Judah, but Bethlehem wasn't included in the list.

THE WALLED-OFF CITY

Today, Bethlehem is a city that looks more like Berlin during the Cold War. In 2000, the Second Intifada, or uprising, began against Israel. Suicide bombers from the West Bank made their way into Jerusalem on an almost weekly basis to blow themselves up in Jewish restaurants, stores, and markets. Israel responded by building a separation barrier to protect its citizens. In most areas the barrier is a fence, but in some areas—including around Bethlehem—something stronger and more permanent was needed. And that's why a wall of concrete slabs greets visitors to the birthplace of the Prince of Peace.

The separation barrier around Bethlehem

The Palestinians refer to the barrier as the apartheid wall. And to most busloads of tourists it does look forbidding and ominous. So is the wall a blessing or a curse? It really depends on which side of the wall you're standing. If you are a Palestinian, the wall can make you feel as if you are in a large prison. You have to pass through a checkpoint to leave Bethlehem for Israel. If you have a job in Jerusalem, the barrier adds additional time to your journey. It stands as a stark reminder that your life is controlled by Israel in ways you find burdensome.

But now step across to the other side of the wall. If you are Jewish, the wall and fence have brought an end to suicide bombings and most other terrorist incidents. You can go to the market, or the mall, or a restaurant without fear that someone will walk in and set off a vest packed with explosives, nails, and ball bearings. Yes, the wall is ugly. But it was the Palestinian leaders' unwillingness to put an end to terrorism that made the barrier necessary.

INSIDE BETHLEHEM

Bethlehem can be a disappointment to tourists, though the tourists themselves are partly to blame. They arrive in Bethlehem with only a vague idea of what to expect. The images they have of Bethlehem are of Ruth harvesting grain, David tending his father's sheep, or Mary, Joseph, and baby Jesus inside a stable with shepherds and wise men crowded around. Then they drive through crowded streets and fight their way through shopkeepers and vendors toward the Church of the Nativity. But instead of reaching a magnificent cathedral, they

Reality seems to fall far short of expectations in Bethlehem.

Entrance to the Church of the Nativity

find themselves standing in front of a rather nondescript building with a very small entrance. Reality seems to fall short of expectations in Bethlehem.

Guides will share different stories about why the entrance to the church is so small. It's clear that the entrance was once much larger, but the original opening was sealed. Was the entrance made smaller to keep out knights on horseback—or marauders trying to squeeze horse-drawn carts through the doorway? Was it to force pilgrims to bow their heads in reverence as they enter? The real reason was lost in antiquity, but that never stops a guide from sharing a good story.

The inside of the church has recently been renovated, which came none too soon. There were times in the past when groups had to make their way around standing puddles of water caused by a leaking roof. The mosaics and paintings on the columns were virtually hidden under years of soot from burning oil lamps. The entire site looked like an aging spinster who had long ago given up caring about her appearance.

Interior of the church following its renovation

For many years the church was virtually empty except on religious holidays. Groups could visit almost any time. As long as a service wasn't being held, access to the grotto, the traditional spot where Jesus was born, was possible. That all changed with the arrival of large numbers of Russian Orthodox pilgrims along with additional busloads of tourists from cruise ships. The church went from quiet to chaotic.

On several occasions the entire nave was packed with jostling pilgrims and tourists, each trying to avoid being trampled or crushed as they shuffled along toward the grotto. The quietness and sanctity of the site was lost to an underlying babble of several hundred people saying to their neighbors, "What did the guide just say?" This constant chatter was then punctuated by harried priests vainly shouting out, "Silence!" I'm not sure if most people could even hear the priests over the rumble. The scene became so chaotic that we stopped visiting the church. It became virtually impossible to visit the grotto, and the entire experience was as spiritually uplifting as standing on a subway platform during rush hour.

When the church was less crowded, groups could enter the grotto and sing a Christmas carol. "Silent Night," "Away in a Manger," and "O Little Town of Bethlehem" were very popular. But the grotto itself is rather small. It can hold a busload of pilgrims, but not many more. And as the lines grew longer, the priests tried to hustle pilgrims through with little more than a photograph while kneeling beside the silver star.

The traditional spot of Jesus' birth in the grotto

Votive candles in the grotto

My biggest concern in the grotto was always the stand with the votive candles. It stood just off to the side at the bottom of the steps. As people backed up to try to get a picture of the star, they forced those behind them to step back as well. I was always watching to make sure no one backed into the candles. We want our people to be on fire for Jesus, but not in a literal sense!

VIEW FROM THE BELL TOWER

During one of my early trips, the church was virtually empty. So, after visiting the grotto, I turned our group loose to explore on their own. A friend and I went up a set of steps into an area usually closed to visitors. As we walked around, we found ourselves at the entrance to the bell tower just as a worker came out the door. I asked if it was possible to see inside. He hesitated, but then rubbed his thumb against his fingers. I took that as the universal sign that he wanted *baksheesh*—a tip for his services. I reached into my wallet and introduced him to Alexander Hamilton. He then held open the door and waved us in. The stairway up to the bells is not for the faint of heart, but once we finally crawled our way up to the top, the scene was magnificent. We hurried back down because we didn't want him to get into trouble on our account.

EXPLORING BETHLEHEM

For most tourists, a visit to Bethlehem revolves around three visual images: the wall, the Church, and the olive wood shop. Then it's off to the next stop on an overcrowded itinerary. But Bethlehem is much more than these three images. Though it's hard to do on a tour, taking time to get to know some of the people who live in Bethlehem pays great dividends. From Elias the peddler

View from the Bethlehem Bell Tower

who turned out to be a Scripture-quoting follower of Jesus, to two brothers who started out selling postcards and trinkets to busloads of pilgrims and ended up owning a large store, to a local pastor who boldly shares his faith in spite of intense persecution, Bethlehem's living stones are far more inspiring than its shrines and monuments. It just takes longer to uncover them.

Bethlehem can also reveal its biblical secrets, though they require a mixture of persistence and luck. I once found myself in Bethlehem during the time of the grain harvest. I kept my camera close by, and happened on a scene right from the book of Ruth. Ruth 1:22 says Naomi and Ruth arrived back in Bethlehem "in late spring, at the

> Bethlehem's living stones are far more inspiring than its shrines and monuments. It just takes longer to uncover them.

Women harvesting wheat in a field in Bethlehem

beginning of the barley harvest." Ruth continued gleaning in the fields "through the wheat harvest in early summer" (Ruth 2:23). Here I was, looking down at a modern-day Ruth harvesting her grain!

One key event in the book of Ruth occurs at the threshing floor. And for those from the West, that part of the story may seem unclear. What's a threshing floor? Why was Boaz spending the night there? And why did Naomi send Ruth to lie at Boaz's feet? On my very first trip to Israel with a group of students, we came across men threshing grain just outside Bethlehem.

It was late afternoon, and a strong breeze had come up from the Mediterranean. The sheaves of grain had been brought to this barren outcropping of bedrock. After running a threshing sledge over the sheaves to separate the heads of grain from the stalks, the men began using wooden pitchforks to winnow the grain, throwing it into the air. The wind blew away the lighter pieces of chaff, while the heavier grain fell back to the ground.

The winnowing process takes place in the late afternoon. But for Boaz, the coming darkness brought with it the threat of thieves. That's why he spent the night with his laborers, guarding what they had just harvested. All that was missing from the scene I saw was Ruth herself.

The last few verses of the book of Ruth serve as the climax of the book. Ruth and Boaz had a son named Obed. And he eventually grew up and had a son named Jesse . . . who eventually grew up and had a son named David. The book began with the heartache and confusion of the times of the Judges, but it ended with the birth of the king who would lead the nation in God's ways.

Winnowing wheat at a threshing floor just outside Bethlehem

And it all came about because one man and one woman were committed to being faithful—and because of a barley harvest in Bethlehem that brought them together.

KEEPING WATCH OVER THEIR FLOCKS

Before leaving Bethlehem it's also helpful to visit the Shepherds' Fields, the traditional spot where the angels appeared to the shepherds "guarding their flocks of sheep" (Luke 2:8). Not surprisingly, different religious groups have their own competing locations. Pilgrims can visit the Greek Orthodox Shepherds' Field, the Roman Catholic Shepherds' Field, or the YMCA Shepherds' Field.

It's likely that *none* of these sites are the actual spot where the shepherds were the night of Jesus' birth. Alfred Edersheim, in his work on *The Life and Times of Jesus the Messiah*, suggests that the shepherds were watching over flocks destined for sacrifice in the temple. "This *Migdal Eder* [watchtower of the flock] was *not* the watchtower for the ordinary flocks which pastured on the barren sheepground beyond Bethlehem, but lay close to the town, on the road to Jerusalem."[1]

On my very first trip to Israel, our instructor took us to the *perfect* spot to focus on the appearance of the angels to the shepherds in Luke 2. The hillside was to the north of Bethlehem, and off the road from Bethlehem to Jerusalem—just as Edersheim had suggested. There was a natural cave at the site, and the front of the cave was blocked off with stones, allowing it to serve as a sheepfold. Unfortunately, I forgot the location of the site when I returned several years later!

I had a new bus driver, the same one I've now used for three decades. I tried to explain to him where I wanted to go, but he didn't understand my pitiful directions. He finally said, "I don't know that spot, but I can take you to the Mormons' Shepherds' Field." I didn't know the Mormons had their own field, but I decided to try it. It turned out to be the very spot where I wanted to go. Evidently it had been named the "Mormons' Shepherds' Field" by drivers who had taken Mormon groups to it. Sadly, that site is no longer available to *any* group. The cave and hillside have disappeared under the Jewish community of Har Homa, which began in 1997 and has since grown to over 25,000 people.

Today, I take groups to the YMCA Shepherds' Field. The site features a natural cave that could have been used as a sheepfold in the past. It's large enough to hold a busload of pilgrims, and it helps visualize how shepherds could have placed their flock inside and then stood guard against predators in the night.

Cave at the YMCA Shepherds' Field

THE "OXFORD SHIRT" SHEPHERD

On another occasion, my radio cohost and I needed to record in Bethlehem. We asked a storeowner there if he could arrange for us to meet a shepherd with his flock. "Sure, sure! No problem!" However, when we arrived in Bethlehem and asked about a specific time to meet, the owner was a little more tentative. Finally, he said it was arranged, and his driver took us on a roundabout drive into the fields beyond the city.

The "shepherd" with his sheep outside Bethlehem

Almost on cue, a rugged-looking shepherd appeared with a small flock of sheep and goats. We recorded both audio and video clips and took a number of pictures. As the expression goes, it was a "Kodak moment." We tried to interview the shepherd but his English was very rough. However, the sheep and goats cooperated, and the shoot went well.

After we finished recording we walked over to the shepherd to thank him for his time. That's when we noticed that under his *thawb*—his traditional outer garment—he was wearing a very stylish blue Oxford dress shirt. So, was he a "real" shepherd, or was he someone the storeowner had talked into dressing up to help out his American friends? We may never know. But I tend to believe that evening, when the man went home to his house in Bethlehem, he said to his wife, "You'll never guess what I was doing today!"

Around Jerusalem

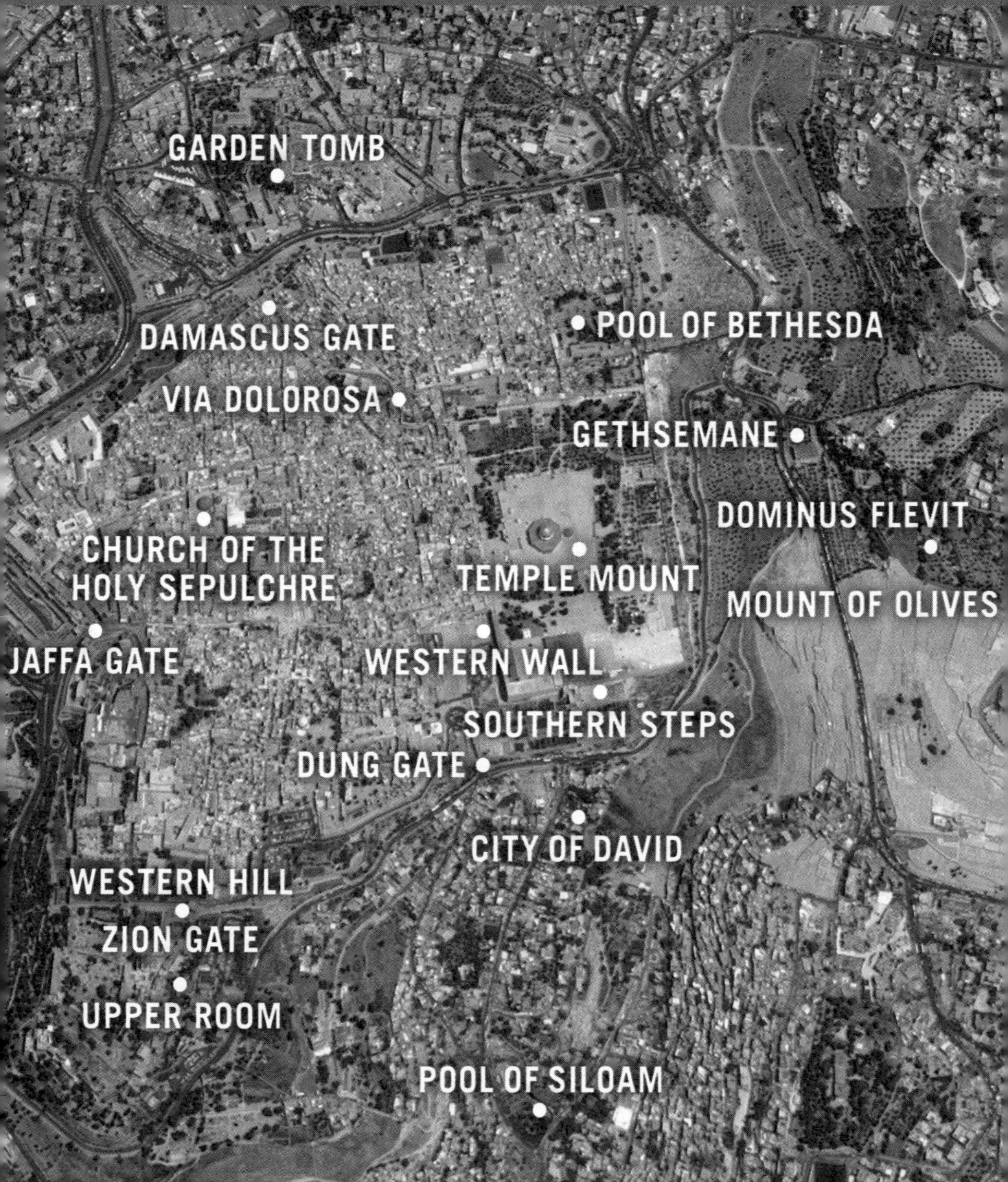

GARDEN TOMB

DAMASCUS GATE

POOL OF BETHESDA

VIA DOLOROSA

GETHSEMANE

DOMINUS FLEVIT

CHURCH OF THE
HOLY SEPULCHRE

TEMPLE MOUNT

MOUNT OF OLIVES

JAFFA GATE

WESTERN WALL

SOUTHERN STEPS

DUNG GATE

CITY OF DAVID

WESTERN HILL

ZION GATE

UPPER ROOM

POOL OF SILOAM

The Old City of Jerusalem

CHAPTER 36

Jerusalem Overview:

The Confusion over Jerusalem

Jerusalem has held a special place in the hearts of many because of its central role in the Bible. Reverend Noyes Miner, a personal friend of Abraham Lincoln, reported that Mary Todd Lincoln told him the President shared with her his desire to visit Jerusalem to "see the places hallowed by the footsteps of the Saviour" while at Ford's Theater the night he died.[1] Even skeptic Mark Twain got excited when he saw Jerusalem for the first time. "At last, away in the middle of the day, ancient bits of wall and crumbling arches began to line the way—we toiled up one more hill, and every pilgrim and every sinner swung his hat on high! Jerusalem!"[2]

THE CONFUSION OVER JERUSALEM

Sadly, a pilgrim's initial sense of excitement and anticipation over visiting Jerusalem can give way to confusion and disappointment. The reality of Jerusalem doesn't always live up to one's expectations. For most visitors, the city of Jerusalem becomes either a confusing maze of narrow, crowded streets, or a scrambled list of disconnected holy sites. The modern city has expanded far beyond the city of the Bible. As a result, it's hard for people to visualize what Jerusalem might have been like in the past, especially during Bible times.

Some look for signs of the past inside Jerusalem's walled Old City, but the current walls were built five hundred years ago. They are relative newcomers to the city. And the streets inside those walls follow a pattern imposed by Hadrian, the Roman ruler who controlled the city a century *after* the time of Jesus. So how can a visitor today hope to understand the history of this incredible city?

THE HILLS OF JERUSALEM

The key that unlocks the city of Jerusalem is its geography. The biblical city of Jerusalem centers on four hills and three valleys. And to remember them all, I tell visitors to picture an ice cream cone inside two halves of a hamburger bun. I know that sounds silly, but it can help first-time travelers visualize the basic geography. The cone underneath the ice cream is the original City of David, and the scoop of ice cream on top is Mount Moriah where Solomon built the temple. The vertical hamburger bun to the left of the ice cream cone is the Western Hill, today mistakenly called Mount Zion. And the hamburger bun to the right is the Mount of Olives, which is always connected to Jerusalem though never actually part of the city itself.

Once someone has mastered the four hills, it's time to focus on the three valleys. Moving from right to left, the first valley is between the right half of the hamburger bun and the ice cream cone. This is the Kidron Valley. The valley between the ice cream cone and the left half of the hamburger bun is the Central Valley. And curving like a large capital letter "L" from the left side of the left hamburger bun down to the tip of the ice cream cone is the Hinnom Valley. At this point most travelers are craving an ice cream or a hamburger!

The four hills of Jerusalem!

The illustration is helpful, but it's important to realize it's not to scale. The City of David—the ice cream cone—is much smaller than the other hills. Its total size was just twelve acres, enough space to build fifty homes in a typical suburban neighborhood today. Mount Moriah—the ice cream on top—covers three times as much space at the City of David. Herod the Great enclosed Mount Moriah with a square platform to provide additional space for the temple complex. The total size of his "sandbox" is thirty-seven acres. The Western Hill—the left half of the hamburger bun—covers twice as much area as the Temple Mount. And the Mount of Olives is the largest of the four hills. All of the area within biblical Jerusalem could fit on the Mount of Olives with room to spare.

It helps to superimpose the four hills on a modern image of Jerusalem.

After placing the hills on the map, three things become apparent. The first is the discrepancy in the size of each hill. The second is the shape of the retaining wall "sandbox" Herod built around Mount Moriah. And the third is the realization that the "Old City" walls today don't correspond to the original shape of the city in history. The walls have migrated north, leaving the original City of David and part of the Western Hill *outside* the current Old City.

ONE FINAL DETAIL

If all this sounds confusing, it is. But remembering the four hills, and the three valleys in between,

The four hills of Jerusalem on a map

347

will help manage that confusion. However, there is still one additional detail that's important. And to understand it, we need to think back to our time at Bet She'an. In that city we saw a main Roman road that cut through the city from north to south. It was the Cardo Maximus. Bet She'an also had an east-west road that intersected the Cardo, which was called the Decumanus Maximus.

Many Roman-designed cities were built with these two roads. They helped organize the city into quadrants. The same design was used to rebuild Jerusalem a century after the time of Jesus. Following the Second Jewish Revolt against Rome (AD 132–135), the Roman emperor Hadrian had Jerusalem rebuilt as a Roman city. He changed the city's name to Aelia Capitolina and reconstructed it with a main north-south and an east-west road. Unfortunately, he couldn't change the geography of the city. He had to add another road down the Central Valley that was still cutting through the city. And the rectangular platform where the temple once stood blocked off the eastern end of his east-

west road. The Cardo, Decumanus, and Valley Street resemble a giant letter "A." And those streets are still the basis for the streets inside the Old City today.

Because of Hadrian's design, I tell visitors that it's impossible to get lost in Jerusalem, though individuals can definitely feel temporarily "misplaced." The two main north-south streets join at the Damascus Gate in the north. The southern end of the Cardo comes out

Hadrian's streets in the Old City

near Zion Gate, and the southern end of the Valley Street brings a traveler to the Dung Gate. The western end of the Decumanus starts at Jaffa Gate and cuts through the city toward the Temple Mount.

I did have one tourist who put my advice to the test. He went exploring in the Old City and got "lost." A feeling of panic set in as the narrow streets and alleyways seemed to become an incomprehensible maze. A local must have spotted his distress because he came up to the tourist and said, "I can show you the way out . . . for $10." Now, this visitor was quite frugal, so he weighed the pros and cons of parting with $10 versus possibly being lost forever in the Old City. He finally decided his life was worth more than $10. His personal "guide" led him up and down countless streets and alleys, until finally reaching one crossroad, the guide pointed up the street and said, "There is your exit." Sure enough, the tourist could see the gate in the distance. He handed over the $10, convinced it was money well spent. But just as he started walking toward the gate, he glanced down a side street and spotted the shop where he had been standing when the guide first approached him. He hadn't been lost after all, just temporarily misplaced—and now a little poorer for the experience.

Hadrian's roads divided the city into four quadrants, which today are known as the Four Quarters of the Old City. The quadrant on the northeast side is the Muslim Quarter since it provided easy access to the Dome of the Rock and Al-Aqsa Mosque. The northwest side is the Christian Quarter because that is where the Church of the Holy Sepulchre is located. The southeast side is the Jewish Quarter, which provided access to the Western Wall, the closest spot Jews could get to where their temple once stood. And the southwest quadrant is the Armenian Quarter. Armenia was the first country to adopt Christianity as a state religion, and many Armenian monks settled in Jerusalem.

Four hills. Three valleys. Two main Roman roads. Got it!

WHICH JERUSALEM IS IN VIEW?

Visiting Jerusalem is like traveling back in time, and it's important to remember that Jerusalem grew, changed, and developed over its four-thousand-year history. So, during the rest of your visit to Jerusalem, it's important to constantly ask one key question: "Which Jerusalem is in view during this time period?"

Jerusalem from the time of Abraham through the time of David was the small ice cream cone that's now *outside* the walls of the Old City. Solomon's Jerusalem expanded to include the ice cream on top of the cone. The city remained like that until the time of King Hezekiah. Following the Assyrian invasion of the northern kingdom of Israel, thousands of refugees fled south to Jerusalem and settled on the Western Hill. Hezekiah built a wall around that hill to protect against a threatened Assyrian invasion against his own kingdom. This greatly expanded the size of the city. The city remained on all three hills until it was destroyed by the Babylonians in 586 BC.

When the Jewish captives returned from Babylon, Jerusalem remained in ruins for almost a hundred years, though the temple was rebuilt. Nehemiah returned to rebuild the walls of Jerusalem, but the walls he built were the ones around the ice cream cone and ice cream. During the intertestamental period the city once again expanded onto the Western Hill, and the walls around it were rebuilt. Herod the Great completed the "sandbox" around Mount Moriah. And that is what Jerusalem looked like in the time of Jesus, though the city continued expanding toward the north. A wall was built around this part of the city just before the Jewish revolt against Rome in AD 70. The Romans destroyed the city and knocked down the walls.

Jerusalem's destruction didn't last long. A hundred years after the time of Jesus, Hadrian defeated the Jewish rebels once again and decided to turn Jerusalem into a Roman city. His attempt to rename the city failed, but his city plan survived. The city underwent several periods of construction and destruction in the subsequent centuries. Its history is fascinating if you're a history major. But for most pilgrims it's a layer of detail and complexity best left for future study. The final piece of the puzzle fell into place five hundred years ago when the Ottoman Sultan Suleiman the Magnificent decided to rebuild the city's walls.

And now that you know Jerusalem's history and geography, we're ready to begin exploring.

The Dome of the Rock from the top of the Mount of Olives

CHAPTER 37

The Mount of Olives:
Jerusalem's Overlook to the East

The bus ride to the top of the Mount of Olives tests the skill and patience of the even the most experienced bus drivers. Cars park on both sides of the narrow road—sometimes two abreast—as children and adults dart into the roadway between them. The remaining space is barely wide enough for the bus to squeeze through.

Now keep in mind this is a *two-way* street.

At several points along the top of the Mount of Olives the road makes a sharp turn. A small car or van can navigate those turns without too much difficulty. However, a forty-five-foot-long tour bus with mirrors extending from the front like giant antennae is an altogether different matter. Watching out the front window, one would expect to find the roadway littered with broken mirrors, but that's not the case. The drivers deserve great credit for handling their behemoths as agilely as if they were operating a small sports car.

ARRIVING ON THE MOUNT OF OLIVES

The roadway ends at a small parking lot in front of a hotel. This hotel controls one of the best locations in all Israel. Sadly, it's now a shadow of its former glory, though no other hotel can match its one-of-a-kind view. On the drive up the Mount of Olives tourists are encouraged to gather everything they will need for their time away from the bus, to be ready to exit the bus *quickly* when it stops, to follow the guide's directions and line up for a group photograph, and to not stop to take pictures. These instructions are repeated, then quickly forgotten as the bus stops and the people look out the window at the magnificent view. Chaos ensues.

As the people slowly make their way off the bus, they're surrounded by a crush of other tourists and peddlers. "Panoramic photos of Jerusalem. Only $2!" "Thirty postcards or ten bookmarks. Only $1!" "Ride the camel. Just $5!" "Genuine silver necklaces for $10!" Meanwhile, the guide and tour hosts are vainly shouting at the bewildered passengers to assemble in front of the bus to have their picture taken by the local photographer.

And all this is happening as buses are trying to enter—and exit—on the same roadway!

A group photograph on the Mount of Olives

Most of the vendors at the overlook have been hawking their wares for years, and each has his own unique schtick to draw attention to what he's trying to sell. I'm reminded of the words of Captain Renault in *Casablanca* when

I see them. "Round up the usual suspects."

One salesman who is no longer with this group was simply known as Mike. Mike would almost assault the tourists before they could even step off the bus. Sadly, once the first person responded by saying, "No, thank you," Mike would begin shouting obscenities worthy of any R-rated film. The overall gist of his message—minus the cursing—was that *all* Americans hated Arabs. I took him aside and kindly tried to help him understand that it wasn't his ethnicity but his rudeness that was the problem. From that point on I would watch for Mike as the bus pulled up. Before he could say anything, I would jump out, call his name, and walk over to shake his hand and ask how he was doing. It caused him to be less hostile, at least with our groups.

Sadly, on a later trip our bus driver said to me, "Do you remember Mike on the Mount of Olives?" "Of course!" I responded. "Well, he was killed," the driver said. Evidently Mike's anger issues were not limited to the tourists. He got into a fight with another Palestinian who pulled out a knife and stabbed him. It was a sober reminder of the truth from Proverbs 29:11. "Fools vent their anger, but the wise quietly hold it back."

THE OVERLOOK

Once the photographer has taken the group picture—and tallied the number interested in purchasing a copy—the goal is to move our group away from those selling the postcards, bookmarks, necklaces, and pashminas to a spot where we can have an unobstructed view of the city. In front of us is one of the world's most iconic panoramas. It's easy to spot the golden Dome of the Rock . . . perhaps the most photographed building in Jerusalem. But my personal goal is to have our group mentally erase that building and the platform on which it rests. I want them to envision this scene as it might have looked in the time of David and Solomon. The Dome of the Rock rests on Mount Moriah. In David's day, a threshing floor stood on top of the hill. Solomon's Temple later stood where the Dome of the Rock is now located.

Just to the left of the modern platform is the tiny slice of land outside the walls of the Old City that was originally the fortified city of Jebus, the place David captured and made his capital. Remember our earlier illustration? We're now standing on the right half of the hamburger bun. Below us is the Kidron Valley. And just on the other side are the ice cream cone and ice cream. Hopefully the geography will soon begin to make sense.

The Mount of Olives is a mixture of the sublime and the silly. It serves as a backdrop to crucial events in both the Old and New Testaments. And yet it almost seems to have a Disney-like atmosphere with its unique cast of characters. The mute selling postcards and panoramic photos. The camel owner who is often as surly as his ride. (For many years he had a camel named Kojak.) The pitiful-looking lame beggar who holds out his hand shouting, "Help me, Father!" (We've seen him jump up and run to another spot in search of a more generous batch of pilgrims.) There is also the occasional pickpocket, though the Tourist Police do a good job of keeping them away. And we can't forget the pashmina salesman who sells from the trunk of his car. The pashminas are often three-for-$10 at the top of the Mount of Olives, four-for-$10 when he reappears halfway down the hill, and five-for-$10 at the bottom.

But by far my favorite character on the Mount of Olives is "Donkey Man." He's getting up there in years, so I'm not sure how long he will remain, but in my mind he's the star of the show. Dressed in a flowing white robe and *keffiyeh*, and sporting a white moustache, he just looks like he walked off the pages of an illustrated Bible. He's also the consummate performer, hamming it up with the busloads of tourists walking by. He is more than happy to have you take a picture of him, or to get your picture taken with him—for a price of course. But he's so affable how can anyone begrudge him a few dollars? Hopefully, "Donkey Man" will train up a new generation to follow in his footsteps. It's hard to imagine the Mount of Olives without his presence.

IMAGINE MEETING SOLOMON ON THE MOUNT OF OLIVES

If encountering the current cast of characters is fascinating, imagine what would it have been like to stand here on the Mount of Olives and encounter

"Donkey Man" on the Mount of Olives

someone like King David or King Solomon. To visualize that, our group must first find a quiet spot away from the crowds. Thankfully, the Jewish cemetery covering a large portion of the hillside offers such a place of solitude. Standing among these silent witnesses to the past, imagine Solomon coming from his grave for a brief visit. It's been three thousand years since he stood on this hillside. But we now have the opportunity to ask the wisest man of his day what he understood to be the meaning of life.

We want him to answer questions like: Why am I here? Where am I heading? What does the future hold? We can't personally have Solomon come from the grave to answer these questions, but I believe he has already shared answers in the book of Ecclesiastes. In that book, the wisest man in the world grappled with the most troubling issues facing humanity. And Solomon's ultimate conclusion—which is still true today—is that much of life is beyond our comprehension or control.

Picture Solomon walking up the hill toward us. He looks much older than what we might have imagined. The burdens of running a vast kingdom, coupled with all his family problems, are resting heavily on his shoulders. Solomon made many mistakes in his lifetime. They're a keen reminder that being wise doesn't always mean a person will make wise choices. The Solomon coming toward us has become more reflective. His realization of his own mortality brought him back to a sharper focus on the God he pursued so passionately in his youth.

Solomon's final work is both his darkest and his most profound. For much of his life Solomon was trying to discern the ultimate riddle of human existence—discovering the purpose for life itself. But his grand experiment didn't go as planned. Every avenue he traveled on his journey ended at the same dead end. Hedonism, human achievement, the pursuit of knowledge . . . they all led to the same conclusion. Life, in and of itself, seems to be meaningless.

As Solomon comes to where we're standing, he pauses and lowers himself to the ground. He motions for us to sit beside him. "Let me share what I discovered. I wanted to discern the ultimate purpose for life, the secret to satisfaction and achievement, but I kept colliding with unexpected realities that make life so unpredictable."

Seeing the puzzled looks on our faces, he continues. "Enigmas—like the reality of death, the fact that one small mistake can undo so much good, the pervasiveness of injustice, and the corrupting influence of wealth and power. Each of these makes life unpredictable. I finally reached this inescapable conclusion: 'The fastest runner doesn't always win the race, and the strongest warrior doesn't always win the battle. The wise sometimes go hungry, and the skillful are not necessarily wealthy. And those who are educated don't always lead successful lives. It is all decided by chance, by being in the right place at the right time'" (Eccl. 9:11).

Solomon continues, "If that's true, how does one live wisely in an unpredictable world? I finally realized we need to submit to those things we can't control—things like human government. That's why I wrote. 'Obey the king' (Eccl. 8:2). We also need to submit to God. After all, 'the actions of godly and wise people are in God's hands' (Eccl. 9:1). Those two principles don't always harmonize, and we can't follow a government that demands we sin against God. But most of the time, life will go better if we follow the laws of the land, and live according to God's Word."

Solomon abruptly stops and looks directly into our eyes. "But remember this, 'If no one knows what will happen, who can tell him when it will happen? No one has authority over the wind to restrain the wind, nor authority over the day of death' [Eccl. 8:7–8 NASB]. Do *you* understand those words?" Our first impulse is to say, "No, we don't!" But then we stop and think about what Solomon just said. If we don't even know *what* tomorrow holds—and we don't—then we can't possibly know *when* specific events are going to happen. And if we can't control the wind, which is just a small part of God's creation, then how can we possibly control the more significant issues of life and death?

> "How does one live wisely in an unpredictable world?"

We turn and ask the king a question. "So, you're saying that part of learning how to live wisely is recognizing the need to trust God for those things beyond our understanding and control?" A smile slips across his lips. "That is indeed one key part of living wisely. But also remember this: 'There is no military discharge in the time of war, and evil will not save those who practice it' [Eccl. 8:8 NASB]. Do you understand this reality of life?"

Solomon's patient gaze causes us to pause and try to think our way through the riddle. "If we joined the army and are under attack in war, the commander won't just let us walk away from our obligation. That makes sense. In the same way you're saying that if we join ourselves to wickedness, thinking that life's uncertainties mean we probably won't get caught, a time will come when wickedness won't let us opt out of the consequences of our choices either. Life might be uncertain, but criminals still get caught and punished for their crimes!"

Solomon smiles, and then stands up to walk back down the Mount of Olives. We watch him go and shake our head in amazement. We live as if life is totally under our control . . . until something comes along to remind us how out of control life really is. Solomon just explained how to live in a world that's beyond our control. It starts by acknowledging that we're *not* the masters of our fate and the captains of our soul. Those are in God's hands, not ours. So how are we to live? We choose to live in obedience to God and try our best to follow the laws of the government God has placed over us. And we also need to remember that actions have consequences, even if those consequences aren't immediately apparent. We can't control our circumstances, but we *can* control how we respond to our circumstances. And that's indeed a wise lesson to learn.

The roadway down the Mount of Olives

And with that thought, it's time for *our* group to begin walking down the Mount of Olives, following in the footsteps of this final "character" who "sought to find just the right words to express truths clearly" (Eccl. 12:10).

Tear bottle on the corner of Dominus Flevit, commemorating Jesus weeping over Jerusalem

CHAPTER 38

Dominus Flevit:
Jesus Wept Over Jerusalem

The roadway down the Mount of Olives is quite steep. I'm always concerned someone might slip on a bit of loose gravel and fall, so we walk at a leisurely pace—or as I like to say to the group, we'll just *mosey* on down the Mount of Olives. After fighting our way through the mob of peddlers on top, things become a little less hectic for at least a short distance. But the next stop is coming up on the right. It's the entrance to Dominus Flevit, the traditional spot where Jesus wept over Jerusalem. The pashmina salesman hasn't yet arrived in his car, but he will likely be at the entrance to greet us as we leave.

THE TOMBS

There's much to talk about at this site, so I'll begin with the tombs discovered just inside the entrance. The Mount of Olives was known for two things historically—trees and tombs. The mountain must have been named for the large number of olive trees growing there. The roadway up the hill was first identified as early as the time of King David (2 Sam. 15:30), and Zechariah specifically said the "Mount of Olives" was the mountain "east of Jerusalem" (Zech. 14:4).

Finding olive trees on the Mount of Olives makes perfect sense, but why is the hill also associated with tombs? This relates to the reality of burial practices in Bible times. Apart from the royal tombs of the kings, people couldn't be buried inside a city or town. At the same time, families didn't want to carry their dead loved ones too far. So graves were located outside the town—but not too far away. The slopes of the Mount of Olives provided an excellent place to carve a family tomb for those living in Jerusalem. It has tombs dating back to both the Old and New Testament eras. There's also a relatively modern Jewish cemetery there today.

Ossuaries, or bone boxes, inside the entrance of Dominus Flevit

Just inside the entrance to Dominus Flevit, on the right, is a small building containing the remains of a New Testament-era family tomb. The basic pattern for Jewish funeral customs remained the same throughout the Bible, though there were some variations. The individual was buried soon after death, on the same day if possible. The body was left in the tomb for a year while the flesh decomposed. Then family members came to the tomb to collect the bones of the loved one and "gather them to their fathers." The imagery of being "gathered to their fathers" (Judg. 2:10 NASB) began in the Bible actually with God's promise to Abraham in Genesis 15:15. When Abraham finally died, he "joined his ancestors in death" (Gen. 25:8).

During the Old Testament, the bones of the individual who died were eventually collected from off the stone slab or shelf on which they had been placed at death and thrown into a repository in the family tomb. They were quite literally "gathered" to their ancestors. By the time of the New Testament, the custom had changed slightly. The person who died was placed in the family tomb for a year, and after that the family came to gather the individual's bones. But instead of throwing the bones into a repository, they were now placed inside a "bone box," known as an ossuary. These boxes were then placed in the tomb with their ancestors.

Numerous ossuaries in varying sizes are visible in this tomb, all hand-carved from limestone. The differences in the size of the boxes makes perfect sense when one thinks about the variations in the height of people within a family. The boxes had to be long enough to hold the femur, the longest bone in the human body. Seeing tiny boxes that once held the bones of very young children is a reminder of the sad reality of death experienced by families who longed for the day when the promise of Isaiah 65:20 would become reality. "No longer will babies die when only a few days old."

THE CHAPEL

The chapel is just a short walk down the pathway. The building was designed by Antonio Barluzzi, the same architect who designed the chapel on the Mount of Beatitudes. In fact, Barluzzi designed all three of the churches and chapels that are my personal favorites. (The third sits at the very bottom of the Mount of Olives and is part of our next stop.) Barluzzi tried to design each building in a way that complemented the event it commemorated. He accomplished this at Dominus Flevit by adding decorative urns on each of the outside corners. These urns represent tear bottles, because the chapel commemorates the place where Jesus wept over Jerusalem.

But why tear bottles? What's the story behind them? Excavators have found numerous small, blown-glass bottles from New Testament times that were used to collect someone's tears. It was as if, by collecting their tears in a bottle, people could hang on to the memories of their loved ones through times of separation and loss. It was a tangible way to demonstrate how much you cared for somebody. Barluzzi placed these bottles on each corner to remember the tears Jesus shed for this city and its people.

The tear bottles help visitors focus on the time when the Son of God wept over Jerusalem. Luke described the scene this way as he pictured Jesus' triumphal entry into Jerusalem on Palm Sunday. "But as he came closer to Jerusalem and saw the city ahead, he began to weep. 'How I wish today that you of all people would understand the way to peace. But now it is too late, and peace is hidden from your eyes'" (Luke 19:41–42). The word for *weep* chosen by Luke is not the word used in John 11:35 (*dakruō*) where John described Jesus weeping at the tomb of Lazarus. That word simply pictured tears streaming down Jesus' face. The word used by Luke (*klaiō*) evokes uncontrollable sobs of sorrow and grief. Why was Jesus sobbing on Palm Sunday while everyone else was so excited?

Jesus was weeping because, as God, He knew the hearts of the people . . . and He knew the future. In just five days this same crowd now welcoming Him as King would shout to Pilate, "Crucify him! . . . We have no king but Caesar" (John 19:15). Jesus could also see the coming destruction of Jerusalem that would take place "because you did not recognize it when God visited you" (Luke 19:44). He was brokenhearted over *their* impending pain, not His.

The interior of the chapel is beautiful in its simplicity. The tile pattern on the floor matches that of a church that stood on the same site during the Byzantine era. At the front of the chapel is a large window looking out over Jerusalem. And if someone stands in just the right spot, the cross on the altar before the window is superimposed over the Dome of the Rock. I can't say Barluzzi deliberately intended this, but it's almost as if he was trying to say, "You might think you have supplanted Christianity, but we know the One who is really in control!"

The chapel once contained a small pump organ to be used for services.

Looking toward Jerusalem from inside the chapel

The Franciscans control the chapel, and it is often reserved for Roman Catholic masses. But others are allowed inside if a mass is not taking place, and the chapel is a wonderful place for a group to sing. On one occasion, our group arrived and found the chapel empty. We hurried in and sat down. While I was sharing the history of the site, the priest in charge—a kind, elderly man—slipped in. I then asked our group if they would like to sing. At that point the priest came forward and pointed to the organ and then to himself. He then wiggled his fingers, letting me know he was volunteering to play the organ for us as we sang. He didn't speak English but I still tried to ask if he knew the song by Bill and Gloria Gaither, "There's Something about That Name." He nodded yes.

The priest took his seat at the organ and pumped away, giving us a single note to indicate the pitch. I'll never forget that moment! I lifted my hands to direct our impromptu choir as we began to worshipfully sing "Jesus, Jesus, Jesus! There's just something about that name . . ." At the same moment, the priest started belting out the tune to "Amazing Grace." He knew we were a Protestant group, and that was the only Protestant hymn he knew.

A CROWN OF THORNS

Just outside the chapel are two *Ziziphus spina-christi* trees. The name means "Christ's thorn," and the trees are one possible candidate for the crown of thorns placed on Jesus' head. The thorns on this tree can grow up to three inches long and are very sharp. It's sobering to gaze at these thorns and imagine what they would do when forced onto someone's head.

Thorns on the Ziziphus spina-christi tree

Is this the *exact* spot where Jesus wept over Jerusalem? No one knows. But we *do* know without a doubt that somewhere on this hill "as he came closer to Jerusalem and saw the city ahead, he began to weep" (Luke 19:41). And Dominus Flevit is as good a place as any to remember that event.

But there is one *additional* thing we can remember while we're here at Dominus Flevit.

JESUS' TWO APPROACHES TO JERUSALEM

Most of our time at Dominus Flevit has focused on the events of Palm Sunday and Jesus' Triumphal Entry into Jerusalem. The crowds were cheering while Jesus was weeping. But the Bible describes a second time when Jesus will ride into Jerusalem. On His first approach, Jesus rode in on a "colt, the foal of a donkey" to fulfill the prophecy of Zechariah 9:9 (NASB). But His final approach to Jerusalem will look much different.

Revelation 19 describes Jesus' return from heaven this way:

> Then I saw heaven opened, and a white horse was standing there. Its rider was named Faithful and True, for he judges fairly and wages a righteous war. His eyes were like flames of fire, and on his head were many crowns. A name was written on him that no one understood except himself. He wore a robe dipped in blood, and his title was the Word of God. The armies of heaven, dressed in the finest of pure white linen, followed him on white horses. From his mouth came a sharp sword to strike down the nations. He will rule them with an iron rod. He will release the fierce wrath of God, the Almighty, like juice flowing from a winepress. On his robe at his thigh was written this title: King of all kings and Lord of all lords. (Rev. 19:11–16)

The prophet Zechariah describes Jesus' final approach to Jerusalem from earth's perspective. "Then the LORD will go out to fight against those nations, as he has fought in times past. On that day his feet will stand on the Mount of Olives, east of Jerusalem. And the Mount of Olives will split apart, making a wide valley running from east to west. Half the mountain will move toward the north and half toward the south" (Zech. 14:3–4). Jesus is coming again, and ground zero for His return is the Mount of Olives. But this time He will be riding the white horse of a conquering hero. And when His feet finally touch the Mount of Olives, the entire mountain will split apart!

Some guides and Bible teachers have said there must be a hidden geological fault line underneath the Mount of Olives that will shudder to life at the exact moment Jesus returns. However, Jesus doesn't need a geological fault line to split this mountain in half. This event will be God's exclamation point on the reality that Jesus is God's Son and Israel's Messiah. As Zechariah writes just a few verses later, "And the LORD will be king over all the earth. On that day there will be one LORD—his name alone will be worshiped" (Zech. 14:9).

I like to remind people that someday God is going to rearrange the entire geography of Jerusalem. The Mount of Olives will become two smaller mountains, with a valley between leading from Jerusalem toward the Jordan River and the Dead Sea. Jerusalem itself will be "raised up" like a flat plateau. And when that happens, those who visit Jerusalem now will be able to say to those born in the coming kingdom era, "You know, when I stood on the Mount of Olives the first time, it looked totally different than it does now!"

And indeed it will!

But now it's time to head toward the exit to see if our pashmina salesman has arrived.

Olive trees inside the Garden of Gethsemane

CHAPTER 39

Gethsemane:

The Three Locations of Gethsemane

The trek down the Mount of Olives has been a success. And by success, I mean no one stumbled and fell while on that steep road, no one was hit by the cars zooming up—and down—the one-lane roadway, and no one had an unpleasant encounter with a brash vendor or the occasional pickpocket looking to separate a tourist from his or her cash.

Our final stop on the Mount of Olives brings us to Gethsemane or, more precisely, to the three locations for Gethsemane. No, this isn't a case of different religious groups each claiming to know the *exact* location of Gethsemane. The Bible itself identifies three separate locations connected with Gethsemane on the night Jesus was betrayed.

> Then Jesus came with them to a place called Gethsemane [location #1], and told His disciples, "Sit here while I go over there [location #2] and pray." He took Peter and the two sons of Zebedee with Him, and began to be grieved and distressed. Then He said to them, "My soul is deeply grieved, to the point of death; remain here and keep watch with Me." And He went a little beyond them [location #3], and fell on His face and prayed. (Matt. 26:36–39 NASB)

THE OLIVE OIL PRESS

The first location is at the very bottom of the Mount of Olives. When most people think of Gethsemane they think of the Garden of Gethsemane. That will be the second stop. But the first place in order of appearance is Geth-semane itself. It's located down the street from the Garden of Gethsemane. Many fail to visit the site because it's hidden down a flight of stairs, at the end of a narrow alleyway. Above the doorway is the word "Gethsemani." It's used as a chapel today, but take away the lights, the seats, and the other modern additions, and it's not too hard to recognize that it was originally a cave. *This* is the olive oil press—Gethsemane!

The olive oil press—Gethsemane—was inside a cave at the bottom of the Mount of Olives

Earlier, on our visit to Guvrin, we discovered that the word "gethsemane" is actually a combination of two Hebrew words—*gath*, which refers to a press, and *shemen*, which is the word for olive oil. When Jesus went with His disciples to Gethsemane, He was literally going to the olive oil press. Olives are harvested at the very end of summer, just as the rainy season is about to begin. As a result, presses were often placed in some type of enclosure like a building or a cave. Here on the Mount of Olives this natural cave was the perfect location for the olive oil press—Gethsemane.

The press would have been active in the fall when olives were being harvested, but the rest of the year the cave served as a convenient shelter or gathering point for those visiting Jerusalem. Very likely, Jesus and His disciples used this cave for shelter on numerous occasions. On the night of His betrayal, Luke said Jesus "went, as was His habit, to the Mount of Olives" and, with His disciples, "arrived at the *place*" (Luke 22:39–40 NASB). The group, minus Judas, came to the cave where the olive oil press was located. The disciples assumed this was where they would bed down for the evening, as they had likely done in the past.

Judas also knew this was the spot where Jesus could be captured. Earlier in the day, Jesus had sent two of His disciples into Jerusalem and told them to watch for a man carrying a jar of water. They were to follow him home and then say to the owner, "The Teacher asks: Where is the guest room where I can eat the Passover meal with my disciples?" (Mark 14:14). Jesus didn't tell the disciples the exact location beforehand because He knew Judas was looking for a place where the authorities could ambush and capture Him. Jesus wanted to guarantee He would be alone with His disciples for the Passover meal. Judas's Plan B was to take the authorities to the olive oil press since he knew that was where Jesus would go afterward.

THE GARDEN OF GETHSEMANE

The second location in this journey through Gethsemane is the spot where Jesus went with Peter, James, and John. Luke actually provides a relative distance between the cave and the place where Jesus took these three disciples. He says Jesus "walked away, about a stone's throw" (Luke 22:41). Of course, the exact distance depends on the person throwing the stone. But assuming we could eliminate the modern stone walls, someone standing at the entrance to the cave and throwing a stone could expect it to land around the area known today as the Garden of Gethsemane.

The present Garden of Gethsemane is well maintained. In addition to the gnarled olive trees, the area also has beautiful flowers. However, at the time of Jesus a "garden" would have referred to a cultivated area—a working agricultural farm, not a flower garden. So Jesus and the three disciples were not making their way through a rose garden. They were walking among olive trees. Some of the trees in the area today are very old. Guides will say they are two thousand years old and were around at the time of Jesus. It's a beautiful, though untrue, story. The oldest trees today are likely less than a thousand years old. But they could be the "children" or "grandchildren" of the trees that once grew here, since the future generations of olive trees can grow from the roots of earlier trees.

It's easy to picture Jesus standing among these trees with the three disciples who formed His inner circle. And what were His instructions to them? "Keep watch and pray, so that you will not give in to temptation. For the spirit is willing, but the body is weak" (Mark 14:38). And what was their response? They fell asleep! Three times! I can almost picture Peter propped against a tree, snoring softly. And yet, we can't be too hard on these disciples. It was late at night. It was dark. And they had just finished eating the Passover seder.

THE CHURCH OF ALL NATIONS

Next to this small grove of olive trees is a modern church, called the Church of All Nations. This is the third of the churches built by Barluzzi that I love. It has a number of wonderful architectural highlights. The colorful mosaic on the exterior focuses on Jesus and His role as mediator between God and man. The church's windows are made from purple-tinted alabaster. They allow some light to enter, but they block enough to make the interior seem dark and foreboding. And at the front of the church is an area where the bedrock is exposed. This is said to mark the spot where Jesus went by Himself to pray. Matthew says Jesus went "a little farther" beyond the three disciples before falling "with his face to the ground" to pray (Matt. 26:39).

Somewhere in this general area—perhaps at the very spot we see at the

The exterior mosaic on the Church of All Nations

front of the church—is the location where Jesus wrestled with the reality of the coming horror of His crucifixion. As He agonized in prayer, Luke records that His sweat became like drops of blood, an indication of the deep emotion Jesus was experiencing. "Father, if you are willing, please take this cup of suffering away from me. Yet I want your will to be done, not mine" (Luke 22:42).

Jesus knew the moment He took on Himself the sin of the world He would experience not just the horrific pain of physical crucifixion. He would also experience all the separation, judgment, and punishment required for our sin. Is it any wonder that as He prayed that night He was in agony? This is a fitting place to pause and imagine the emotions Jesus was experiencing . . . and to realize that, in the end, He was willing to submit to all that was to come because of His love for you.

As each of us walks out of the darkness inside the church and into the bright sunlight, it's important we pause and reflect on the immense significance of this site. This is where Jesus agonized in prayer over the personal

Interior of the Church of All Nations

cost required of Him to pay for *our* sin. And having agreed to submit to the Father's will, Jesus walked back to the three slumbering disciples, awakened them, and headed back to the olive oil press to meet Judas and the mob—and begin the sequence of events that would lead to the cross.

Before we leave this hallowed spot, I do need to ask you life's most important question. Have you placed your trust in Jesus as your personal Savior? He died on the cross to pay the penalty for *your* sin . . . and He did so willingly because of His love for you. You can receive Him today by speaking to God and saying something as simple as "Dear God, I know I've done wrong. I believe Jesus died on the cross to pay the penalty for my sin, and I now want to open my heart and receive Him as my Savior. Please forgive me of my sin and have Jesus take control of my life."

ONE FINAL STOP

As we step out into the street from the Garden of Gethsemane all the buses are lined up along the road to the left. But before heading to the bus we have one final stop to make. It's right across the street, inside a private garden. The attendant is unlocking the iron gate, so follow me inside.

The calmness and sanity of this quiet refuge is a welcome change. The honking horns and shouts of peddlers can still be heard, but they're muted by the stone walls. This enclosure, with its grove of olive trees, is an island of peace. But I want to point out something that most visitors miss. Just beyond this iron grate along the back wall is the entrance to an ancient tomb carved into the bedrock. This wasn't an elaborate tomb like some of those at the bottom of the Kidron Valley. It's a rather simple affair, likely the tomb of an average family.

Just inside the tomb, on the right, is a bench where a body would have been laid. Normally, a stone would cover the opening to the tomb, but for some reason the stone is no longer here. Instead, we're able to look directly into the grave, where we can see part of a human skull, and a pile of bones. This is another reminder that the Mount of Olives, even in Jesus' day, was known for two things—olive trees and tombs.

Looking inside a tomb on the Mount of Olives

379

Tombs, like this one, created something of a problem. A person traveling to Jerusalem to visit the temple and participate in the annual festivals didn't want to become ceremonially unclean by accidently touching a tomb. The Jewish people came up with a solution to this problem. They would white-wash or plaster the outside of the tombs so they would stand out, even in the dark. By the time of Jesus, some of the tombs had become quite elaborate, with cone-shaped roofs and intricately carved designs. But whether a tomb was plain or fancy, the whitewash on the outside made the tomb stand out, indicating a location to be avoided.

Take a closer look at this tomb. The pile of bones helps explain Jesus' description of the Pharisees in Matthew 23:27. "What sorrow awaits you teachers of religious law and you Pharisees. Hypocrites! For you are like white-washed tombs—beautiful on the outside but filled on the inside with dead people's bones and all sorts of impurity."

Jesus was comparing the false righteousness of these individuals with the reality of what they were on the inside. They put on a good appearance, but with His divine x-ray eyes Jesus could see beneath the exterior into their hearts. He knew their inner thoughts, their motives, and their true feelings. They might look good to others, but Jesus saw them for what they were—walking, talking graves filled with uncleanness, hypocrisy, and lawlessness.

It's easy to dress up something on the outside. With enough whitewash, even a tomb can look downright beautiful. But it still contains the stench of death. And sadly, that's what Jesus saw in the self-righteous religious leaders of His day. Others were impressed by the outward appearance these individ-uals gave of following God. But Jesus looked on the inside and saw it was all a sham. God has always been infinitely more concerned about what we look like on the inside than how we might appear to others on the outside.

As we head to the bus to continue our tour, we can see more of the tombs at the base of the Mount of Olives. Some are modern, and some were standing in the time of Jesus. But each one represents an illustration to help us in our walk with Christ. They are reminders that God sees not just our actions, but also our motives and attitudes. He looks beyond the whitewash to what's really inside. As God said to Samuel when he was searching among Jesse's sons for Saul's replacement as king, "Don't judge by his appearance or height . . . The LORD doesn't see things the way you see them. People judge by outward appearance, but the LORD looks at the heart" (1 Sam. 16:7).

Ancient and modern tombs on the Mount of Olives

Jewish men gather to pray at the Western Wall

CHAPTER 40

The Western Wall and Dung Gate:
The Holiest Site in Judaism

The holiest site in Judaism today is the Western Wall. Yet many non-Jewish visitors don't quite know what to expect when they visit. The confusion begins with the name itself. Some assume it's the western wall of Israel's ancient temple. But when asked about the temple itself, Jesus made it clear it would be destroyed. "Do you see all these buildings? I tell you the truth, they will be completely demolished. Not one stone will be left on top of another!" (Matt. 24:2). The Romans tore down the temple when they destroyed Jerusalem in AD 70.

The Western Wall is actually part of the retaining wall built by Herod the Great to expand the size of the temple platform on Mount Moriah. If the Temple Mount is the ice cream in our diagram of Jerusalem, then the Western Wall is part of the "sandbox" built around the ice cream to turn it from a rounded scoop into a rectangular box. The Western Wall is the holiest place in Judaism because for centuries it was as close as Jews were allowed to come to the site of their ancient temple. Many Jewish people believe God's divine presence never left the area.

Even the name of the site causes confusion. It's sometimes referred to as the Wailing Wall because individuals gathered there to weep over the destruction of the temple. The name of the site in Hebrew is *HaKotel HaMa'aravi*, which simply means "the Western Wall." But that's often shortened to the *Kotel*—the wall. Yet according to Muslims, the site has nothing to do with the Jewish people. They refer to the wall as *Al-Buraq*, the name of the winged horse they say Muhammad tied there on his night journey to Jerusalem before ascending to paradise.

One final bit of confusion centers on the relatively small size of the area. The entire space visible from the plaza is about 160 feet long and sixty feet high. It's divided into men's and women's sections, with the men having about twice as much space as the women. However, this public area is only a small portion of the actual retaining wall, which extends for over 1,600 feet. The wall also continues below the current ground level for an additional seventeen courses of stone.

VISITING THE WALL

Christians are sometimes unsure if they're permitted to visit the Western Wall. They are, as long as they're respectful and modestly dressed. For men, this means heads must be covered. Both men and women can walk up to the wall, pray, and even take pictures—except on the Sabbath when photography is prohibited. A good rule of thumb is to treat other worshipers at the site as you would want them to treat you if they were visiting your church.

On one visit I was embarrassed when I saw a young man walk up to the wall wearing short pants and no head covering. I could tell he was a Christian because on the back of his T-shirt, in bold letters, was the name JESUS with the phrase "It's All about Him" printed above. As he walked up beside an Orthodox Jewish man and began to pray, I waited for someone to interrupt him and ask him to leave. I can only hope his in-your-face actions were the result of ignorance, because he *didn't* demonstrate Christ's love, care, or concern for those around him by his actions.

On certain days of the week, bar mitzvahs are celebrated at the Western Wall. The family assembles outside the walls of the Old City and the young boy is marched toward the Western Wall under a canopy while musicians play and family members clap and cheer. The groups that organize these run a brisk business, so if you miss one parade going by just wait for the next one!

Once the family reaches the Western Wall, the son is taken to the men's side where he puts on his tallit—his prayer shawl—binds phylacteries on his arm and forehead, and then reads aloud from a Torah scroll brought out for the occa-

The procession for a young man arriving for his bar mitzvah

sion. The women lean over the dividing wall and watch. The son is then hoisted on a family member's shoulders and paraded around while the women cheer and throw candy.

Celebrating at a bar mitzvah

Reading a prayer book at the wall

PRAYING AND STUDYING AT THE WALL

Leaving the energy and excitement of the bar mitzvah, one can walk just a few paces to discover an elderly Jewish man reading a prayer book next to the wall. He seems lost in thought as he works his way down the page. Standing next to the wall is another man wearing his prayer shawl and reciting his prayers. All around him the wall is filled with tiny slips of paper pressed into every conceivable crevice and crack. These are the prayers left by recent visitors as well as prayers carried to the wall on behalf of others.

Watching everyone praying and studying brings to mind the words of the apostle Paul in Romans 10:2–4. "I know what enthusiasm they have for God, but it is

Praying at the wall

misdirected zeal. For they don't understand God's way of making people right with himself. Refusing to accept God's way, they cling to their own way of getting right with God by trying to keep the law. For Christ has already accomplished the purpose for which the law was given. As a result, all who believe in him are made right with God." It's a sobering reminder that religious zeal alone doesn't bring someone into a right relationship with God.

PEOPLE-WATCHING AT THE WALL

The Western Wall is a wonderful spot to watch people: the Jewish men— young and old—who come to pray, the young children brought by parents who hope to teach them devotion at an early age, the religious and the secular, the devout and the curious. There are Jews who turn to leave after praying

Israeli soldiers praying at the wall

and those who back away, lest they "turn their back on God." And occasionally one can spot an Orthodox Jew pause in the middle of his prayers to answer his cellphone. (I wonder if the words Samuel spoke to God when God called out to him in the tabernacle ever come to mind: "Speak, your servant is listening" [1 Sam. 3:10].) Perhaps the most unusual sight I ever witnessed was a group of Israeli soldiers praying with their rifles slung over their backs.

On one of my earlier trips—in the days of Super 8mm cameras—we had a fellow traveler who was fascinating. He brought along his Super 8, but he only packed three rolls of film. Each roll would shoot three minutes of soundless video. His apparent goal was to compress the entire trip into nine minutes. He did this by shooting a series of five-second panoramas. He would start at one end, rapidly pan toward the other, pause, and then rapidly pan back before turning off the camera. I believe anyone watching his recording would be convinced Israel was nothing more than a dizzying blur of motion. All the excitement of the Western Wall—in five seconds!

That same tourist also brought along a regular camera, and he had a habit of asking people to take his picture. (This was before smartphones and selfies. Someone else had to actually hold the camera and look through the viewfinder.) He would walk up to a stranger, talk briefly with the person, and then hand them the camera as he stepped back to have his picture taken. What made this interesting is that the real subject of interest *should* have been the person to whom he was handing the camera. I pictured him returning home and sharing his photos with his friends.

Tourist: "This picture of me was taken by an Israeli soldier at the Western Wall."

Friend: "Where's the soldier?"

Tourist: "He's the one taking the picture."

Friend: "Then where's the Western Wall?"

Tourist: "It's right behind the soldier."

THE DUNG GATE

The gate that leads through the walls of the Old City to the Western Wall is the Dung Gate. It got its name because it was the gate that led out toward the Hinnom Valley, the garbage dump of antiquity. In biblical times, the gate was located farther south, right along the edge of the Hinnom Valley, but the city walls have "migrated" north, so the valley is now some distance away. And yet, neither the name of the gate nor its overall purpose ever changed. It doesn't take a great deal of imagination to picture what was hauled out of the city to the dump through this gate.

In addition to refuse, people would use this gate to take other items of trash to the valley. The amount of trash discarded would have been much less than we generate today. After all, people had far fewer material possessions, so most items were repurposed. A torn garment was mended. A broken wooden handle became fuel. One of the few items that became totally useless when broken was pottery. If a cup, bowl, jar, or oil lamp broke, it was worthless and simply discarded. Perhaps that's why Jeremiah refers to this gate as the "Gate of the Broken Pots" or "Potsherd Gate" (Jer. 19:2)—the gate someone used when taking broken pottery to the dump.

I remind people to watch their step when leaving Jerusalem by the Dung Gate. My concern has little to do with the two-way traffic crowding through the gate, or the busy street outside. I'm more worried about their reputation. Who wants to go home and tell their friends they slipped and fell at the Dung Gate? That could be embarrassing.

A friend actually fell and broke his leg at the Dung Gate. He was one of our group leaders, and his particular role that day was to position himself outside the Dung Gate to point people toward the bus. Unfortunately, his wife had stopped to shop, and he remained with her. Instead of being at the front of the line, he and his wife were AWOL. I ran back to find him and reminded him where he was *supposed* to be. He apologized and took off running to get into position. But just as he exited the gate he slipped on a section of slick, smooth limestone paving. After a trip to the emergency room, he spent the

The Dung Gate

The Southern Steps led to the Temple Mount

CHAPTER 41

The Southern Steps:
I Walked Today Where Jesus Walked

The next stop on our tour is the Southern Steps. These are two-thousand-year-old steps that brought worshipers up to the temple at the time of Jesus. Many visitors enjoy this spot because it is one of the places where they can actually sing, "I walked today where Jesus walked" and have it be true!

In addition to the Southern Steps, a number of other archaeological discoveries have been made in this area. For example, a section of the city wall dating back to the time of King Solomon was uncovered near the roadway by the Kidron Valley. Since Solomon built the temple on Mount Moriah, it makes sense that he also constructed a wall around the hill to protect the temple and connect it to the original City of David. We don't have time to visit all that has been uncovered in this general area, but we will explore several items of interest.

SOME HYSSOP

On the walk across the plaza to the steps, few notice as I step over a low stone wall beside the walkway and begin breaking off small sprigs from bushes growing among the stones. A few from our group eventually stop to see what I'm doing, but I slip back over the wall and onto the path before most realize what I've done.

"Okay, everyone, gather around. Rub your fingers over these small sprigs and tell me what food comes to mind." The group begins passing the small

Hyssop growing among the rocks

twigs from person to person. As each one rubs the tiny leaves and takes in the fragrance, I see the wheels turning in their mind. The smell is familiar, but it seems out of context here in Israel, next to the Temple Mount. It *does* smell like something I like, but what *is* it? Finally, someone shouts out "Pizza! It reminds me of pizza!" And then someone else chimes in. "Of course! It's oregano!"

It *is* oregano. Well, actually it's hyssop, which is from the oregano family. And suddenly this unimposing bush sprouting next to these stones takes on new meaning for our band of tourists. First Kings 4:33 says Solomon focused his interest on all sorts of plants, "from the great cedar of Lebanon to the tiny hyssop that grows from cracks in a wall." From the most majestic of trees to the most humble and common of shrubs . . . that's the idea behind the verse. And yet this humble shrub played a rather dramatic role in Bible history.

In Exodus 12, the Israelites were to dip hyssop in the blood of the Passover lamb and apply it to the doorposts and lintel of each home. In Leviticus 14, hyssop was used with cedar wood and scarlet yarn as part of the ritual after someone had been cleansed of leprosy. And in Psalm 51, David admitted there was no sacrifice in the Mosaic Law that could cover the guilt of his sin. But he then cried out and asked God to "purify me with hyssop, and I will be clean" (v. 7 NASB).

Why did God choose hyssop? Perhaps it was because hyssop symbolized *humility*. Many believed leprosy was God's judgment on the sin of pride. Certainly that was the case when Moses's sister Miriam was struck with leprosy (Num. 12:1–15). And that's why it's no accident that the ritual following someone being cleansed of leprosy involved cedar wood and hyssop. It's as if the one being cleansed was saying, "I was once as proud as a cedar, but now I'm humble like the hyssop."

The opposite of pride is humility, just as the opposite of the cedar was the hyssop. Both Peter and James understood the importance of avoiding pride and striving for humility. Peter called on everyone to "dress yourselves in humility as you relate to one another, for 'God opposes the proud but gives grace to the humble.' So humble yourselves under the mighty power of God, and at the right time he will lift you up in honor" (1 Peter 5:5–6). And James quotes the same verse from Proverbs as Peter, but adds that as a result we need to "humble [ourselves] before God" and "resist the devil" (James 4:7).

Powerful lessons from a small plant. But it's time to continue on to the steps.

THE STEPS

The Southern Steps have been partially restored. Many of the steps are new, but some are original. They led through two passageways in the retaining wall surrounding Mount Moriah and up to the temple courts. Today, those passages are blocked to prevent access.

One interesting aspect of these steps is that they vary in width. This

The restored Southern Steps that once led to the temple

forced pilgrims to pay careful attention to each step they took—as opposed to uniform "OSHA-approved" steps today, which allow people to ascend and descend without having to focus as carefully on the width of each step. Some believe this was a very deliberate design on the part of the builders. Those ascending to God's house needed to do so deliberately, with their minds focused on the reality that they were entering the very presence of God. Having to look down at each step helped keep the worshiper's mind from wandering.

Near the steps are a number of Jewish ritual baths, called a *mikveh* (singular) or *mikva'ot* (plural). These baths were used for ritual purification. Before

ascending to the Temple Mount, each worshiper had to immerse in a *mikveh* to become ritually pure. Scores of *mikva'ot* have been uncovered in this general area. They were needed to handle the thousands of worshipers who came to the temple each day.

The discovery of these ritual baths helps explain the events that

A mikveh, or ritual bath, at the Southern Steps

took place in the book of Acts on the day of Pentecost. After preaching to the multitude, Peter issued a call to action. "Each of you must repent of your sins and turn to God, and be baptized in the name of Jesus Christ for the forgiveness of your sins. Then you will receive the gift of the Holy Spirit" (Acts 2:38). Luke continues his account of that day by explaining what happened next. "Those who believed what Peter said were baptized and added to the church that day—about 3,000 in all" (v. 41). It's almost certain these ritual baths were used to baptize those three thousand new converts.

ROBINSON'S ARCH

At the southwest corner of the Temple Mount is a protrusion from the wall. It's the spring of an arch that once extended out from Herod's retaining wall. Today it's called Robinson's Arch after the American scholar and explorer who first described it two hundred years ago. "The courses of these immense stones, which seemed at first to have sprung out from their places in the wall in consequence of some enormous violence, occupy nevertheless their original position; their external surface is hewn to a regular curve; and being fitted one upon another, they form the commencement or foot of an immense arch, which once sprung out from this western wall . . ."[1]

Robinson's Arch

When Robinson first spotted the spring of this arch, it was only slightly above ground level. Archaeologists have now excavated down to a street that passed below the arch in the time of Jesus. Small shops, and additional ritual baths, were uncovered along this roadway. Robinson thought the arch was part of a bridge connecting Mount Moriah to the Western Hill, but subsequent excavations show that it was actually part of a massive stairway that led up to the temple. This stairway and the underground passages by the Southern Steps were the main entry points to the temple from the south.

A model of what this area must have looked like during the Second Temple period is on display in the Citadel of David museum just inside Jaffa Gate. It shows the spring of the massive arch jutting out from the retaining wall and the monumental stairway that extended down from the corner of the Temple Mount to the street below.

Model of the monumental staircase and Robinson's Arch

NOT ONE STONE LEFT ON ANOTHER

Before leaving this area, look down at the first-century street that has been uncovered. Much of the rubble has been removed, but some of the blocks that were found have been left in place. These are the remains of the temple and other buildings that once stood atop the Temple Mount. When the Romans destroyed Jerusalem and the temple in AD 70, they dismantled the buildings on top of the platform and pushed the stones over the edge. Those stones came crashing down on the street below. The Romans also tried to dismantle the retaining walls of the platform, but that proved too difficult and they gave up—which is why the spring of the arch and courses of stones still remain in the wall.

Stones thrown off the Temple Mount by the Romans

I mentioned it once before, but this massive pile of stones is a vivid reminder of Jesus' words to His disciples when they pointed out the beautiful temple buildings to Him. "Do you see all these buildings? I tell you the truth, they will be completely demolished. Not one stone will be left on top of another!" (Matt. 24:2). This jumbled pile of stones once graced the buildings above. They cracked and broke as they crashed down onto the street below . . . and then other stones smashed down on them from above.

THE PLACE OF TRUMPETING

As archaeologists dug their way through the rubble that had filled the Central Valley next to the temple, they discovered two stones that fit together perfectly. One was the stone that stood on the very southwest pinnacle of the temple. On the left side of the stone was a carved niche that provided a place for someone to stand. The second stone was a piece of the left side that had broken off when it hit the pavement below. And on that piece was an inscription in Hebrew. Part of the inscription was destroyed, but the part remaining says "to the place of trumpeting."

The niche cut into this pinnacle was the place where a priest would stand to sound the trumpet announcing the beginning and end of the Sabbath. Think of this inscription as the original "For Dummies" publication. Imagine it's your first day on the job as the new temple trumpeter. You're a bit nervous, so you ask someone more experienced what to do. "No problem! Just head up to the roof and find the spot marked 'Stand here and blow!' And once you find it—STAND THERE AND BLOW THE TRUMPET."

The original inscription is in the Israel Museum, but an exact copy has been reproduced and fastened to the stone that was once the corner pinnacle.

The pinnacle of the temple with a copy of the Trumpeting Place inscription

The Dome of the Rock on the Temple Mount

CHAPTER 42

The Temple Mount:
Ground Zero in the Current Conflict

The major question at the heart of the ongoing struggle between Israel and the Palestinians is this: Who has the right of ownership to the Holy Land? The most contested piece of real estate in the dispute has been Jerusalem, and the very center of that geographical bull's-eye is the thirty-seven-acre plaza now sitting on Mount Moriah. To the Jewish people, this is the Temple Mount, the spot where their First and Second Temples once stood. To the Muslims, it is Haram al-Sharif, the noble sanctuary and the third holiest site in Islam.

The Dome of the Rock sits over a section of bedrock in the middle of the plaza. And while some Christians mistakenly refer to this building as the Mosque of Omar, it is neither a mosque nor the third holiest site in Islam. Those honors belong to the somewhat nondescript building with a dark dome at the *southern* end of the plaza—the Al-Aqsa Mosque.

The Temple Mount has been under Israeli control since 1967. However, after capturing Jerusalem in the Six-Day War, Israel handed administration of the site back to the Muslim religious leaders. Technically, Jordan holds custodianship over the site while Israel maintains security control, but the relationship between the two is often tense. The only entrance to the site for non-Muslims is through a gate at the southwest corner. In 2004, the earthen ramp up to that gate collapsed. Three years later a temporary wooden bridge was built to provide access until a new, permanent bridge could be constructed. But Muslims objected to Israel building the bridge, even though it is located *outside* the site, so the temporary bridge has now become "permanent"—at least until it also collapses!

MARK TWAIN ON THE TEMPLE MOUNT

Mark Twain visited the Temple Mount and Dome of the Rock during his trip to the Holy Land. In writing about his experiences, he referred to the Dome of the Rock as the Mosque of Omar, and he wasn't impressed. "I need not speak of the wonderful beauty and the exquisite grace and symmetry that have made this Mosque so celebrated—because I did not see them."[1]

Part of Twain's disappointment was his reaction to some of his guide's more outlandish statements. For example, in describing his visit to the Foundation Stone inside the Dome of the Rock, Twain added the following snide comments. "This rock, large as it is, is suspended in the air. It does not touch any thing at all. The guide said so. . . . In the place on it where Mahomet stood, he left his foot-prints in the solid stone. I should judge that he wore about [size] eighteens."[2]

Twain's cynical impressions continued as the guide pointed out the different buildings around the Dome of the Rock. "Just outside the mosque is a miniature temple, which marks the spot where David and Goliath [*sic*] used to sit and judge the people."[3] Twain includes a footnote at the bottom of the page helping his readers to understand the absurdity of that explanation. "A pilgrim informs me that it was not David and Goliath, but David and Saul. I stick to my own statement—the guide told me, and he ought to know."[4]

THE THRESHING FLOOR

We need to begin our visit to the site by remembering the history of Mount Moriah. This hill, just to the north of the city, was the spot where Abraham bound Isaac and prepared to sacrifice him to God (Gen. 22). Isaac was spared when God provided a substitute. The next time the site appears in history, it was the threshing floor of Araunah, also called Ornan, the Jebusite (2 Sam.

24:18; 1 Chron. 21:15). Both chapters begin with David making a foolish mistake. Either from pride in how great he had become or because of a lack of trust in God's ability to protect the nation, David decided to take a census of all the fighting men in Israel. His rash act displeased God, who brought judgment on Israel. A plague sent from God decimated the very army David had sought to number.

After David confessed his sin, the angel of the Lord had the prophet Gad tell him to "build an altar to the LORD on the threshing floor of Araunah the Jebusite" (1 Chron. 21:18). This incident took place in late May or early June because Araunah was "busy threshing wheat" when David arrived (v. 20). David requested the threshing floor, and Araunah willingly obliged. "Take it, my lord the king, and use it as you wish" (v. 23). He was willing to suffer financial loss to help David.

David's response must have shocked him. "No, I insist on buying it for the full price. I will not take what is yours and give it to the LORD. I will not present burnt offerings that have cost me nothing!" (v. 24). David was not about to make one of his subjects pay for David's mistake. The compiler of 1 Chronicles reports that David paid "600 pieces of gold in payment" for the site (v. 25).

At first there appears to be an apparent discrepancy in the purchase price. While 1 Chronicles 21 says David paid six hundred pieces of gold, 2 Samuel 24:24 says David paid "fifty pieces of silver" for the property. That's quite a difference! But a careful reading of both passages shows how they can be harmonized. In 2 Samuel 24, David paid fifty pieces of silver—nearly two months' wages—for "the threshing floor and the oxen" which he used as a sacrifice. In 1 Chronicles 21:25, David paid six hundred shekels of gold for "the site" (NASB). The threshing floor was just a small part of the area. Evidently David also purchased all the land that surrounded the threshing floor. This likely included all the wheat fields since the threshing floor would have been located near the area where the wheat was grown.

Why is David's purchase so important? The answer is found in two additional passages of Scripture. Second Chronicles 3:1 says, "So Solomon began to build the Temple of the LORD in Jerusalem *on Mount Moriah*, where the LORD had appeared to David, his father. The Temple was built on the threshing floor of Araunah the Jebusite, the site that David had selected." Much earlier, in Genesis 22:2, God had commanded Abraham to take Isaac "to the land of Moriah" where he was to offer him as a sacrifice "on one of the mountains, which I will show you." Mount Moriah—the land purchased by David and where Solomon later built the temple—was the very mountain to which God sent Abraham and Isaac.

Standing here on the spot where Abraham and David offered sacrifices to the God of Israel makes this a wonderful place to focus on one key aspect of worship. True worship demands that we place God above all that we value most. For Abraham, it was the willingness to offer his only son. For David, it was his insistence on personally paying full price for the threshing floor and surrounding land. The real test of our love for God is our willingness to give Him that which we value most. Worship, at its core, is *worth*-ship . . . acknowledging the worth and supreme authority of the God we claim to love.

THE AL-AQSA MOSQUE

At the very southern end of the Temple Mount platform, near where non-Muslim visitors are allowed to enter, stands the Al-Aqsa Mosque. This rather modest-looking building with the dark dome was built to commemorate Muhammad's night ride to heaven. *This* is the third holiest site in Islam. On the eastern side of the mosque is a flat plaza. Underneath this plaza is where the stairways from the Southern Steps ascended up to the Temple Mount.

Herod's architects designed the underground space using a series of arches to support the plaza above. For two thousand years those arches stayed firmly in place, standing against all natural disasters, including earthquakes. But in 1999, the Muslim authorities removed several of these arches and carted away tons of soil and debris to create an entryway to a massive underground mosque. Removing the supporting arches caused the outer portion of Herod's

The Al-Aqsa Mosque

retaining walls in that area to begin bowing outward, and the entire south-eastern corner of the Temple Mount was in danger of collapse. Workers from Jordan were brought in to make repairs on the walls, preventing what could have been an international incident.

THE REAL "ZION"

We've already discovered on this tour that Jerusalem is confusing. The city is over four thousand years old, but the walls of the "Old City" were built less than five hundred years ago. And the original city of Jerusalem is now *outside* those walls. If a couple were to hop in a cab and ask the driver to take them to Mount Zion, their final destination will actually have nothing to do with the Mount Zion of the Bible. Modern "Mount Zion" is the Western Hill—the left half of the hamburger bun. The name Zion somehow got attached to the wrong hill during the Middle Ages. But that raises some questions. What does the word "Zion" mean? And how did "Zion" become synonymous with Jerusalem?

The name "Zion" was originally applied to the city of Jebus, the city captured by David. The word focused on the physical defenses of the city and conveyed the idea of *castle* or *fortress*. Second Samuel 5:7 says, "David captured the fortress of Zion." But in spite of the city's impressive fortifications, David understood that its real protection came from the God who dwelt in its midst, not in the stone walls that surrounded it. The city was a fortress and refuge because of God's presence. That becomes very clear in the parallelism of verses like Psalm 20:2: "May He send you help from the sanctuary, and support you from Zion" (NASB). When David wrote those words, the temple hadn't yet been built. The "sanctuary" was just a tent holding the ark of the covenant. But it represented God's presence among His people.

The Dome of the Rock with the Mount of Olives standing guard in the background

Zion came to refer to the city where God dwelt among His people. It included the original City of David and, eventually, Mount Moriah. The author of Psalm 125 captured the sense of strength and security that the God who dwelt in Mount Zion promised to give to His people. "Those who trust in the LORD are as secure as Mount Zion; they will not be defeated but will endure forever" (v. 1). He continued by providing an object lesson, using the geography of the area to remind them of God's protection. "Just as the mountains surround Jerusalem, so the LORD surrounds his people, both now and forever" (v. 2).

The author of Psalm 48 stresses the reality that God is the ultimate strength and protection for Jerusalem. He begins in verses 1–3 by announcing that God is worthy of our praise. Look closely at how he identifies Mount Zion as the city where God dwells—and where He offers protection.

> Great is the LORD, and greatly to be praised
>> In the city of our God,
>>> His holy mountain.
>>>> Beautiful in elevation, the joy of the whole earth,
>>> Is Mount Zion in the far north,
>> The city of the great King.
> In its palaces, God, has made Himself known as a stronghold. (NASB)

The psalmist used a literary style we call a chiasm, where the first and last lines are parallel, as are the subsequent lines. The idea is that God is to be praised for what He has done (first and last lines). He is to be praised in His city, where He rules as the ultimate King. The holy mountain from which He rules is Mount Zion, which is the joy of all the earth.

In what way had God shown Himself to be a stronghold? Psalm 48 was likely written following Assyrian king Sennacherib's invasion of the land in 701 BC. His army had come right to the outskirts of Jerusalem, but God spared the city by killing 185,000 Assyrian soldiers. The psalmist ends by encouraging the people to "Go, inspect the city of Jerusalem. Walk around and count the many towers. Take note of the fortified walls, and tour all the citadels, that you may describe them to future generations" (Ps. 48:12–13). What was the purpose for this tour of the city's defenses? It was to show them that the physical walls hadn't been touched by the enemy. No stones had been knocked out of place, no siege ramps had been constructed, no arrows had been shot inside. The walls were untouched because God had defeated Jerusalem's enemies before they could even launch an attack. He had indeed shown Himself to be the city's stronghold and protection.

REMAINS OF THE SECOND TEMPLE

The Muslim authorities will not allow any archaeological activity to take place at Haram al-Sharif, and they insist that no Jewish temple ever stood on the site. But if tourists explore some of the remains near the entrance, they will see pieces that are almost certainly from the temple that stood here in the time of Jesus.

A capital that once stood atop a column in Herod's Temple

Seeing these few scattered remains gets one to wondering what else might be resting just beneath the surface, waiting to be uncovered. Sadly, such excavations are very unlikely anytime soon. Having already declared that a Jewish temple *never* existed on the site, Muslim religious leaders won't allow explorations that could prove them wrong. In fact, if too many people show an interest in the artifacts already on display, I fear that even they will be hidden away. So, before we draw too much attention to ourselves, it's time to walk across the plaza and exit to the north.

The ruins of a Crusader church at the Pool of Bethesda

CHAPTER 43

The Pool of Bethesda:

Does God Help Those Who Help Themselves?

According to George Barna, 75 percent of Americans believe that the statement "God helps those who help themselves" is found in the Bible.[1] More disturbingly, 52 percent of practicing Christians *also* believe the statement matches what the Bible teaches.[2]

Spoiler alert: the statement itself was popularized in America when Benjamin Franklin published it in his *Poor Richard's Almanac* in 1733. But it is *not* found in the Bible.

Why do so many believe that statement *is* found in the Bible? Perhaps it's because the statement does seem to have a patina of truth about it and reminds us of other pithy statements in the Bible. Or it might be due to the fact that the statement sounds so American. In a land that has historically prided itself on self-reliance, Americans assume such a virtue *must* have the blessing of the Almighty.

But you might be wondering what this statement has to do with the Pool of Bethesda. Well, we need to visit there to find out. Thankfully, it's the next stop on our tour of Jerusalem.

A VISIT TO THE POOL OF BETHESDA

The Pool of Bethesda is north of the Temple Mount on the northeastern side of the Old City. It's located about a hundred yards inside a gate known today as both St. Stephen's Gate and the Lions' Gate, but in the time of Jesus it had a different name. "Inside the city, near the Sheep Gate, was the pool of Bethesda" (John 5:2). The gate was called the Sheep Gate because it was the gate through which sheep destined for temple sacrifice were brought into the city.

The walk from the northern end of the Temple Mount to the Pool of Bethesda is fairly straightforward, though the site itself could easily be missed. A nondescript doorway leads from the roadway into a courtyard and beautiful garden. At the far end of the garden is St. Anne's church, and just beyond is the partially excavated Pool of Bethesda. The name "Bethesda" originally comes from two Hebrew words—*beth hesed*—which can be translated as "house of mercy." John reports that the pool was surrounded by "five covered porches" (John 5:2).

Archaeologists have helped confirm John's description. The pool area was divided into two sections by a dam. All four sides of the pool were bounded

Pool of Bethesda at the model of Second Temple Jerusalem

by covered walkways, while a fifth walkway extended across the dam in the middle. Each of the pool's two halves was up to forty feet deep, and together they held up to sixteen million gallons of water.

But how does the Pool of Bethesda connect with the expression, "God helps those who help themselves"? After all, even though the Bible stresses personal accountability and individual responsibility, it does *not* present self-reliance as a virtue. In fact, just the opposite is true. Proverbs 28:26 says, "Those who trust their own insight are foolish," while Proverbs 3:5 exhorts God's followers to "trust in the LORD with all your heart; do not depend on your own understanding." The problem with self-reliance is that it can result in the prideful belief that we are the masters of our fate and the captains of our souls—which is *not* true.

And maybe that's why the miracle at the Pool of Bethesda in John 5 makes us feel just a little uneasy.

THE DISTURBING INCIDENT AT THE POOL

The Pool of Bethesda must have been impressive. Certainly, that much water served as a visible reminder of God's mercy in a land so dependent on rain from heaven. Yet the scene that unfolds in John 5 seems to be anything but merciful. The entire area around the pool was a sea of human suffering. "Crowds of sick people—blind, lame, or paralyzed—lay on the porches" (v. 3).

At this point there's a textual problem that has resulted in a debate over whether the rest of verse 3 and all of verse 4 were written by John or added later. Why is there a problem? It's because the verses in question say the people were "waiting for a certain movement of the water, for an angel of the Lord came from time to time and stirred up the water. And the first person to step in after the water was stirred was healed of whatever disease he had."

In other words, God helped those who helped themselves! When the waters began moving, the first person who was able to drag himself or herself into the water got healed. With the depth of the pool, it makes me wonder what happened to the *second* person into the water—someone who was also disabled but *wasn't* healed. It's easy to see why people have had a problem with these verses. It sounds like God is willing to heal the person with the least amount of disability, while the most needy and helpless are doomed to remain in their pitiful state.

And yet, I tend to believe these verses *were* part of John's original manuscript. So, how do I reconcile what was happening here with the character of God? I'm able to do so by challenging one assumption. We assume that the "angel of the Lord" who stirred the pool was a good angel, but we know from Scripture that a third of the heavenly angels originally created by God joined with Satan in his rebellion against God. What if this was one of the fallen angels?

Holding people captive to such false hopes seems to have Satan's fingerprints all over it. Archaeologists discovered that in the century before the time of Jesus an area by the pool had been dedicated to the worship of Asclepius, the Greek god of healing. They also found that about a hundred years after the time of Jesus a large temple to Asclepius was built at the site. Why was this particular area connected with Asclepius? Perhaps because there had indeed been healings here, though not from the hand of God.

In contrast to the false promises of healing held out by Satan, Jesus entered the place and demonstrated the healing power of God. He approached one of the most hopeless of those packed into the colonnaded area—an individual who had been an invalid "for thirty-eight years" (John 5:5). Jesus' question to the man went straight to the point. "Would you like to get well?" (v. 6).

The man explained his pitiful plight. He had no one to assist him when the waters were stirred. "Someone else always gets there ahead of me" (John 5:7). He was too seriously disabled to make it into the water first. Yet, it seemed as if this was his only hope for healing, so he was held captive to the Pool and to the fickle promise held out there by some supernatural being.

In contrast to the false hope from the angel associated with this pool, Jesus demonstrated the true healing power of God. "Stand up, pick up your mat, and walk!" (John 5:8). God's healing was instantaneous . . . and came through no effort on the part of the lame man. "Instantly, the man was healed!

Looking down into a small section of the pool

He rolled up his sleeping mat and began walking!" (v. 9).

But there was a problem. "This miracle happened on the Sabbath" (John 5:9). Since the Pool of Bethesda was just to the north of the temple, it didn't take long for the man to be spotted by some of the religious leaders on their way to worship. They accosted him for violating the Sabbath. As they questioned the man, it became obvious that he was *not* healed because of faith in Jesus. In fact, he had no idea who had healed him. In the initial excitement, as the man stood up and cried out to those around him that he had been healed, Jesus had slipped away.

Later, Jesus found the man in the temple and issued a warning. "Now you are well; so stop sinning, or something even worse may happen to you" (John 5:14). The fact that he was *now* well could suggest he hadn't always been sick. And because Jesus warned him to "stop sinning, or something even worse may happen to you," we know Jesus was even more concerned about the man's spiritual condition than his physical paralysis.

The miracle at the "house of mercy" is a reminder that God *doesn't* help those who help themselves, but He does extend mercy to the helpless and seeks a relationship with any willing to acknowledge their sin and come to Him.

CHURCH OF SAINT ANNE

Next to the Pool of Bethesda is the Church of Saint Anne. Most Protestants don't have a clue who Saint Anne is, so I have to ask any Catholics on our tour to help them out. Saint Anne is the *mother* of the Virgin Mary. But since she's not mentioned anywhere in the Bible, how do we know her name? As Tevye said in *Fiddler on the Roof,* "That I can tell you in one word—tradition!" She was first identified in the apocryphal gospel of James, written about a century after the time of Jesus.

Since I lead Protestant groups to Israel, we don't go into Saint Anne's Church to focus on the tradition of this being the childhood home of Mary. Our groups go into the church because of its incredible acoustics. It's a *terrible* church for speaking, but a *wonderful* church for singing. As long as a mass isn't in progress, we're able to go in and sing. And I always ask my groups to sing "It Is Well with My Soul." Sadly, the number of Christians who know the words to this song is declining. I can envision a day when few will remember the lyrics. But until then, I believe it's the perfect song for this church—sung slowly, in parts, and with dramatic pauses

Entrance to the Church of Saint Anne beside the Pool of Bethesda

between lines to allow the group to hear their voices reverberate off the stone walls and ceiling. Even a small group can sound like a mighty choir inside this church.

On one particular trip, I was helping lead a large multi-bus tour for a ministry. The goal was to arrange the tour so the buses didn't become one long convoy snaking its way through the land. I was looking forward to our time at Saint Anne's because I had purchased a new video recorder and was anxious to try it out. As our group approached at the site, I was surprised to see another group from our tour arriving from the opposite direction. I might have been surprised, but I was also quite delighted.

The teacher on the other bus is one of my best friends. And in his group was the featured soloist on the trip, a nationally known gospel artist. The church was empty, so both groups went in and sat down. After a brief explanation we asked the soloist if he would lead us all in singing the first and last verses of "It Is Well." Nearly a hundred voices sang in full-throated harmony, led by this amazing musician.

As the final strains of the song echoed away, someone asked if *he* would sing for the group. He chose Martin Luther's "A Mighty Fortress Is Our God." (I did momentarily wonder if the Roman Catholic priest overseeing the church might object to having this hymn of the Protestant Reformation sung, but nothing was said.) The artist sang the song *a cappella*, in perfect pitch, modulating up on each verse. The acoustics of the church amplified his magnificent voice, and all of us sat transfixed. As he sang the final line, "His kingdom is forever . . . and ever," I don't believe there was a dry eye in the church.

I remained still for a moment, completely overwhelmed by the powerful time of worship we all had just experienced. And then I looked down—and realized I had forgotten to turn on my video recorder!

Street sign on the Via Dolorosa

CHAPTER 44

Via Dolorosa:

The Way of Sorrow . . . and Confusion!

The Via Dolorosa is a fraud! There, I've said it. Those looking forward to the Via Dolorosa as a highlight of their time in Israel will not have their expectations met on the trips I lead. Part of the reason is my deeply embedded passion for authenticity and accuracy. (Remember back when I had you climbing guardrails and tramping through weeds in the Elah Valley?) I just don't get excited about something that has little basis in historical reality.

I have three personal problems with the authenticity of the Via Dolorosa. First, we don't know how streets were laid out in the time of Jesus. The main streets in the Old City of Jerusalem today date back to the time of Hadrian, a century *after* the time of Jesus. The city had been destroyed twice between the time of Jesus and the time it was redesigned as a Roman city with a main north-south and east-west roadway grid.

Second, we don't know where Jesus' trial before Pilate actually took place. Tradition says it happened in the Fortress of Antonia on the northwest side of the temple. But the Fortress of Antonia was a Roman army barracks. What if Pilate chose instead to stay in the luxurious palace built by Herod the Great on the west side of the city, near today's Jaffa Gate? It would have been more suitable for the Roman leader, and it had its own protective fortress. The palace would also allow for an easier escape from the city should any trouble arise.

Finally, we don't know for certain where Jesus' crucifixion and burial took place. Two places currently compete for this possibility. This happens to be a case where my *head* tells me the Church of the Holy Sepulchre is probably the correct location. However, my *heart* loves the Garden Tomb. But in any case, there is at least some debate on the exact location.

With two possible starting points and two possible ending points, we technically end up with four potential routes for the Via Dolorosa. Perhaps we need to refer to all of them as the Viae Dolorosa—the "*ways* of sorrow." And as if these issues aren't enough to create doubt, who came up with the fourteen stations of the cross, the supposed locations where fourteen events leading up to the crucifixion—not all of which are even mentioned in the Bible—occurred? No one from the time of Jesus scratched a little X on the side of a building to say, "Simon of Cyrene took up Jesus' cross *here*."

As you can tell, I simply don't get too excited about the Via Dolorosa. But before you skip to the next chapter, bear with me for just a few moments. There are *some* truths we can glean as we walk along these streets.

THE TRADITIONAL VIA DOLOROSA

As we walk down the traditional Via Dolorosa, the sun reflects off the limestone walls, creating a sharp contrast between sunlight and shadows. Even though it's the middle of the day, the streets are alive with activity. A group of pilgrims—carrying a cross—snake their way down the street following the route they believe Jesus traveled on His final journey to Calvary. They walk carefully because the roadway's limestone blocks have been worn to a slippery smoothness. Every few yards they gingerly step around a discarded box or pile of garbage—leftover reminders that people still live and work in the houses and shops crowding in on each side.

> As the soldiers marched Jesus through Jerusalem, the streets were lined with vendors hoping for a profitable holiday shopping season.

The pilgrims try to focus on the events that unfolded here twenty centuries ago. They want to experience what it was like for the Lamb of God as He journeyed to Calvary to pay for the sins of the

Pilgrims carrying a cross down the Via Dolorosa

world. They try to imagine the physical pain He felt, the anguish and fear of His followers, and the harsh shouts of the guards marching this group of condemned prisoners to the place of death. But the cries of vendors calling from shops along the route seem to shatter the sacred moment. "Hand-carved olive wood crosses!" "You are my first customer. I'll make you a special deal!" "Get your 'Stations of the Cross' map here!"

My wife has one vivid memory from her first experience on the traditional Via Dolorosa. Our group turned the corner at the third station of the cross, only to have the roadway temporarily blocked by a Coca-Cola truck making deliveries. At first, the commercialism all along the route jars the senses of those seeking to make this a sacred journey. And yet, delivery vehicles and the profane hawking of religious trinkets by vendors is probably very close to what really happened the day Jesus hung on the cross. As the soldiers marched Jesus through Jerusalem, the streets were also lined with vendors hoping for a profitable holiday shopping season. They shouted at those passing by to "stop and shop" at their store—offering the latest in lamps, olive oil, spices, cloth, leather, and any other items needed by pilgrims who had made the long journey to Jerusalem for Passover.

Most likely, shopkeepers and shoppers retreated into the stores, as the brutal parade passed by, not wanting to block the way, or attract the attention, of those soldiers. But scarcely had the condemned criminals shuffled past when the bargaining began anew. That Friday morning people were so busy shopping, cleaning, and preparing for Passover that they scarcely paid attention to this group of prisoners on their way to be executed. The shoppers never heard the hammer blows as iron nails punched through human flesh and embedded in wood.[1]

Walking the Via Dolorosa *can* help someone visualize what Jerusalem might have been like two thousand years ago. The streets are somewhat cleaner and the shops brighter—thanks to electric lights—but the shopkeepers are just as aggressive in trying to make a sale. We might be uncertain about the specific route of the Via Dolorosa, but this can help provide a close approximation. However, someone seeking authenticity might want to try an *alternative* Via Dolorosa.

THE "OTHER" VIA DOLOROSA

The other Via Dolorosa has no street signs identifying it as the road to Calvary. Nor does it have any "stations of the cross" dotting the route. And yet, the starting and ending points seem to have greater historical validity. This "unofficial" Via Dolorosa begins just inside the Jaffa Gate at the Citadel of David and ends at the Church of the Holy Sepulchre.

Like so much in Jerusalem, the Citadel of David is misnamed. It actually has *nothing* to do with King David. It sits on the Western Hill—the left half of the hamburger bun. The original City of David was the ice cream cone. The Citadel of David is actually the site of a luxurious palace and fortress built by Herod the Great. The fortress included three massive towers built to guard his palace from the very people he governed. The base of one tower is still standing.

Next to Herod's palace is a site known as the *Kishle*, a name that means "barracks" or "dungeon." It was built by the Ottoman Turks and served as part of the barracks for their soldiers. Later it was used as a prison by the British.

Inside the Citadel of David at Jaffa Gate

Recent excavations have uncovered remains at the site that also date back to the time of Herod the Great. If Pilate chose to stay at Herod's palace in Jerusalem—rather than in the Fortress of Antonia—the Kishle could be near the spot where Jesus appeared before him. This would also then be the barracks where the Roman guards tortured Jesus before taking Him out to be crucified.

The most direct route from the Citadel of David to the Church of the Holy Sepulchre led down David Street—later Hadrian's Decumanus—to Christian Quarter Road. Several hundred yards down Christian Quarter Road is Saint Helena Street, which leads directly to the Church of the Holy Sepulchre. The exact route taken by the soldiers isn't known, but this is a close approximation of the course they might have followed.

SHOPPING ON THE VIA DOLOROSA

No matter which Via Dolorosa a pilgrim chooses, all roads to Calvary lead through the Old City with all its shopping. Based on what I've seen over the years, many trips to Israel are little more than extended shopping tours. Visit a shrine, then "stop at my good friend's olive wood shop." Visit an ancient church, then "stop at my good friend's pottery store." Walk the Via Dolorosa, then "stop at my good friend's T-shirt shop." Instead of singing "I walked today where Jesus walked," visitors might wonder if the theme song for such trips ought to be "I shopped today where Jesus walked."

Walking on David Street in the Christian Quarter

Don't get me wrong. Most people want to shop for souvenirs while in Israel, and there are many unique and beautiful items for sale. But some tours seem to visit more stores than sites. I realize I live on the other end of the shopping spectrum, and I've come to understand that *some* opportunities to shop are important. But not *too* many.

The key to successful shopping is to learn the "shopping proverb"—Proverbs 20:14. The book of Proverbs gives wisdom on how to live life successfully, and Proverbs 20:14 comes right from the streets and markets of ancient Israel. "'Bad, bad,' says the buyer, but when he goes his way, then he boasts" (NASB). The thought behind the proverb was that the smart shopper never expressed too much enthusiasm over an item being offered for sale. If the buyer appeared too excited, the price would stay high. But if the shopper didn't seem too interested, the seller would be more willing to reduce the price. So as a wise shopper began bargaining, he or she wanted to appear disinterested, or at least less than enthusiastic. Later they could boast to their friends about the great deal they got on their purchase.

426

While Solomon's proverb might help a pilgrim walking and shopping on the Via Dolorosa today, can it have any practical significance in that pilgrim's life back home? After all, very few stand in the checkout line at Walmart and bargain with the cashier over the price they're willing to pay for their purchases. So, does Proverbs 20:14 have any relevance for today?

Actually, it does! This proverb says far more about *life* than it does about shopping. Solomon was reminding his listeners not to believe everything they hear. Sometimes people might say one thing while really believing something else. Only later will their true feelings be known. They might claim something is "worthless," but their words might not reflect what they really think about it.

Let me move the truth of this proverb off the Via Dolorosa and into life. As you share your faith with others, they might seem to reject the message, and perhaps even get upset with you. But don't believe everything you hear. Their reaction might be their way of hiding fears and insecurities. They haven't necessarily rejected you or your message. As the shopkeepers of old learned, don't get discouraged by their apparent lack of interest. It might

Some of the many baubles on sale in the Old City

just be a mask hiding a heart that is searching for spiritual treasure.

Remember, "The buyer haggles over the price, saying, 'It's worthless,' then brags about getting a bargain!" Don't believe everything you hear. And don't get discouraged if people appear to be uninterested in Jesus. Just keep sharing the good news!

Entrance to the Church of the Holy Sepulchre

CHAPTER 45

The Church of the Holy Sepulchre:

A Clash of Expectations

The Church of the Holy Sepulchre confounds expectations, and often not in a good way. Jerome Murphy-O'Connor, the late Roman Catholic scholar who lived in Jerusalem and taught at the École Biblique, explained why the church could be both disappointing and disturbing to visitors from the West.

> One expects the central shrine of Christendom to stand out in majestic isolation, but anonymous buildings cling to it like barnacles. One looks for luminous light, but it is dark and cramped. One hopes for peace, but the ear is assailed by a cacophony of warring chants. One desires holiness, only to encounter a jealous possessiveness: the six groups of occupants—Latin Catholics, Greek Orthodox, Armenian Orthodox, Syrians, Copts, Ethiopians—watch one another suspiciously for any infringement of rights. The frailty of humanity is nowhere more apparent than here; it epitomizes the human condition. The empty who come to be filled will leave desolate; those who permit the church to question them may begin to understand why hundreds of thousands thought it worthwhile to risk death or slavery in order to pray here.[1]

While He was here on earth, Jesus gave His followers a key command. "This is my commandment: Love each other in the same way I have loved you" (John 15:12). On His way to the Garden of Gethsemane—just before His arrest, trial, and crucifixion—Jesus paused to pray for His disciples and for those who would come to faith through them. "I am praying not only for these disciples but also for all who will ever believe in me through their message. I pray that they will all be one, just as you and I are one—as you are in me, Father, and I am in you. And may they be in us so that the world will believe you sent me" (John 17:20–21). Jesus commanded love . . . and prayed for unity. Sadly, those two words are seldom connected with the history of the Church of the Holy Sepulchre.

THE STATUS QUO AGREEMENT

In 1970, during Easter prayers, the Coptic monks left their monastery located on the roof of the church. Ethiopian monks slipped in, changed the locks, and claimed the space for themselves. The police had to intervene to restore the status quo. In 2002, a Coptic monk moved his chair into space claimed by the Ethiopians. Eleven people were hospitalized after the fighting ended. In 2008, Israeli police had to enter the church to break up a fistfight between Greek and Armenian monks over an apparent infringement of rights. And these are just some of the *recent* incidents! The Crimean War in the 1850s was fought, in part, over the reassignment of rights in the church between the Roman Catholic and Eastern Orthodox groups.

The different religious groups have fought each other during much of the time they have occupied this church. The problems became so severe that in 1757 the Turkish authorities issued a royal decree dividing the church among its different occupants and declaring that no change could be made by one sect unless the other five agreed. The Greek Orthodox, Roman Catholic, and Armenian Apostolic churches were allowed to actually share the church, while the Syrians, Copts, and Ethiopians were only given rights to use some parts of the building. Following the Crimean War, the status quo was reestablished and received international recognition in the 1856 Treaty of Paris.

The tension and conflict within the church is visualized by a ladder standing in front of a window above the entrance. The ladder was first placed there in 1728 and has—with just a few minor exceptions—remained in place since 1757, when the status quo was established. Whether one views a sketch of the church from the 1700s or a photograph from the 1850s, the ladder can be seen perched in front of the window. In 2009, all the sects agreed to move the ladder temporarily to accommodate scaffolding for renovations. But once the renovations were completed, the ladder was put back in place.

The entryway into the Church of the Holy Sepulchre

The power struggles within the church ultimately dictated who controls the key to the front door. None of the groups trusted the others. They were concerned that if one group kept the key, that group would lock the others out. So since 1192, a Muslim family has kept the key to the front door. They open the door each morning and lock it again at night. They also serve as "peacekeepers" to help settle frequent quarrels between the sects. It seems the Christian groups have more faith in these Muslims than they do in each other!

WHERE EAST CLASHES WITH WEST

The Church of the Holy Sepulchre is also the spot where the spiritual credulity of the East clashes most dramatically with the modern cynicism of the West. Visitors from the West coming to see Calvary and Joseph of Arimathea's tomb struggle when they are also shown the tombs of Adam, Melchizedek, Nicodemus, and John the Baptist—as well as the "navel stone" that's said to be the center of the world.

Tourists trying to look beyond the external nonsense and focus on the reality of what might have actually occurred at this place are bothered by all the extraneous sideshows connected with the site. Over 150 years ago, Rev. Norman MacLeod gave voice to his concerns. "But as these poor pilgrims gazed on the spot where, as they believed, the Lord lay, how one longed to make them also believe, and rejoice much more in the thought 'He is not here, but risen!' and to be able, in the strength of His resurrection-life, to rise with Him and to set their affections on things above, where He sitteth on the right hand of God!"[2]

> A visitor needs to search carefully to find the historical reality hidden behind all the excess religious baggage.

Less devout tourists find much of the religious paraphernalia and activity to be little more than superstitious balderdash. Mark Twain certainly fits this profile as he described his reaction to being shown the tomb of Adam. "The tomb of Adam! How touching it was, here in a land of strangers, far away from home and friends and all who cared for me, thus to discover the grave of a blood relation. True, a distant one, but still a relation. The unerring instinct of nature thrilled its recognition. The fountain of my filial affection was stirred to its profoundest depths, and I gave way to tumultuous emotion. I leaned upon a pillar and burst into tears."[3] Twain's guffaws were tears of derisive laughter, not sorrow!

A TOUR OF THE CHURCH

Intellectually, I believe the Church of the Holy Sepulchre marks the location of Jesus' crucifixion, burial, and resurrection. When Hadrian came to Jerusalem a hundred years after the time of Jesus, he discovered the site was venerated by Christians, so he constructed a pagan temple there to claim it for his gods. But the early tradition never died, and the temple was eventually torn down to build the church. Still, a visitor needs to search carefully to find the historical reality hidden behind all the excess religious baggage.

With that in mind, let's tour the church!

Immediately inside the doorway, on the right, is a steep set of stairs leading up to the traditional site of the crucifixion. The reality is that Jesus wasn't crucified on top of the hill. The Romans carried out their crucifixions just outside the city, beside the road, so those traveling by could see the ugly horror of capital punishment—and think twice about defying the government

The traditional spot, under the altar, where the cross of Jesus was said to have been placed

of Rome. They wanted the criminal charges posted over the head of the condemned individual so they could be read by those passing by.

The steps might not lead to the actual place of the crucifixion, but they *are* taking the visitor to the top of a natural rock outcropping. Perhaps the hill was named Golgotha (in Aramaic) or Calvary (in Latin) because the shape of the rock gave the hill the appearance of a skull. Or perhaps the name came from its use as a place of execution and burial. Unfortunately, the rock outcropping is virtually invisible under all the religious trappings, unless one knows where to look.

Look carefully at the pilgrims waiting in line to touch the spot where the cross was said to have been placed. On both sides of that spot are glass panels, and just below them one can see bedrock. The steps we climbed led to the *top* of the rocky outcropping. This isn't where Jesus was crucified, but it is the rock that could have given the site its name.

Another set of steps takes visitors back down to ground level. Both sets of steps are extremely steep, so hold on to the handrails. At the bottom of the steps is the next stop on this tour—the Stone of Unction. This is the traditional spot where Jesus' body was placed, after being taken from the cross, and anointed for burial. Matthew 27:59 simply says that Joseph took the body and "wrapped it in a long sheet of clean linen cloth." The gospel of John adds additional details. Joseph was accompanied by "Nicodemus, the man who had come to Jesus at night. He brought about seventy-five pounds of perfumed ointment made from myrrh and aloes. Following Jewish burial custom, they wrapped Jesus' body with the spices in long sheets of linen cloth" (John 19:39–40).

The current Stone of Unction is not the actual stone on which Joseph and Nicodemus prepared Jesus' body for burial. But it is likely that they prepared the body close to the place of crucifixion for one obvious reason. It would take two men to carry the body, but they were also carrying seventy-five pounds of spices. Unless they wrapped the body in the spices first, it's hard to envision how these two could have carried both the body and the spices separately.

The traditional Stone of Unction

After wrapping Jesus' body, Joseph and Nicodemus carried it to a new tomb that was nearby. Actually, John 19:41 says, "The place of crucifixion was near a garden, where there was a new tomb, never used before." The tomb was in the garden, and the garden was at the place where He was crucified. That means the tomb must have been relatively near the place of crucifixion. How near? Someone from the West might envision the tomb being within a half-mile, or perhaps a kilometer, of the crucifixion site. But here in the church the distance from Calvary to the tomb is about a hundred feet! It's much "nearer" than most imagine.

Two additional details about the tomb are important. First, the tomb wasn't just any unoccupied tomb nearby. Matthew 27:60 says Joseph of Arimathea placed Jesus "in his own new tomb, which had been carved out of

The Aedicule built over the place of Joseph of Arimathea's tomb

the rock." The tomb belonged to Joseph, which is an amazing "coincidence" orchestrated by God. Second, don't actually expect to see Joseph's tomb when you walk around the corner. The tomb has disappeared.

Instead of coming to a tomb, pilgrims discover a small stone structure encircled by a long line of pilgrims waiting to peer inside. This is the Aedicule, literally a "little house," that marks the spot where Joseph's tomb was once located. Emperor Constantine's mother searched out the authentic tomb and then had all the stone around it quarried away. Then in 1009, a Muslim ruler named Al-Hakim ordered the destruction of both the tomb and the church. The tomb was hammered apart until only the base remained under the rubble.

Today, the Aedicule is built over the spot where the tomb used to be located. Inside is a bench where the body of Jesus was said to have been placed. This stone shrine is most dissatisfying to those who expect to see an actual tomb, but this is still the likely spot where the crucifixion, burial, and resurrection happened. It might not look the way we want, but that doesn't take away from the historicity of the site. Both early church tradition and archaeology offer their support for this location.

Follow me to a rather deserted area behind the Aedicule. Queen Helena quarried out all the stone around the one tomb that became the central focus underneath the building's massive dome. We're now far enough away from where that tomb was located to find remnants of the bedrock left behind by the builders.

In this out-of-the-way room, carved into the bedrock, are remains of other first-century tombs. They look very similar to the tombs we saw at the entrance to Dominus Flevit on the Mount of Olives. In Jesus' day these tombs would have been *outside* the city walls. But around AD 41–44, King Agrippa I started build-

Tombs carved into the bedrock

ing another wall around the northern suburbs of Jerusalem. These graves would then have been *inside* the city walls, which means they would have gone out of use at that time.

Why is this important? It's archaeological proof that this area was being used as a place of burial in the time of Jesus! And yet, within a decade after that time it ceased being used for burial. Joseph of Arimathea's tomb could very well have been in this area.

It's time to end our abbreviated tour of the Church of the Holy Sepulchre. The church is not to everyone's liking, but it is still important. And yet, I want to end our tour with Jesus' words to His disciples that I quoted earlier. He called on His followers to love one another and to display unity. This church, by itself, isn't holy. Its significance comes from events that occurred over three days and that changed the course of history. Our real focus shouldn't be on a shrine, it should be on Jesus—His death, burial, and resurrection. And if we love Jesus, then we need to become the light to the world He has commanded us to be.

Mark Twain toured the Holy Land, including this church. But the tour didn't change Twain's spiritual life. One reason is that he was keenly aware of the disconnect between beliefs and actions he saw in the lives of those who claimed to follow Christ. He knew what Christians professed, but he didn't see it lived out in a winsome way in many lives. Some of the saddest comments Twain made in his travelogue are his closing remarks on the Church of the Holy Sepulchre. They're both profound, and troubling.

And so I close my chapter on the Church of the Holy Sepulchre—the most sacred locality on earth to millions and millions of men and women and children, the noble and the humble, bond and free. In its history from the first, and in its tremendous associations, it is the most illustrious edifice in Christendom. With all its claptrap sideshows and unseemly impostures of every kind, it is still grand, reverend, venerable—for a god died there; for fifteen hundred years its shrines have been wet with the tears of pilgrims from the earth's remotest confines; for more than two hundred, the most gallant knights that ever wielded sword wasted their lives away in a struggle to seize it and hold it sacred from infidel pollution. Even in our own day a war that cost millions of treasure and rivers of blood was fought because two rival nations claimed the sole right to put a new dome upon it. History is full of this old Church of the Holy Sepulchre—full of blood that was shed because of the respect and the veneration in which men held the last resting place of the meek and lowly, the mild and gentle, Prince of Peace![4]

Inside Jaffa Gate in the Old City of Jerusalem

CHAPTER 46

The Old City of Jerusalem:

Walking through Time

It's hard to explain the feelings one experiences walking through the Old City of Jerusalem. The deep spiritual and emotional connection one already feels to people and events in the Bible becomes more visceral and intense. In fact, the impact can become so overwhelming that it has at times resulted in psychological problems for those unable to handle the emotional overload. The phenomenon is known as "Jerusalem Syndrome," and it can cause individuals to experience intense religious feelings to the point where they believe God is speaking directly to them or they see themselves becoming a character from the Bible.[1]

We've never had anyone on our trips actually experience Jerusalem Syndrome, but I know of other tours that have. It might sound humorous, but it's really quite serious because the person could potentially harm himself or herself. Thankfully, relatively few travelers actually suffer Jerusalem Syndrome, but almost everyone who walks Jerusalem's streets understands the emotional impact the city can have on a visitor.

We have already visited some areas within Jerusalem, so today we'll explore other sites in and around the city, beginning at Zion Gate.

ZION GATE

Zion Gate received its name because it sits on top of the Western Hill—the hill that today is mistakenly called Mount Zion. The gate is not only misnamed, it's also misplaced. When Hezekiah built his wall around the Western Hill, he positioned the wall on the edge of the Hinnom Valley. The enemy would need to fight its way uphill. At the time of Jesus, the walls were also along the edge of the Hinnom Valley. But when Suleiman the Magnificent commissioned his architects to build the wall, they took a shortcut across the top of the hill. A story has circulated that

A van driving out Zion Gate

when Suleiman saw what they had done he had them beheaded. It's uncertain if this is true, especially since the architects were honored by being buried in tombs just inside Jaffa Gate.

Two things impact me as I stare at this gate. First, I'm shocked at the many bullet holes in and around it. In 1948, Jewish forces tried, and failed, to break into the city here to rescue the inhabitants of the Jewish Quarter. The Jewish Quarter fell, and Jerusalem was ethnically cleansed of its Jewish inhabitants. For nineteen years, Jews were denied access to the Western Wall, until Israel captured Jerusalem in the 1967 Six-Day War. Those bullet holes speak to the desperation and ferocity of that original failed attack.

The second thing that impacts me is the reality that this five-hundred-year-old gate is now used as an exit point by cars and vans. What isn't obvious from the outside is that the gate makes a sharp turn inside. Less experienced drivers need to repeatedly pull forward and then back up to get their vehicles around the tight corner. And a careful inspection of the vehicles shows that all too often drivers have scraped against the side on their way out!

THE JEWISH QUARTER

Once inside Zion Gate, it's a short walk to the Jewish Quarter. The area was almost completely demolished by the Jordanian army during the battle for the Old City. But as heartbreaking as that was, it also provided Israel with a unique opportunity. After capturing the Old City in 1967, Israel was able to conduct a large-scale archaeological excavation of the Jewish Quarter before beginning to rebuild. And what they uncovered is amazing.

One of the most spectacular discoveries was the foundation of the Broad Wall dating back to the time of King Hezekiah. The remains of this wall

The Broad Wall that dates back to the time of King Hezekiah

actually extended beyond the section still visible today. Hezekiah began building this wall in about 705 BC as part of a major project to extend the walls of Jerusalem around the entire Western Hill. In one spot, architects discovered the remains of houses that were here before the wall. When the wall was built, the houses were in the way and had to be torn down.

The prophet Isaiah predicted the coming invasion of Judah by the Assyrian army. In Isaiah 22 he pictured a time when "Chariots fill your beautiful valleys, and charioteers storm your gates. Judah's defenses have been stripped away" (vv. 7–8). In Isaiah 36 that time arrived. "In the fourteenth year of King Hezekiah's reign, King Sennacherib of Assyria came to attack the fortified towns of Judah and conquered them" (Isa. 36:1).

Knowing an invasion was coming, Hezekiah prepared to defend Jerusalem. He built the Broad Wall to protect the part of the city on the Western Hill that was outside the original walls. Knowing a reliable water supply was essential, he dug a tunnel to bring water from the Gihon Spring into the city, collecting it in the Pool of Siloam. We'll visit those locations later.

It's always wise to try to prepare for threats in advance—to be ready before disaster strikes. Building this wall and providing an adequate supply of water seemed like wise actions. In fact, Isaiah continued describing all the preparations made by Hezekiah. "You run to the armory for your weapons" (Isa. 22:8). The army of Judah went into the palace built by King Solomon and counted all the *weapons* stockpiled in the armory.

Isaiah continued. "You inspect the breaks in the walls of Jerusalem . . . You survey the houses and tear some down for stone to strengthen the walls" (Isa. 22:9–10). Hezekiah's architects looked carefully at the *walls* of Jerusalem to determine where new walls might be needed, and where the current walls had to be repaired.

The prophet then focused on their third concern. "You store up water in the lower pool. . . . Between the city walls, you build a reservoir for water from the old pool" (Isa. 22:9, 11). They paid careful attention to the *water* supply for Jerusalem.

It's almost as if the people of Jerusalem ticked off all the boxes on their to-do list of final preparations. Are all the weapons ready? Check. Are the defensive walls in place? Check. Have we taken care of providing an adequate water supply to withstand the siege? Check. Weapons, walls, water. It looks like we thought of everything!

That's when Isaiah pointed out the one thing they had *failed* to consider when preparing for the coming invasion. "But you never ask for help from the One who did all this. You never considered the One who planned this long ago" (Isa. 22:11). Oops. In their haste to prepare for the coming battle the one thing they forgot to focus on was the God of the universe. They were so busy seeing what *they* could do, they neglected to ask God what *He* could do.

In the end, the nation was almost destroyed. Isaiah reports that King Sennacherib of Assyria "came to attack the fortified towns of Judah and conquered them" (Isa. 36:1). Sennacherib left his own account of the campaign. In it, he claims to have captured forty-six strong, walled cities and countless villages and to have deported over 200,000 captives as slaves. Hezekiah, he says, was shut up in Jerusalem "like a bird in a cage."[2] Only after Hezekiah and the leaders of Jerusalem humbled themselves before God did God intervene and rescue the nation by sending the angel of the Lord to put to death 185,000 Assyrian soldiers. Jerusalem was spared, but it wasn't the weapons, walls, or water that saved them. It was a miracle that came directly from the hand of God.

> We become so busy seeing how we can solve our own problems that we forget to look to God.

This wall can teach us an important lesson. When faced with problems and difficulties in our lives, often our first thought is to look within ourselves to see what *we* can do to overcome them. We count the weapons, collect the water, and strengthen the walls of our lives. We become so busy seeing how we can solve our own problems that we forget to look to God. And yet, He should be our *first* place of refuge, not our *last* line of defense.

A short distance from Hezekiah's Broad Wall is a modern plaza in front of a now-restored synagogue that had been destroyed by the Jordanians. This is our next stop.

The synagogue is beautiful, but we're actually stopping to view a reproduction of the menorah from the Second Temple period that is currently located in the plaza. We might call this the peripatetic menorah because it has moved around inside the Jewish Quarter over the years. For several years it stood on the ancient Roman Cardo, the street from the time of Hadrian that was uncovered during the excavations. Then the menorah was moved to a spot overlooking the Western Wall and Temple Mount. Most recently it was placed in this plaza. Who knows where it might turn up next!

A reproduction of the menorah from the Second Temple in the Jewish Quarter of the Old City

A woman playing her harp inside Jaffa Gate

The design is based on research by the Temple Institute, a group preparing materials to use in a new temple once it is rebuilt. This model also resembles the menorah on the Arch of Titus in Rome, which is no surprise since that arch commemorates the destruction and looting of Jerusalem in AD 70. This model is *not* made of gold, although the final menorah will need to be cast from pure gold. It's an excellent visual reminder that there are a small but growing group of individuals who believe God wants Israel to rebuild the temple.

JAFFA GATE

Our final stop in the Old City is Jaffa Gate. This is an ideal place to do some people-watching. Tourists from around the world. Orthodox Jews on their way to the Western Wall. Arab shopkeepers heading to work. A convoy of Segways touring Jerusalem. Money changers shouting from their shops to those passing by. They can all be found at Jaffa Gate.

Riding a Segway at Jaffa Gate

My all-time favorite image from Jaffa Gate was a Hasidic Jew riding a Segway while using his cellphone. Only in Jerusalem! A short distance inside the Old City one can shop for anything from scarves and rugs to sandals, antiquities, jewelry, and olive wood. Just be prepared to bargain!

Shopping near Jaffa Gate

OUTSIDE THE OLD CITY

We have one more stop to make on this part of the tour, and it's actually *outside* the Old City. Thankfully, it's not too far from Jaffa Gate, though we do need to cross the Hinnom Valley. This is a bonus stop on our trip—a place we can visit if the group is ahead of schedule. I like it because it's somewhat interactive, though not in a high-tech way. We're going to visit a 2,600-year-old family tomb!

We talked about New Testament–era

447

tombs on the Mount of Olives. The tomb we're about to visit is a family tomb from the Old Testament era. The location is called Ketef Hinnom, the shoulder of Hinnom. It's the spot where the ridge opposite the city of Jerusalem forms something of a saddle, a low spot where it was easiest for travelers on the Way of the Patriarchs to drop into the Hinnom Valley and make their way over to the City of David. Over time the city of Jerusalem expanded onto the Western Hill, just across the Hinnom. But this low spot on the ridge remained the easiest crossing point.

Volunteers "resting" in a family tomb from Old Testament times

Seven adventuresome volunteers lie down on the burial benches—this particular tomb could hold up to seven bodies at one time. This tomb was *not* open to the sky. It was a cave carved into the hillside. The top of the cave was hacked away in the not-too-distant past, exposing the tomb itself. Imagine standing inside the flat area at the far end. The family brought the body into that area of the burial cave through a small opening and then carried the body into the inner chamber to be placed on one of the seven spots carved into the benches that extended around three sides. A repository was carved into the rock underneath the longest bench. After allowing the body to decay for a year, the bones were collected and placed in that repository as the deceased literally "joined his ancestors in death" (Gen. 25:8, 17; 35:29; 49:33).

But as fun and educational as the site might be, an amazing discovery also came from this very tomb. In 1979, an Israeli archaeologist led an excavation at the site. Though it first appeared as if the site had been looted in the past, they discovered that a layer of limestone inside the repository had dislodged and fallen from the ceiling, completely hiding everything below. The slab was removed, and the treasures from the tomb came to light.

Now, it wasn't like uncovering King Tut's tomb. There were no chariots, or golden masks, or alabaster jars. But in addition to the bones, they discovered about a thousand small objects. Most were clay lamps and jars, along with needles and pins, glass bottles, jewelry, and even some arrowheads. But the most remarkable objects discovered were two small silver items that looked . . . well, they looked something like cigarette butts. The archaeologists determined they were rolled up pieces of silver that had once been worn as necklaces or amulets. It took years of careful work to unroll the tiny scrolls and discover what was written inside.

Once the scrolls were opened, they found carefully inscribed ancient Hebrew letters. These thin pieces of silver had then been rolled up and worn as part of a necklace. When the owner died, he or she was buried with this prized possession. What was written on these tiny silver scrolls? The larger of the two begins by talking about "Yahweh the great, who keeps the covenant and who is gracious toward those who love Him and who keep His commandments." Then it goes on to say, "For redemption is in Him. For Yahweh is our restorer and rock. May Yahweh bless you, and may He keep you, May Yahweh make His face shine" . . . and that's where the bottom of the scroll was broken away.

The smaller amulet has a line or two that aren't clearly legible at the very beginning, though it may have given the person's name and family identity. Then it goes on to say "May you be blessed by Yahweh, the warrior and rebuker of evil: May Yahweh bless you, keep you. May Yahweh make His face shine upon you and grant you peace."

Sound familiar? Both amulets end by quoting from Numbers 6, the passage where Moses told Aaron how he and his sons were to bless Israel. "Then the LORD said to Moses, 'Tell Aaron and his sons to bless the people of Israel with this special blessing: "May the LORD bless you and protect you. May the LORD smile on you and be gracious to you. May the LORD show you his favor and give you his peace"'" (Num. 6:22–26).

In this family tomb, archaeologists discovered *two* references to this very blessing assigned to Aaron and his descendants by Moses. Pretty amazing! And it's even more amazing to realize this is the earliest written quotation of Scripture ever uncovered by archaeologists. It's a good reminder that we *can* trust the Bible . . . and the God who wrote the Bible. He's the one who has promised to bless, keep, make His face shine on, be gracious to, and grant peace to His followers. The people buried in this tomb more than 2,600 years ago knew that to be true—and so can we.

Interior of the Upper Room

CHAPTER 47

The Upper Room:
Site of the Last Supper?

The Upper Room is another site that epitomizes everything confusing about Jerusalem. For example, Jesus told His two disciples to "go *into* the city" and meet a man carrying a jar of water who would lead them to the owner of a house with a "large room" upstairs (Mark 14:13–15). But the Upper Room most people visit today is *outside* the walls of the Old City, and it sits directly *above* the so-called tomb of David. It's hard to envision Jesus having His Last Supper in a room just above a tomb.

The confusion only gets worse when visitors actually walk into the Upper Room, and discover the arched ceiling dates back to the time of the Crusades—a thousand years *after* the time of Jesus. They also learn the entire room had at one point been turned into a mosque. Discovering a *mihrab*, a niche in the wall facing toward Mecca, is *not* what one expects in the Upper Room.

Then, as soon as someone begins to speak, the final flaw appears. The stone floor, walls, and ceiling make the room one large echo chamber. Every whisper, cough, click of a hard-soled shoe, and rip of Velcro from someone's bag bounces off the walls and ceilings, joining together to form a noisy rumble that makes it almost impossible to hear a distinct human voice. If Jesus had delivered the message of John 13–14 in *this* Upper Room, the disciples would have had no idea what He was saying. ("In Your Father's house are *what*? Could you repeat that? I said, COULD . . . YOU . . . REPEAT . . . THAT!")

This room is *not* the room where Jesus met with His disciples the night

He was betrayed, but at least it's located in the right part of town. We're on the left half of the hamburger bun, and in Jesus' day the entire area *was* enclosed within the city's walls. In fact, this upper portion of the Western Hill would have been filled with large houses that had spacious upper rooms.

THE LAST SUPPER

When most people think of the Last Supper, Leonardo da Vinci's fifteenth-century mural painting comes to mind. We envision a long table filled with plates, bowls, and cups with Jesus seated in the center, surrounded by His disciples on both sides. But the Passover celebration with Jesus would have looked much different. The table was low and U-shaped, with cushions extending out from the three outside edges. The guests would have reclined on the cushions, resting on their left elbow, with their feet extending away from the table. Jesus and the disciples "were *reclining* at the table and eating" (Mark 14:18 NASB).

The gospel accounts even allow us to reconstruct where key individuals were arranged around the table. As the host, Jesus reclined at the second spot from one end. He would then invite two honored guests to recline on His right and left. The apostle John must have been reclining just to the right of Jesus. As he rested on his left elbow he would have been leaning against Jesus Himself. Surprisingly, Jesus invited Judas Iscariot to recline at the other place of honor—the cushion just to His left.

How do we know this is where John and Judas were positioned? After reporting that Jesus told the disciples one of them would betray Him, the apostle John then adds, "Lying back on Jesus' chest was one of His disciples, whom Jesus loved" (John 13:23 NASB). John describes himself elsewhere as the disciple loved by Jesus, so he was next to Jesus. But on which side? "He then simply leaned back on Jesus' chest and said to Him, 'Lord, who is it?'" (v. 25 NASB). For John to be able to lean back against Jesus, he had to be reclining on Jesus' right side.

John 13 also helps establish the location of Judas. When John leaned back and quietly asked Jesus "Lord, who is it?" Jesus must have whispered the answer to John. "It is the one to whom I give the bread I dip in the bowl" (John 13:26). Then Jesus dipped the bread and handed it to Judas. For this to take place, Judas must have been next to Jesus, on His left side.

Finally, other details in the account suggest Peter was at the opposite end of the table. He had to be positioned where he could make eye contact with John in a room lit only by flickering oil lamps. Just after Jesus announced that one of the Twelve was about to betray Him, "Simon Peter motioned to [John] to ask, 'Who's he talking about?'" (John 13:24). This makes most sense if Peter were directly across from John. From here he could get John's attention and encourage John to ask Jesus without arousing the curiosity of the other disciples.

Why would Peter—one of the inner circle of disciples—have been seated at the far end of the table? Perhaps he was offended at not being offered one of the places of honor. Rather than selecting another cushion near Jesus, Peter deliberately went to the opposite end. It's almost as if he were trying to make a statement about his displeasure by choosing the seat farthest from the host. Perhaps that's also why Peter responded as he did when Jesus came to wash his feet (John 13:5–10).

An oil lamp similar to the type used at the time of Jesus

Matthew presents several specific elements from a typical Jewish Passover in his account. First, Jesus broke the bread *during* the meal rather than before, which was the normal custom at a regular meal. *"As they were eating,* Jesus took some bread and blessed it. Then he broke it in pieces and gave it to the disciples, saying, 'Take this and eat it, for this is my body'" (Matt. 26:26). In the Passover Seder, two blessings are recited over the matzah before it's broken and eaten.

Second, Jesus told John that the one who would betray Him was the one "who has just eaten from this bowl with me" (Matt. 26:23). John added another detail in his account. Jesus told him that the one about to betray him was "the one to whom I give the bread I dip in the bowl" (John 13:26). In the Passover Seder, matzah is dipped into the bitter herbs and then eaten. It appears that Jesus handed Judas this bite of matzah.

Finally, Jesus then took a "cup," and after giving thanks gave it to the disciples and said, "Each of you drink from it, for this is my blood, which confirms the covenant between God and his people. It is poured out as a sacrifice to forgive the sins of many" (Matt. 26:27–28). The third cup of wine at the Passover meal is the "cup of redemption," and Jesus connected this cup to the New Covenant promised in Jeremiah 31.

The disciples didn't fully appreciate the events of that night. They didn't understand Satan hoped to use Judas to thwart God's plan of redemption. They didn't understand Jesus was the ultimate Passover Lamb about to die to pay the penalty for sin. They hadn't yet grasped that the New Covenant promised by the prophets required a sacrifice only God Himself could pay. This Passover Seder would be followed by the ultimate sacrifice of the Lamb of God on Calvary.

This is a good place to pause and once again ask yourself life's most important question. Have you come to the realization that it's our sin that separates us from God? Thankfully, God loves us so much that He sent His only Son to earth as the divine Passover Lamb who willingly died to pay the eternal price for our sin. But that gift of eternal life that God now offers still needs to be accepted. If you've not yet done so, why not make a decision today, right now, to place your trust in Messiah Jesus, God's Son, as your Savior? "For this is how God loved the world: He gave his one and only Son, so that everyone who believes in him will not perish but have eternal life" (John 3:16).

THE BIRTH OF THE CHURCH

Following Jesus' ascension to heaven, the disciples returned to Jerusalem from the Mount of Olives and "went to the upstairs room of the house where they were staying" (Acts 1:13). It's not too great a jump in logic to assume the Upper Room used by the disciples as a gathering place following Jesus' resurrection was the same room used by them for the final Passover. While Luke used two different words for "upper room" in Luke 22:12 and Acts 1:13, the two words are synonymous.

If the disciples met in the same Upper Room after Jesus' ascension where they had earlier met to celebrate Passover, then this would also be the place where the Holy Spirit was poured out on the day of Pentecost. "On the day of Pentecost all the believers were meeting together in one place. Suddenly, there was a sound from heaven like the roaring of a mighty windstorm,

Olive tree sculpture in the Upper Room

and it filled the house where they were sitting" (Acts 2:1–2).

The sculpture on the stone platform here in the Upper Room symbolizes the outpouring of the Holy Spirit on the day of Pentecost. It's easy to recognize by its leaves that the tree is an olive tree. However, on top of this olive tree

457

are bowls or lamps. The entire sculpture symbolizes God's message in Zechariah 4. The olive oil represents God's Holy Spirit, and the bowls connected to the tree picture a continuous supply. The olive oil within the bowls will never run out. God interpreted the vision to Zechariah. "It is not by force nor by strength, but by my Spirit, says the LORD of Heaven's Armies" (v. 6). The artist used imagery from Zechariah's vision to picture the pouring out of God's Holy Spirit on the Day of Pentecost.

THE "ALTERNATIVE" UPPER ROOM

Like so much else in Jerusalem, there is an "alternative" Upper Room. A few of us came across the site by accident as we were exploring in the Old City. We climbed a staircase that led to a walkway across the roofs of houses. We

The Upper Room at the Monastery of St. Mark

were just about to turn back when we came to St. Mark's Monastery, associated with the Syrian Orthodox Church. We were intrigued by a sign identifying the site as both "The Upper Room" *and* "The House of St. Mark." So we went in.

A nun asked us to be seated and began to share the history of the church. Though the nun was small in stature, she commanded attention and respect. "And it's important to remember . . . HELLO! KEEP YOUR FEET OFF THE BENCH! Now, where was I? . . ."

We discovered this was the home of John Mark's mother, Mary, and that the apostles themselves declared it to be the first church. There can be no doubt of this fact because a sixth-century inscription discovered at the site says, "This is the house of Mary, mother of John, called Mark. Proclaimed a church by the holy apostles under the name of the Virgin Mary, mother of God, after the ascension of our Lord Jesus Christ into heaven. Renewed after the destruction of Jerusalem by Titus in the year AD 73."

Two amazing facts impressed me as the nun lectured us. First, since the church at this site dates back to the time of Pentecost, its upper room *must* be the true Upper Room. And we were allowed to go *down* a flight of steps to view it. The room is smaller than the more traditional Upper Room we had visited earlier, but the acoustics remained the same thanks to the stone floor, walls, and ceiling. I appreciated the fact that this room didn't have Crusader-era arches holding up the roof. Of course, I felt the need to deduct authenticity points for having to walk *down* to reach the *Upper* Room!

The icon of Mary and Jesus supposedly painted by Luke

The second amazing fact was the realization that this monastery contains the only known "authentic" portrait of Mary and Jesus that was actually painted by Luke. I had no idea Luke was both a doctor *and* an artist. I wanted to take a picture of the icon, but I was informed that pictures weren't allowed. ("HELLO! SIT DOWN! NO PICTURES! Now, where was I? . . .")

However, I could *purchase* a postcard containing a photograph of the icon, which I did. If you look carefully, you can even see the resemblance between Mary and Jesus.

The moral of this story is to take time to explore Jerusalem, if you can. There are countless discoveries that are sure to add a touch of fun and adventure to any trip. ("HELLO! I DIDN'T SAY YOU COULD LEAVE! Now, where was I? . . .")

Model of Second Temple Jerusalem at the Israel Museum

CHAPTER 48

The Israel Museum:

Seeing Everything That Was Discovered

Visiting the many historical sites throughout Israel is fascinating. Unfortunately, when describing the wonderful discoveries found at the different sites I find myself repeating the same phrase over and over: "The object is on display at the Israel Museum." Want to see the inscription from Pontius Pilate? Israel Museum. The Tel Dan stele that mentions the "house of David"? Israel Museum. The Dead Sea Scrolls? Israel Museum!

As a result, no trip to Israel would be complete without a visit to this storehouse of national treasures. Our time is limited, so we will only be able to explore some of the highlights found here.

MODEL OF SECOND TEMPLE JERUSALEM

Our first stop at the museum is the outdoor model of Second Temple Jerusalem. Created in 1966, the model was originally on display at the Holy Land Hotel in West Jerusalem. Forty years later, it was sawed apart and trucked to the Israel Museum. Visitors are surprised by the size of the model—more than ten thousand square feet—and by how helpful the model is visually. The model places the various sites in Jerusalem into their proper geographical context. Even the ice cream cone and hamburger bun (minus the Mount of Olives) can be clearly seen.

How accurate is the model?

The archaeologist who designed the model based it on several factors. He tried to take into account archaeological discoveries that had been made. He consulted written sources, including the Bible, rabbinic writings, and historical texts like those of Josephus. He also used other historical literature to help fill in details like the design of houses. Unfortunately, in a few spots he did surrender to tradition, even if that tradition isn't correct. For example, he placed the tomb of David on the wrong hill to match the spot where the Orthodox Jews believe it was located.

The temple complex

The large amount of space the temple took up in Jerusalem becomes clear in the model. The temple *dominated* the city. Surrounding the temple building itself is the court of the Gentiles, and on the southern end is the so-called portico of Solomon or Solomon's Colonnade (John 10:23; Acts 3:11; 5:12). This structure had nothing to do with King Solomon, but it was associated with him because of its immense size and its location on the Temple Mount.

A smaller enclosure wall surrounded the temple building itself. Just in front of this wall was a small barrier with signs written in Greek that said, "No man of another nation to enter within the fence and enclosure round the temple. And whoever is caught will have himself to blame that his death ensues."[1] This barrier was the dividing line between Gentiles and Jews. Jews were able to enter the enclosure, but Gentiles were not. The barrier was as close to the presence of God as Gentiles were allowed to come.

The barrier, and its signs, helps visualize the events in Acts 21. The apostle Paul took a group of Jewish followers of Jesus to the temple to help complete their Nazirite vow. After going through ritual purification in a nearby *mikveh*, Paul and the four entered the temple area. At that point a case of mistaken identity occurred. As Luke so kindly puts it, some of those in the temple "had previously seen Trophimus the Ephesian in the city with [Paul]" (v. 29 NASB). They recognized Paul, but not his companions, and they assumed Paul had brought a group of Gentiles into the temple. They began crying out, "Men of Israel, help us! This is the man who preaches against our people everywhere and tells everybody to disobey the Jewish laws. He speaks against the Temple—and even defiles this holy place by bringing in Gentiles" (v. 28).

The mob grabbed Paul and dragged him out of the inner court, back to the court of the Gentiles. They shut the doors to the temple area and, Luke says, "they were trying to kill him" (Acts 21:31). Had the Roman soldiers not intervened when they did, Paul would have been put to death—just like the sign warned. Thankfully, a guard in the Fortress of Antonia on the north side of the temple saw the commotion and reported it to his commander. A squad of soldiers rushed down to the Court of the Gentiles and rescued Paul.

Beyond visualizing this amazing story, seeing the model can also serve as a reminder of all that Jesus did to open up the way to God. Gentiles could only approach up to the separation barrier. Jewish women could get a little closer. Jewish men were allowed up to the altar of sacrifice. Priests could minister before the temple building, but only a select few were allowed inside the Holy Place to perform the sacred rituals. And then, just one day a year, the High Priest was allowed to briefly step behind the curtain into the holy of holies to sprinkle the sacrificial blood on the mercy seat. The closer one got to God, the more restricted the access. But Jesus opened the way to God through His own sacrificial death on the cross. Using the barrier in the temple as an illustration, Paul described the impact of Christ's death as he wrote to Gentile believers in Ephesus. "Once you were far away from God, but now you have been brought near to him through the blood of Christ. For Christ himself has brought peace to us. He united Jews and Gentiles into one people when, in his own body on the cross, he broke down the wall of hostility that separated us" (Eph. 2:13–14).

THE SHRINE OF THE BOOK

Right beside the model of Second Temple Jerusalem stands the Shrine of the Book, a section of the Museum that houses the Dead Sea Scrolls. A white dome, visible above ground, represents the top of the clay jars that held some of the Dead Sea Scrolls. Across from the white dome is a black basalt wall. The contrast between the two represents the war between the Sons of Light and the Sons of Darkness, an account contained in one of the scrolls found at Qumran.

Visitors can descend a set of stairs and enter the Shrine of the Book. Inside are artifacts from the excavations at Qumran, including sandals, pieces of cloth, lamps, and other objects from daily life. But the most significant objects are some of the jars in which the scrolls were discovered as well as an exact reproduction of the complete scroll of Isaiah. The scroll encircles the very center of the display. The discovery of this Isaiah scroll, dating to the second century BC, is very significant for those who believe the Bible is God's Word.

Beginning in Isaiah 40, the prophet predicts the deliverance of Israel from captivity in Babylon by a king named Cyrus. The prophecy is so dramatic—and so

The white dome on the Shrine of the Book

specific—that many scholars have concluded the second half of the book must have been written by someone else . . . someone living long after the original Isaiah had died. This otherwise unknown writer then either assumed Isaiah's identity—putting words into his mouth, so to speak—or else penned his message anonymously only to have a still-later generation mistakenly attach it to the original book of Isaiah. Over the many centuries, the two books came to be viewed as a single work from the hand of one author. At least that was the theory.

The discovery of this complete copy of Isaiah creates serious problems for that theory. In the scroll, Isaiah 39 ends on the next to last line of

The copy of the Isaiah scroll on display inside the Shrine of the Book

a column. If Isaiah 40–66 was a separate book, penned by a different author living two centuries after the original Isaiah, then the person copying this manuscript had the perfect way to show that break. All he needed to do was begin chapter 40 at the top of the next column. Instead, chapter 40 begins on the last line of the previous column, immediately after the end of chapter 39. There is *no* break, nothing in the scroll that even remotely hints at the idea of separate authors. The book was written by one author, Isaiah the son of Amoz, who prophesied during the reigns of Uzziah, Jotham, Ahaz, and Hezekiah.

The Knesset from the Shrine of the Book

The Shrine of the Book is also an excellent place to view the Knesset, Israel's parliament building. The Knesset building is a reminder that since its rebirth in 1948 Israel has considered Jerusalem to be its capital. In fact, Jerusalem has remained the epicenter of Israel's political and religious life for three thousand years.

And now it's time to visit the archaeological section of the Israel Museum.

ARCHAEOLOGICAL TREASURES

During my early visits to the Israel Museum, I had mixed emotions. I loved seeing all the antiquities, but I was frustrated by the museum's policy of not allowing photography. I understood not allowing flash photography, but taking photos without using a flash didn't harm the objects. Thankfully that policy has changed, and photography is now permitted.

Let me take you to just a few of the many objects on display in the archaeological section of the museum. I'm sure you will want to take more time to wander through all the priceless historical artifacts on display.

Herod the Great was the king who killed the babies in Bethlehem. He's also the king who built the temple, the Herodium, Masada, and the city of Caesarea—to name just *some* of the places he built that we have visited. At the Herodium we saw where archaeologists had uncovered the remains of Herod's mausoleum. In those remains they discovered a beautiful sarcophagus that had been smashed to pieces. Though his name wasn't inscribed on the box, it's almost certainly the sarcophagus of King Herod. The craftsmanship was intended to be fit for a king.

Sarcophagus of Herod the Great

Speaking of boxes that held bones, here's the ossuary (bone box) of Caiaphas, the high priest when Jesus was crucified. We know this is his ossuary because the name "Caiaphas" was incised on the side. John 11:50–52 records the one prophecy made by this wicked high priest. "'You don't realize that it's better for you that one man should die for the people than for the whole nation to be destroyed.' He did not say this on his own; as high priest at that time he was led to prophesy that Jesus would die for the entire nation. And not only for that nation, but to bring together and unite all the children of God scattered around the world."

Jesus did die, but He rose from the dead. Caiaphas also died, and his bones ended up in this intricate, limestone box. Someday Caiaphas will also rise and stand before God. Sadly, his resurrection won't be to eternal life (Rev. 20:11–15).

Ossuary of Caiaphas the high priest

In 1961, archaeologists were excavating the theater at Caesarea. They pulled off a stone seat and discovered writing on the other side. The writing was from an inscription for a building in Caesarea. The building had deteriorated, and some enterprising stonemason had rescued the plaque to use as a replacement seat while making repairs on the theater.

The plaque contained parts of four lines. The first referred to the "Tiberium," possibly a temple dedicated to Tiberias Caesar. The second line contained two words: ". . . tius Pilatus"—the Latin form of Pontius Pilate's name. The third line had Pilate's official title. Though much of the wording is missing, the remaining

Inscription with the name of Pontius Pilate

letters spell out ". . . ectus Iuda . . ."—Prefect of Judah. The fourth line is not legible. We know of Pontius Pilate from the role he played during Jesus' crucifixion, but seeing his name inscribed on a stone plaque brings him to life in a unique way.

If the Pilate inscription offers that sense of historicity, then the next item on our tour opens our eyes to the horrors endured by Jesus during the crucifixion. A portion of a heel bone was found inside an ossuary during an excavation in Jerusalem. The name of the man scratched onto the side of the ossuary was Yehohanan, the Hebrew equivalent of the New Testament name John. What made this discovery unique was the fact that the man's heel bone had an iron nail driven through it. This was the first tangible evidence of Roman crucifixion uncovered in Israel. Evidently the nail bent as it was being driven into the wooden cross. When the victim was finally removed from the cross, the nail couldn't be pulled from his body, so it was left in place.

The nail is large, and the force required to pound it through bone and into wood had to have been great. Crucifixion was designed to be brutal and

painful. Looking at this gruesome arti-
fact is a graphic reminder of what Jesus
went through for us. As Jesus Himself
said, "The Son of Man must be betrayed
into the hands of sinful men and be crucified, and . . . rise again on the third
day" (Luke 24:7).

Heel bone of a man who was crucified with the iron nail still imbedded in the bone

We've reached the final stop on this
whirlwind tour of the museum. In the
previous chapter we visited an Old Testament family tomb. Inside the repository of that tomb archaeologists found
two small silver amulets. Once the pieces of silver were unrolled, they discovered writing inside—a quotation from Numbers 6. This is the larger of the
two unrolled amulets while being viewed through a magnifying glass. The
writing is virtually invisible, even when examined closely. Yet this misshapen
piece of silver is still another reminder of the
reliability of God's Word.

Silver amulet discovered at the Ketof Hinnom excavations

Some scholars believe the Aaronic
blessing in Numbers 6 wasn't written until
the Babylonian Captivity, nine hundred
years after the time of Moses. However, this
tomb and its contents date to *before* the
Babylonian Captivity. Discovering a Scripture quotation from a portion of God's
Word that supposedly hadn't yet been written is a problem for that theory. But it's *not*
a problem for those who accept the reality
that the Bible is God's Word—and that
Moses wrote this blessing.

Entrance to Yad Vashem

CHAPTER 49

Yad Vashem:
Israel's Holocaust Museum

Yad Vashem isn't directly connected with Bible history, but it's a site that needs to be included in every visit to the Holy Land. I say that because one key purpose for a trip is to help visitors gain a greater understanding of Israel and the Middle East. And Yad Vashem, Israel's Holocaust Museum, helps people appreciate why the modern State of Israel responds as it does to terror threats and attacks. Israel knows only too well what can happen if governments fail to hold evil in check.

THE MEANING OF THE NAME

Yad Vashem appears in English as two words, but in Hebrew it's actually three. The first word is *yad*, which is the Hebrew word for "hand." However, the word can also refer to a "memorial" or a "monument." For example, King Saul "set up a monument [*yad*] to himself" after defeating the Amalekites (1 Sam. 15:12). The word *yad* is being used in the sense of "memorial" at Yad Vashem. The second word in Hebrew is actually the single Hebrew letter *vav*. The *va* sound in the word *Vashem* is the Hebrew word for "and." The last part of the word, *shem*, is the Hebrew word for "name." So *Yad Vashem* in Hebrew means "a memorial and a name."

> Israel knows only too well what can happen if governments fail to hold evil in check.

The phrase comes right from Isaiah 56:5. There, the prophet recorded God's message of hope and comfort to Israel, "I will give them—within the walls of my house—*a memorial and a name* far greater than sons and daughters could give. For the name I give them is an everlasting one. It will never disappear!" A memorial and a name. Yad Vashem is Israel's memorial to the millions of Jews who perished in the Holocaust. The Nazis first tried to erase the names of their victims, reducing their identity to numbers tattooed on their arms. And then the Nazis tried to erase their very lives . . . to annihilate the Jewish race.

The entrance to Yad Vashem is flanked by gates designed to look like the barbed wire at a Nazi concentration camp. After passing through the Visitors' Center, visitors can go in several directions. The Holocaust History Museum is the central feature of the site with its nine galleries that take visitors on an emotional journey through the horrors of the Holocaust. The tour is self-guided, and no photography is permitted. It's an intensely personal trek through a horrifying time in world history.

THE LITTLE TREE

But before heading into the Museum, I want us to visit one other spot. To reach it, we must first walk down the Avenue of the Righteous among the Nations. Carob trees have been planted all along this pathway. Each carob tree represents a Gentile who risked his or her life to save a Jewish person during the Holocaust. At the base of each tree is a sign identifying the individual and his or her country of origin. These trees are a wonderful tribute to brave individuals like Oskar Schindler. But it's also sad to realize how few trees there are. Most Gentiles stood by and did nothing during that dark period—including many who claimed to be followers of Jesus. That reality forces us to ask a disturbing question: Would we have risked *our* lives to help?

Up ahead is the Warsaw Ghetto Square and Wall of Remembrance. The red brick wall and two sculptures commemorate the Warsaw Ghetto uprising when Jewish fighters rose up to resist the Nazi attempt to clear the Warsaw

Ghetto. Just off to the side of this monument stands a rather small carob tree. It's so much tinier than the scores of beautiful carob trees we passed along the way. In fact, it almost seems out of place—at least until we know its history. The tree is small because it's relatively new. The original tree died and had to be replaced. Thousands of visitors had loved it to death!

Carob tree for Corrie ten Boom's family

Look carefully at the sign near the base of the tree. It reads: "Corrie ten Boom & father Casper & sister Elisabeth." This tree was planted in honor of Corrie ten Boom and her family. These natives from Holland risked their lives to protect a group of Jews fleeing Nazi persecution. Sadly, someone turned the family in to the authorities. They were arrested and sent to a concentration camp. Corrie survived, but her father and sister perished.

Sign at carob tree for Corrie ten Boom's family

After the war, Corrie ministered in Holland and Germany. In her book *The Hiding Place*, she wrote about an experience she had after the war when she met one of the guards from the concentration camp.

It was at a church service in Munich that I saw him, the former S.S. man who had stood guard at the shower room door in the processing center at Ravensbruck. He was the first of our actual jailers that I had seen since that time. And suddenly it was all there—the roomful of mocking men, the heaps of clothing, Betsie's pain-blanched face.

He came up to me as the church was emptying, beaming and bowing. "How grateful I am for your message, *Fraulein*," he said. "To think that, as you say, He has washed my sins away!"

His hand was thrust out to shake mine. And I, who had preached so often to the people of Bloemendaal the need to forgive, kept my hand at my side.

Even as the angry, vengeful thoughts boiled through me, I saw the sin of them. Jesus Christ had died for this man; was I going to ask for more? *Lord Jesus, I prayed, forgive me and help me to forgive him.*

I tried to smile, I struggled to raise my hand. I could not. I felt nothing, not the slightest spark of warmth or charity. And so again I breathed a silent prayer. *Jesus, I cannot forgive him. Give Your forgiveness.*

As I took his hand the most incredible thing happened. From my shoulder along my arm and through my hand a current seemed to pass from me to him, while into my heart sprang a love for this stranger that almost overwhelmed me.

And so I discovered that it is not on our forgiveness any more than on our goodness that the world's healing hinges, but on His. When He tells us to love our enemies, He gives, along with the command, the love itself.[1]

Take one last look at Corrie ten Boom's tree . . . and remember her lesson on forgiveness. Few will ever experience the horrors she went through in that concentration camp, but at some point in their lives, *many* will experience the pain of rejection and loss. Others will feel the sting of anger, prejudice, and hatred. And it's during times like these when we struggle with extending forgiveness to others. That's why we need to turn our focus back to Jesus, just like Corrie. Jesus instructed us to pray, "Forgive us our sins, *as we have forgiven* those who sin against us" (Matt. 6:12).

Jesus demonstrated His own ability to extend such forgiveness. While on the cross He prayed, "Father, forgive them, for they don't know what they are doing" (Luke 23:34). Though it might sound impossible, forgiveness actually releases an individual from the cancer of anger and vengeance that can gnaw away at their very soul. The next time you struggle to forgive, remember Corrie's little tree. Lewis B. Smedes expressed the power of forgiveness this way: "To forgive is to set a prisoner free and discover that the prisoner was you."[2]

THE CHILDREN'S MEMORIAL

Visitors to Yad Vashem can spend an entire day looking through the exhibits, art museum, learning center, visual center, and bookstore. Unfortunately, time is usually a limiting factor. But one spot everyone should visit before leaving is the Children's Memorial, dedicated to the 1.5 million children who were killed during the Holocaust.

Entrance to the Children's Memorial

At the entrance is a relief of Uziel Spiegel, whose eyes seem to direct the visitor toward the doorway leading inside. Uziel was one of the children murdered by the Nazis, and his family donated funds to build this memorial. Inside, the memorial itself is haunting in its simplicity. Five lit candles are reflected by mirrors in a way that gives visitors the feeling of being suspended in space among millions of stars. Meanwhile, the name, age, and country of origin for each child killed is being read aloud by disembodied voices.

On the way to Yad Vashem, tourists are normally talking, laughing, and sharing impressions from the last stop. But after Yad Vashem, they're quiet and subdued. On one trip we had a woman who had lived in Germany as a child during the war. Almost apologetically, she kept repeating, "They never told us this was happening."

Yad Vashem forces visitors to ask life's hard questions. Questions like: Is the human heart really capable of such evil? Sadly, the answer is yes. Or as Jeremiah wrote, "The human heart is the most deceitful of all things, and desperately wicked. Who really knows how bad it is?" (Jer. 17:9). Thankfully, in the very next verse God supplies His answer to this disturbing question. "But I, the LORD, search all hearts and examine secret motives. I give all people their due rewards, according to what their actions deserve" (v. 10).

Entrance to the City of David excavations

CHAPTER 50

The City of David:
Exploring Jerusalem's Roots

The original City of David—the ice cream cone in our diagram of Jerusalem—is located outside the current walls of the Old City. The real challenge today in visiting the City of David is deciding what to visit. A group could easily spend most of a day walking through all the tunnels and channels and visiting the different sites archaeologists have uncovered. That assumes, of course, the group is physically fit, and *not* claustrophobic.

DAVID'S PALACE

Our tour begins just inside the main entrance. Descending a flight of steps below the main floor, we see the outline of a massive building that once stood at this spot. The archaeologist who uncovered the building is convinced she found the palace that was built by King David after he captured the city. "Then King Hiram of Tyre sent messengers to David, along with cedar timber and carpenters and stonemasons, and they built David a palace" (2 Sam. 5:11).

The palace was constructed on the upper side of the city—at the top of the ice cream cone—and likely outside the original city walls. This could help explain an otherwise unusual incident in 2 Samuel 5:17. When David heard the Philistines were coming for him, he "went *down* to the stronghold" (NASB). As the New American Standard Bible makes clear, in 2 Samuel 5 the writer refers to the "stronghold" three times. In verse 7 David "captured the stronghold of Zion, that is, the city of David," and in verse 9 David "lived in the stronghold, and called it the city of David." So, it seems almost certain verse 17 is also referring to Jerusalem, the "stronghold" he captured and made his capital city. David had to leave his palace and go *down* to the stronghold, likely because the palace wasn't yet protected by Jerusalem's defenses.

The stepped stone structure that might have supported a corner of David's palace

Just to the side of David's palace, archaeologists uncovered a massive stepped stone structure. Originally thought to be built by the Canaanites, it's now assumed to be a structure that supported the palace built for David. This could be the elusive "Millo" first mentioned in connection with David's building projects in Jerusalem. David "extended the city, starting at the supporting terraces [*millo'* in Hebrew] and working inward" (2 Sam. 5:9). The word Millo comes from a Hebrew verb that means "to fill up," suggesting the structure was a supporting wall built from stone and dirt. Evidently this terrace-like structure, which is almost sixty feet high, later had to be reinforced and repaired by both Solomon (1 Kings 9:15, 24; 11:27) and Hezekiah (2 Chron. 32:5).

In the area of the Millo, archaeologists also discovered remains of houses and other buildings from the time of the Judean monarchy. One of the buildings must have been used to store official documents because fifty-one clay seal impressions, called bullae, were discovered there. They bore names from the Bible, including "Gemariah, son of Shaphan" (Jer. 36:10), "Jehucal son of Shelemiah" (Jer. 37:3), and "Gedaliah son of Pashhur" (Jer. 38:1). Those are the names of royal officials that we struggle to pronounce . . . and seldom remember.

WARREN'S SHAFT

Following a modern set of stairs down the hillside, we come to the entrance of an underground tunnel dug by the Jebusites to solve a major defensive problem with their city. The Gihon Spring was the main water supply, but it was located near the bottom of the hill in the Kidron Valley. If the city were under siege, enemy archers would shoot at anyone trying to reach the spring. So, the inhabitants built massive walls around the water supply to protect it from attack and then carved this tunnel enabling them to reach the spring without being seen.

The underground passageway to the Gihon Spring

Near the bottom of this passageway is a natural shaft that reaches down to the Gihon Spring. The shaft is called Warren's Shaft after Sir Charles Warren, a British explorer who discovered it in 1867. Some initially thought this shaft was used by the city's inhabitants to lower buckets into the spring below, and that it was also the "water tunnel" or "water shaft" Joab climbed up to break into Jerusalem (2 Sam. 5:8; 1 Chron. 11:6). But later excavations have disproved both theories. The shaft is simply a natural fissure in the limestone.

481

THE GIHON SPRING

The Canaanite tunnel extended down to the massive fortifications that surrounded the Gihon Spring. A pool carved into the rock held water from the spring, with additional water then directed through channels to irrigate plants and trees in the Kidron Valley. "Gihon" comes from a Hebrew word that means "to gush forth." The Gihon Spring is an intermittent spring whose rate of flow varies during the day. Solomon was anointed king at the Gihon Spring (1 Kings 1:38–39). Later, King Hezekiah blocked up the entrance to the spring after carving his tunnel to divert the water to the Pool of Siloam. We'll visit both the tunnel and the pool shortly, but we first need to take a slight detour.

Gihon Spring and entrance to Hezekiah's tunnel

THE CANAANITE TUNNEL

Just to the left of the entrance into the Gihon Spring is a doorway that leads into a narrow tunnel. The tunnel was carved by the Jebusites eight hundred years before the time of David. It extended for over six hundred feet, with the water then flowing into a pool. Openings along the side of the tunnel allowed water to be diverted into the valley to irrigate crops. It was an ingenious system that allowed the Jebusites to turn the Kidron Valley into productive farmland. But this tunnel also proved to be their Achilles' heel.

For four hundred years the Jebusites proved to be a thorn in Israel's side. Their massive fortifications made the city seem impenetrable, even as they enticed Israel to abandon the one true God and embrace idolatry. Multiple attempts to dislodge the Jebusites had failed. The city was just too strong to be taken. Or so it seemed.

That's when thirty-seven-year-old King David arrived on the scene. After defeating the forces of Saul's son Ish-bosheth, David was finally acknowledged as king of all Israel. This new king needed a new capital, one that would unite all the tribes. Real estate is all about location, location, location. And David's real estate agent had just the place for him. It only had one *slight* problem. It was controlled by the Jebusites. David's first challenge as king was one that would define his reign and that could make or break his fragile nation. Capture the stronghold of the Jebusites and turn it into the capital of all Israel.

The "dry" Canaanite tunnel from the Gihon Spring

The compiler of Chronicles provided a concise summary of what happened. "Then David and all Israel went to Jerusalem (or Jebus, as it used to be called), where the Jebusites, the original inhabitants of the land, were living. The people of Jebus taunted David, saying, 'You'll never get in here!' But David captured the fortress of Zion, which is now called the City of David" (1 Chron. 11:4–5).

Unfortunately, that account doesn't explain *how* David captured the city. Thankfully 2 Samuel 5:8 does. David told his men, "Whoever attacks them should strike by going into the city through the water tunnel." That is, they would need to slip into the city through its water system tunnels. This tunnel along the Kidron Valley, along with the tunnel that led past Warren's Shaft, became the pathway to victory for David's forces, led by Joab.

Had Joab and his men been discovered, their assault would have become a suicide mission. But the audacity of the plan is what made it so brilliant.

A city that could withstand a direct assault by thousands of warriors fell after a select group slipped into the city through the water system to open the gates from the inside. Over the course of a single evening the city of the Jebusites became the stronghold of David and the capital of Israel. Hopefully, focusing on that story also kept you preoccupied as you squeezed through this very *narrow*—though dry—tunnel!

HEZEKIAH'S TUNNEL

If you enjoyed the Canaanite dry tunnel, you'll *love* sloshing through Hezekiah's Tunnel. This 1,800-foot-long tunnel snakes its way under the City of David from the Gihon Spring to the Pool of Siloam. The tunnel and a major wall placed around the Western Hill were part of Hezekiah's preparations for the threatened attack by the Assyrians. The purpose for the tunnel was to divert the water from the Gihon Spring into the Pool of Siloam, providing an easily accessible water supply for the people of Jerusalem.

Walking through Hezekiah's Tunnel

Today, the depth of the water in Hezekiah's Tunnel varies from just a few inches to mid-thigh deep. Before starting through, it's important to make sure you have a flashlight. It's also helpful to have a knapsack to carry your shoes and socks. And bring water shoes or flip flops to wear on your feet. The water will feel cold at first, but you'll quickly get used to it. The tunnel itself is somewhat narrow, and there are a few places where the ceiling is a bit low. But you'll do just fine.

Hezekiah's Tunnel was an amazing engineering marvel. Two teams of workers started at opposite ends and snaked their way toward each other, ultimately carving the channel through solid rock. In fact, the compiler of 2 Kings summarized the reign of Hezekiah this way: "The rest of the events in Hezekiah's reign, including the extent of his power and how he built a pool and dug a tunnel to bring water into the city, are recorded in *The Book of the History of the Kings of Judah*" (2 Kings 20:20). The book of 2 Chronicles repeats this theme as it records that Hezekiah "blocked up the upper spring of Gihon and brought the water down through a tunnel to the west side of the City of David" (2 Chron. 32:30).

Once the tunnel was completed, the workmen chiseled a plaque into the wall to record the event. "The water flowed from the spring toward the reservoir for 1,200 cubits, and the height of the rock above the heads of the quarrymen was 100 cubits!"[1] This plaque was discovered in the 1800s. Sadly, it was chiseled from the rock and taken to the Istanbul Archaeology Museum, where it's still on display today. However, a modern copy has been affixed to the wall of the tunnel, near the exit to the Pool of Siloam.

The biggest difficulty for visitors walking through the tunnel today is fighting off claustrophobia. But during some of my early trips through the tunnel we faced even greater challenges. The tunnel wasn't always kept as "clean and clear" as it is now. On one trip, the water reached up to my neck in parts of the tunnel. I had to hold my knapsack over my head with one hand, hold my camera up with the other, and hold my flashlight in my mouth. That was a challenging trek through the tunnel! But my experience pales in comparison to the original explorers. Captain Charles Wilson led a group through the tunnel on December 12, 1867. Here's a partial summary of his report.

> At 850 feet the height of the channel was reduced to 1 foot 10 inches, and here our troubles began. The water was running with great violence, 1 foot in height, and we, crawling full length, were up to our necks in it.
>
> I was particularly embarrassed: one hand necessarily wet and dirty, the other holding a pencil, compass, and field-book; the candle for the most part in my mouth....

When we came out it was dark, and we had to stand shivering for some minutes before our clothes were brought us; we were nearly four hours in the water.[2]

Today's forty-minute walk through the tunnel seems mild by comparison.

THE POOL OF SILOAM

Those who slosh their way through Hezekiah's Tunnel finally exit at the Pool of Siloam. For many years this was the end of the journey—a place to dry one's feet, put on one's sneakers, and occasionally purchase an "I Survived Hezekiah's Tunnel" T-shirt. On one student trip, a participant brought along his wife's single-lens reflex camera. She had given him strict orders to take good care of it, and for most of the trip he had been quite careful. But then came the Pool of Siloam!

As we exited from the tunnel, the water in the pool was quite high, actually covering the stone walkway from the exit to the stairs with several inches of water. The individual decided to take a photo of the tunnel exit. He was a little too close so he stepped back . . . and back . . . and then stepped right off the walkway, falling backward into the pool. The water was only a few feet deep, but that's all it took to submerge both him and his wife's camera.

Group exiting Hezekiah's Tunnel at the Pool of Siloam

Several years ago, a ruptured pipe led to another amazing discovery—the actual Pool of Siloam from the time of Jesus. The pool at the exit from the tunnel dates to the Byzantine era. But just a short distance away were these remains of a much earlier—and much larger—pool.

The Pool of Siloam from the time of Jesus

Only a small segment of the pool has been excavated, but it's clear that it would have been quite large. Having started our journey through the City of David, just below the Temple Mount, this is a good place to stop and focus on the events in John 8 and 9. Following a confrontation with the religious leaders, Jesus "left the Temple" (John 8:59). John 9 then picks up the story. "As Jesus was walking along, he saw a man who had been blind from birth" (v. 1). The disciples used the blind man as an object lesson for a theological discussion, wanting to know if his blindness was the result of his parents' sin, or perhaps something he had done while in his mother's womb.

Jesus responded by saying that neither option was correct. After giving His explanation, Jesus "spit on the ground, made mud with the saliva, and spread the mud over the blind man's eyes. He told him, 'Go wash yourself in the pool of Siloam'" (John 9:6–7). We often skip over verses like that, but now they take on new meaning. The walk from the temple area to the Pool of Siloam was quite a long walk. Downhill. With many steps. A roadway extended from the Pool of Siloam to the temple, and that roadway will be our next stop on this journey. But right now it's important to realize that the road was made from limestone blocks, and those blocks can become smooth and slippery from people walking on them. For this man to follow Jesus' directions was a journey of faith.

Thankfully, by the end of the journey this man possessed both physical *and* spiritual sight.

THE PILGRIM ROADWAY

The most recent discovery at the City of David is the roadway that went from the Pool of Siloam to the Temple Mount. Archaeologists have spent years tunneling under the homes on the west side of the City of David, shoring up the houses above while uncovering the two-thousand-year-old roadway and drainage system below. It has been a slow, methodical process, but the results are spectacular. To walk on a street that existed in the time of Jesus brings a sense of tangibility to the Bible. For example, the man born blind could have inched his way down the very spot where your feet are now standing!

The words "To Be Continued" need to close our journey through the City of David because the process of discovery there goes on. What incredible find is waiting to be uncovered behind the next stone, or in the next bucket of dirt to be sifted? Only time will tell.

Looking down the Pilgrim Roadway by the City of David

THE GARDEN TOMB

بستان قبر السيد المسيح

גן הקבר

Entrance to the Garden Tomb

CHAPTER 51

The Garden Tomb:

The Protestant Holy Site

Every religious group in Israel has its own special list of "holy sites." For Ultra-Orthodox Jews it would be the Western Wall, or perhaps David's Tomb. For Catholic or Orthodox Christians it might be the Church of the Annunciation in Nazareth, the Church of the Nativity in Bethlehem, or the Church of the Holy Sepulchre in Jerusalem. But for most Protestant Christians, the two "holy sites" would be the Sea of Galilee and the Garden Tomb in Jerusalem. We've sailed across the Sea on a boat, and our journey today takes us to the Garden Tomb.

The Garden Tomb is located just north of the Damascus Gate in Arab East Jerusalem. Normally, the area isn't a problem, though it can be difficult for tour buses to find a nearby place to park. The site is situated between two bus stations, and there are times when the street in front of the entrance can become crowded. We discovered how crowded during the first Friday of Ramadan!

Muslims use a lunar calendar, so the month of Ramadan moves forward about ten days every year relative to our calendar. The following mix-up only happened once during all my trips, but on that particular trip the first Friday of Ramadan coincided with the final day of our tour. The group was scheduled to spend most of the day in the Old City before driving to the Garden Tomb in the afternoon. As our driver took us to the initial drop-off point, we learned that all the streets around the Old City would be closed by midmorning because of the large crowds coming to the Al-Aqsa Mosque for Friday services. We would not see our bus or driver again until *after* our visit to the Garden Tomb.

We spent the morning and early afternoon trying to avoid the crowd surging into the Muslim Quarter and onto the Temple Mount. In midafternoon, we started walking toward the Garden Tomb. Unfortunately, at the same time thousands of Muslims began streaming north out of the Muslim Quarter of the Old City to connect with public transportation to take them home.

The crowd—and barrier—blocking the entrance on the left!

Our group zigzagged its way through the Christian Quarter of the Old City, hoping to outflank the surging crowds. Then we saw police barriers set up near Damascus Gate, blocking our way! We made a wide loop around the area, hoping to circle back to the Garden Tomb from the north. It was a *great* plan, but with one tiny flaw. The police had set up barricades across the street that runs in front of the Garden Tomb to help queue up the mass of people so they could be herded onto buses. Unfortunately, they had set up the barrier just *above* the entrance to the site! A wall of humanity, guarded by police and soldiers, was jammed against the barrier stretched across the roadway, effectively blocking us from our destination.

After some animated discussions with those in charge, we were able to persuade them to temporarily open the side of the barrier next to the Garden Tomb so our group could squeeze its way through and enter. After all the crowds and walking, we were ready for the peaceful solitude of the Garden Tomb.

THE TOUR OF THE GARDEN TOMB

The Garden Tomb is controlled by an evangelical organization from the United Kingdom. Their guides are volunteers from around the world who travel to Israel and donate their time to lead groups through the site. And like the water of life in Revelation 22:17, the Garden Tomb is available to all groups "without cost" (NASB).

> The Garden Tomb offers everything Protestant Christians want when they think about the events connected with Jesus' death and resurrection.

I need to start this section by reaffirming that my head tells me the Church of the Holy Sepulchre is likely the location where Jesus was crucified, buried, and rose from the dead. However, that site leaves me unsatisfied spiritually. It's a mass of conflict and confusion. In contrast, the Garden Tomb offers everything Protestant Christians want when they think about the events connected with Jesus' death and resurrection. We want to see Calvary, and here they have "Skull Hill." We want an actual tomb, like the one found here. We want a garden nearby, and the remains of a grape press and cistern were discovered at this site. The Garden Tomb Association has developed the area to give it a warm, inviting, beautiful feel. My head tells me the events happened at the other site, but my heart helps me understand those events more clearly here.

Looking at Skull Hill just above an Arab bus station next to the Garden Tomb

The first stop on the tour is an overlook where the group can see "Skull Hill." It is just above another of the Arab bus stations that bracket the Garden Tomb. The guide points out the indentations that give the impression of eye sockets. The mouth is now covered by pavement, but the guide displays an old photograph where the shape can be seen more clearly.

Skull Hill is often called Gordon's Calvary after Major General Charles Gordon, who visited Jerusalem in 1883. While staying at the home of Horatio and Anna Spafford, he looked out from their roof and saw the site. He wasn't the first to propose it as the location of Calvary, but his popularity in England—especially following his death in Khartoum defending the city against an invading Islamic army—helped popularize the site among British evangelicals who formed the Garden Tomb Association and gathered funds to purchase the land in 1894.

Dwight L. Moody visited the Holy Land in the spring of 1892 and preached at the site. Actually, he nearly caused a riot by preaching there! Above Skull Hill is a Muslim cemetery. Mr. Moody used one of the graves as a platform as he stood to preach. He later responded to the anger and criticism. "I don't blame them. I wouldn't want any man to stand on my father's grave to preach a sermon."[1]

From Skull Hill, the guide takes us to the garden area. The apostle John wrote, "The place of crucifixion was near a garden, where there was a new tomb, never used before" (John 19:41). When those from the West think of a garden, we envision a place for cultivating flowers and perhaps some vegetables. But in

Jesus' day, the word referred to a working garden like an olive grove, orchard, or vineyard. The discovery of a large water cistern and grape press at this site suggests the area might have once been a working vineyard.

The highlight of the tour, though, is the visit to the tomb. The guide stresses one key point that every visitor must remember. Whether this is the tomb in which Jesus was laid or not is not important. We don't worship the tomb, we worship the Son of God who died for our sins, was placed in a tomb, and then rose from the dead!

The entrance to the tomb

The signage throughout the Garden Tomb is quite helpful. Different plants and flowers are labeled, and appropriate Scripture passages can be found at key points. But the most profound sign was the one that hung on the wooden doorway into the tomb. Since the door remained open during the day, some visitors missed it as they stepped inside. But the quotation, adapted from Luke 24:6, summarized the entire focus of the Garden Tomb Association: "He is not here—for He is Risen." Sadly, the sign—and the door on which it was fastened—were removed from the tomb entrance because visitors kept closing the door to take a picture, creating long lines for those

Sign that was affixed to the door into the tomb

wanting to enter. The new arrangement might help "speed up the queue," but I hope the door and sign are eventually restored. They are probably as close as most Protestants will ever come to having an actual religious icon with deep spiritual significance.

But don't despair. Replicas of the sign are available for purchase in the gift shop!

One sign that is not for sale—and, in fact, no longer even on display—is one that was once affixed to the wall just outside the entrance to the Garden Tomb. I walked past this sign many times without ever pausing to read the smaller print underneath. That is, until Jerry Jenkins pointed it out to a group. I suppose we should all be thankful it wasn't posted when Peter, John, and the women went to the Garden on that first Easter Sunday.

THE
GARDEN
TOMB

Opening Hours 08:30am- 5:30pm
Closed on Sunday

Sign that once marked the entrance to the Garden Tomb

COMMUNION AT THE GARDEN TOMB

Following the tour, many groups arrange to have a communion service. The Garden Tomb Association will reserve a location and prepare the elements for any group who requests it. The groups—large and small—then gather for their own special time of remembrance.

One of the most memorable experiences at the Garden Tomb is to hear groups from around the world singing the same songs of worship, but in a myriad of languages. Some are accompanied by guitars while others sing *a cappella*.

A tray prepared with the elements for the communion service

Hearing people from a myriad of nations gather to praise God is a foretaste of heaven and a reminder that a day is coming when a new song will be sung: "You are worthy to take the scroll and break its seals and open it. For you were slaughtered, and your blood has ransomed people for God from every tribe and language and people and nation" (Rev. 5:9).

Many tour groups bring small olive wood cups for their communion service. Following the service, I encourage our participants to write that date on the bottom of the cup and then to take the cup home as a souvenir of their time in the Holy Land—and this special time of remembering Jesus' death, burial, resurrection, and promised return. This is when I want to breathe back the words of the apostle John in Revelation 22:20. "Amen! Come, Lord Jesus!"

The Garden Tomb is significant because it reminds us of the reality of the events that occurred here in Jerusalem. But always remember, our hope rests in a living Savior—not in a cold slab of limestone that once served as the temporary resting place for His human body!

The empty tomb

The branch and flowers of a mustard tree growing beside a wall

CHAPTER 52

Conclusion

After a year or more of anticipation—and weeks of preparation—your tour of the Holy Land is now over. The days in the land, especially the last few days in Jerusalem, flew by in a blur of sites and experiences. So now it's time to pack, head to the airport, bid a tearful goodbye to our guide and driver, and board the plane for the long flight home.

For the next several days you will be fighting jet lag as you try to resume your normal routine. The trip will begin to fade into the background, becoming just a fond memory. Then at some point you will be reading your Bible, and a place name will jump off the page. It might happen at home or in church. But at that instant a mental picture of the site will flash in your mind. You'll see, feel, even smell that spot in a new, visceral way. And as you continue reading through the passage, other details you never noticed before will suddenly stand out.

Instead of reading *about* an event, you will suddenly feel as if you are *experiencing* the event in a fresh, new, and exciting way. The expression used most often by those who've been to Israel is that the Bible suddenly seems to "come alive." Actually, the Bible hasn't changed, you have. The Bible has always been God's living, breathing Word. But you're now experiencing the visual details that were always there but previously unnoticed because you didn't have the proper geographical context for appreciating their significance.

On this trip together I hope you have grown in your understanding of, and appreciation for, God's Word. Experiencing these sites will now allow you to read God's Word with a fresh pair of eyes. And your appreciation for all the many details will grow stronger, not weaker, as the months and years go by.

For some of you, this book has helped you review a past trip to Israel. Hopefully, reading through the text and viewing the pictures has brought back vivid memories of your time in the land. Others might have read this book in preparation for an upcoming trip. If so, I hope I've encouraged you to pack your sense of adventure—and your sense of humor—for that upcoming trip. Seek out new experiences and allow God to use your time in the land to help you grow in your faith. For still others, this book might be the only opportunity you will have to "visit" Israel during your lifetime. And if that's the case, then I trust the book has allowed you to experience a virtual tour of the Holy Land.

Many vacations can be summarized in one sentence: Been there, done that, got the T-shirt. It was fun, but I don't need to do it again. For me, that has *never* been true of Israel. Every visit is an opportunity to learn something new. Sites change and develop over time. But more importantly, I change. Visiting the different locations gives me a greater understanding of God's Word. And that greater understanding of God's Word then helps me more fully grasp what I'm seeing when I revisit the sites. This spiral of understanding never ends. That's one reason people keep going back to Israel. And for those of you who will never be able to go on an actual trip, I would encourage you to read through this book again in the future. Over time, you will experience the same spiral of understanding.

THE LESSONS FROM THE MUSTARD SEED

I want to end by sharing one final lesson from the land. In Matthew 13, Jesus used a mustard seed to make an important comparison to the kingdom of heaven. "The Kingdom of Heaven is like a mustard seed planted in a field" (v. 31). Unfortunately, that's where most modern readers get lost. For us, mustard comes out of a jar or bottle. The mustard we spread on sandwiches has no seeds! We miss whatever point Jesus is trying to make because our train of thought just jumped the tracks.

What was mustard used for in ancient times? And what does a mustard

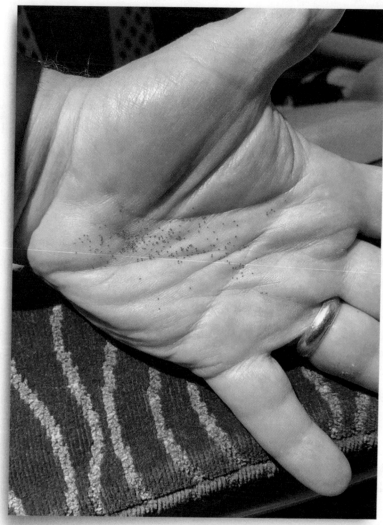

A handful of tiny mustard seeds

seed even look like? Mustard is an irritant, and in the past it was used more as medicine than as a condiment. The ancient physician Galen said mustard was applied to sores to promote healing and was also part of a mixture used to promote vomiting.[1] (The ipecac of its day!)

There's even a question as to what sort of mustard seed Jesus was referring to when He compared it with the kingdom of heaven. Many assume He was referring to the black mustard plant, which does grow in the Middle East. But its seeds aren't particularly small. And though the plant can grow to over ten feet tall, it's really more like a large shrub than a small tree. Others believe He was describing the *Nicotiana glauca* plant, often called a tobacco tree or a mustard tree. It looks more like a spindly tree with yellow flowers, and it can grow to a height of fifteen feet or more. More importantly, its seeds are incredibly tiny. The plant is toxic, so if this is the plant Jesus was describing, it was definitely *not* grown for food. But it was used in poultices and for other medicinal purposes. Personally, I believe this is the plant and seeds Jesus was describing.

The most amazing part of this mustard tree is the small size of its seeds. I love to stop the tour bus when I see some growing along the road and grab a few of the small brown seedpods. I can usually find seeds still inside the pods. I shake the seeds into my hand and then walk through the bus holding out my hand to show people the seeds. It's another of the aha moments as people look at the scores of tiny seeds. They then look outside at the small trees that sprouted from these tiny seeds, trees that are large enough, as Jesus said, for birds to "come and make nests in its branches" (Matt. 13:32).

People have tried to read a great deal more meaning into the parable than Jesus intended, like trying to find significance in the birds that perch in the branches. But when interpreting parables, it's best to stick with the main point of the story—unless Jesus Himself goes out of His way to explain other details. In the parable of the mustard seed He doesn't tell us that there's any deeper significance to the birds.

What is the point of the story? Jesus' point is that God's kingdom program may appear to start small, but God will still be at work in almost mysterious ways to bring about its growth. The seed might have been the tiniest of all those in use by farmers in Jesus' day, but the end result is the largest plant growing in the garden. And in the same way, the kingdom program announced by Jesus will someday fill the earth, when He returns as "King of all kings and Lord of all lords" (Rev. 19:16).

Jesus also used this same plant to teach a lesson on faith. Having just come down from the Mount of Transfiguration, Jesus explained to His disciples why they had been unable to heal a boy possessed by a demon. "'You don't have enough faith,' Jesus told them. 'I tell you the truth, if you had faith even as small as a mustard seed, you could say to this mountain, "Move from here to there," and it would move. Nothing would be impossible'" (Matt. 17:20). The "mountain" to which He was alluding at that moment was very likely Mount Hermon, the tallest mountain in Israel. And the mustard seed was the smallest of seeds. In other words, it doesn't take much faith to accomplish great things.

So, what lessons from the mustard seed can we take home as we wrap up this trip to Israel? Here are two that are related to what Jesus taught about these small seeds. First, don't get discouraged when life doesn't miraculously change following your trip. God's kingdom itself started out small, but God is still working to accomplish all He set out to do. The acronym PBPGINF-WMY is still true—Please be patient, God is not finished with me yet! Your investment of time in Israel will continue paying spiritual dividends in the weeks, months, and years ahead.

> The mustard seed teaches us that the greatest mountain can be moved by the tiniest seed of faith.

The second lesson is that we don't need to be "giants of the faith" to be used by God. The mustard seed teaches us that the greatest mountain can be moved by the tiniest seed of faith. Remember, God isn't looking for *ability*; He's far more concerned about your *availability*.

Hopefully this journey to the land of the Bible has helped you in your walk with God. We visited *real* places where *real* men and women of the Bible exercised *real* faith in God's promises and discovered the *real* impact He could make through them. May you discover that to be true in your life as well.

Shalom!

ACKNOWLEDGMENTS

This book might have my name on the cover, but it did not spring *ex nihilo* from my mind or pen. It's the product of taking groups to Israel for four decades and observing those fellow travelers interact with, and get excited about, the land. As I wrote out my thoughts and impressions, I filtered them through a host of friends as well as the wonderful staff at Moody Publishers. This book is a byproduct of *all* of their input.

I struggle when personally acknowledging everyone who helped bring this book to fruition because I'm fearful of leaving some out, so I apologize in advance for any omissions. And yet, I can't finish this manuscript without singling out the following individuals to whom I'm especially grateful.

Thank you, Amy Simpson and Randall Payleitner, for shepherding the manuscript through the acquisition process at Moody Publishers. You graciously put up with my personal requests—and eccentricities—and found a way forward.

Thank you, Betsey Newenhuyse, for serving as editor on the project. Working with you has *always* been a joy! I learned in the past to listen carefully to your suggestions. Your insightful edits helped shape and sharpen the final copy.

I also want to extend a special thank-you to everyone who traveled with me to Israel over the years. Your unbridled enthusiasm at seeing the land for the first time helped guarantee the sites would never become old for me . . . because I could always see them afresh through your eyes!

I end by once again thanking my wife, Kathy. Those who really know me understand the role Kathy has played in nearly every trip I have taken and every book I have written. She was the guide to the restrooms, the keeper of the nonprescription medication bag, and the companion of those unable to do all the hikes. She has also been my in-house editor and proofreader who always makes the initial manuscript look polished and professional. I might have traveled to Israel more times, but your seventy-plus trips is a record seldom matched by others!

NOTES

Introduction
1. Mark Twain, *The Innocents Abroad* (Hartford, CT: American Publishing Co., 1869), 22.
2. Ibid., 582.
3. Ibid.

Chapter 3: Megiddo: The Site of Armageddon
1. Mark Twain, *The Innocents Abroad* (Hartford, CT: American Publishing Co., 1869), 523.
2. Carl G. Rasmussen, *The NIV Atlas of the Bible* (Grand Rapids: Zondervan, 1989), 36.

Chapter 4: Nazareth: Jesus' Hometown
1. Mark Twain, *The Innocents Abroad* (Hartford, CT: American Publishing Co., 1869), 528.

Chapter 6: The Sea of Galilee: The Little Lake with a Big History
1. Mark Twain, *The Innocents Abroad* (Hartford, CT: American Publishing Co., 1869), 497–98.

Chapter 8: Capernaum: The Village of Nahum
1. Flavius Josephus, *The Wars of the Jews, The Works of Josephus,* trans. William Whiston (Peabody, MA: Hendrickson Publishers, 1987), 3.3.2.
2. Mark Twain, *The Innocents Abroad* (Hartford, CT: American Publishing Co., 1869), 580.

Chapter 9: Chorazin: Capernaum with a View
1. Jerome Murphy-O'Connor, *The Holy Land*, 5th ed. (New York: Oxford University Press, 2008), 257.
2. Nogah Hareuveni, *Tree and Shrub in Our Biblical Heritage* (Kiryat Ono, Israel: Neot Kedumim, 1984), 60–62.

Chapter 10: Bethsaida: The City That Went Missing
1. Flavius Josephus, *Antiquities of the Jews, The Works of Josephus,* trans. William Whiston (Peabody, MA: Hendrickson Publishers, 1987), 18.2.1.
2. Flavius Josephus, *The Wars of the Jews, The Works of Josephus,* trans. William Whiston (Peabody, MA: Hendrickson Publishers, 1987), 3.10.7.

Chapter 11: Tabgha: Site of the Misplaced Miracle
1. Mendel Nun, *The Sea of Galilee and Its Fishermen in the New Testament* (Ein Gev, Israel: Kibbutz Ein Gev, 1989), 14.
2. Ibid.

Chapter 17: Banias: Site of Peter's Great Confession
1. Charles H. Dyer, *30 Days in the Land with Jesus: A Holy Land Devotional* (Chicago: Moody Publishers, 2012), 117–18.
2. Mark Twain, *The Innocents Abroad* (Hartford, CT: American Publishing Co., 1869), 465.
3. Ibid., 472.
4. "Mark Twain's Journey to Jerusalem: Dreamland," PBS Documentary, 2017.

Chapter 24: En Gedi: David's Encounter with Saul
1. Howard Hendricks speaking to tour group at En Gedi, May 27, 1993.

Chapter 25: Masada: Herod's Doomsday Fortress

1. Flavius Josephus, *The Wars of the Jews, The Works of Josephus,* trans. William Whiston (Peabody, MA: Hendrickson Publishers, 1987), 7.8.4.
2. Ibid., 7.9.1.

Chapter 26: The Dead Sea: You Can't Sink, But You Can Drown!

1. Pliny, *Natural History,* trans. Philemon Holland (London: Barclay, Castle Street, Leicester Square, 1848), 5.15–16.
2. Ibid.
3. Mark Twain, *The Innocents Abroad* (Hartford, CT: American Publishing Co., 1869), 595.
4. Ibid., 595–96.

Chapter 28: Beersheba: From Dan to Beersheba

1. Stanley Ellisen, *Who Owns the Land?,* updated and revised by Charles H. Dyer (Wheaton, IL: Tyndale House Publishers, 2003), 157.

Chapter 29: Lachish: Israel's Archaeological Gem

1. James B. Pritchard, *Ancient Near Eastern Texts Relating to the Old Testament,* 3rd ed. (Princeton, NJ: Princeton University Press, 1969), 322.

Chapter 33: The Aijalon Valley: The Front Door to Jerusalem

1. Eusebius, *The Onomasticon,* trans. G. S. P. Freeman-Grenville (Jerusalem: Carta, 2003), 53.
2. Norman MacLeod, *Eastward,* 4th ed. (London: Strahan & Co., 1869), 178–79, 186.

Chapter 34: The Herodium: Herod's Funeral Monument

1. Flavius Josephus, *The Wars of the Jews, The Works of Josephus,* trans. William Whiston (Peabody, MA: Hendrickson Publishers, 1987), 1.21.10.
2. Flavius Josephus, *Antiquities of the Jews, The Works of Josephus,* trans. William Whiston (Peabody, MA: Hendrickson Publishers, 1987), 14.13.8.
3. Ibid., 14.13.9.

Chapter 35: Bethlehem: O Little Town of Bethlehem?

1. Alfred Edersheim, *The Life and Times of Jesus the Messiah* (New York: Longmans, Green, and Co., 1906), 186.

Chapter 36: Jerusalem Overview: The Confusion over Jerusalem

1. Peter Baker, "Unveiling a Lincoln Bible That Was Sitting in Plain Sight All These Years," *New York Times,* June 20, 2019, Section A, 23.
2. Mark Twain, *The Innocents Abroad* (Hartford, CT: American Publishing Co., 1869), 556.

Chapter 41: The Southern Steps: I Walked Today Where Jesus Walked

1. Edward Robinson, *Biblical Researches in Palestine* (London: John Murray, 1841), 1:425.

Chapter 42: The Temple Mount: Ground Zero in the Current Conflict

1. Mark Twain, *The Innocents Abroad* (Hartford, CT: American Publishing Co., 1869), 578.
2. Ibid., 579.
3. Ibid., 580.
4. Ibid.

Chapter 43: The Pool of Bethesda: Does God Help Those Who Help Themselves?

1. Bill Broadway, "You May Swear on the Bible, but It's Not in the Bible," *Los Angeles Times,* September 11, 2000.
2. George Barna, "Competing Worldviews Influence Today's Christians," Barna Group, May 9, 2017, https://www.barna.com/research/competing-worldviews-influence-todays-christians/.

Chapter 44: Via Dolorosa: The Way of Sorrow . . . and Confusion!

1. Charles H. Dyer, *30 Days in the Land with Jesus: A Holy Land Devotional* (Chicago: Moody Publishers, 2012), 227–30.

Chapter 45: The Church of the Holy Sepulchre: A Clash of Expectations

1. Jerome Murphy-O'Connor, *The Holy Land*, 5th ed. (New York: Oxford University Press, 2008), 49.
2. Norman MacLeod, *Eastward*, 4th ed. (London: Strahan & Co., 1869), 224.
3. Mark Twain, *The Innocents Abroad* (Hartford, CT: American Publishing Co., 1869), 567.
4. Ibid., 573.

Chapter 46: The Old City of Jerusalem: Walking through Time

1. Chris Nashawaty, "The Jerusalem Syndrome: Why Some Religious Tourists Believe They Are the Messiah," *Wired*, February 17, 2012, https://www.wired.com/2012/02/ff-jerusalem syndrome/.
2. James B. Pritchard, *Ancient Near Eastern Texts Relating to the Old Testament*, 3rd ed. (Princeton, NJ: Princeton University Press, 1969), 288.

Chapter 48: The Israel Museum: Seeing Everything That Was Discovered

1. C. K. Barrett, ed., *The New Testament Background: Selected Documents* (New York: Harper & Row, Publishers, 1961), 50.

Chapter 49: Yad Vashem: Israel's Holocaust Museum

1. Corrie ten Boom with Elizabeth and John Sherrill, *The Hiding Place*, 35th anniversary edition (Bloomington, MN: Chosen Books, 2006), 247.
2. Lewis B. Smedes, *Forgive and Forget: Healing the Hurts We Don't Deserve* (New York: Harper & Row, 1984).

Chapter 50: The City of David: Exploring Jerusalem's Roots

1. James B. Pritchard, *Ancient Near Eastern Texts Relating to the Old Testament*, 3rd ed. (Princeton, NJ: Princeton University Press, 1969), 321.
2. Charles Wilson and Charles Warren, *The Recovery of Jerusalem*, ed. Walter Morrison (New York: D. Appleton & Co., 1871), 188–89.

Chapter 51: The Garden Tomb: The Protestant Holy Site

1. William R. Moody, *The Life of Dwight L. Moody* (Chicago: Fleming H. Revell Co., 1900), 391.

Chapter 52: Conclusion

1. Galen, *Method of Medicine, Volume 1: Books 1–4*, ed. and trans. Ian Johnston and G. H. R. Horsley, Loeb Classical Library (Cambridge: Harvard University Press, 2011), 393–403.

CHARLES H. DYER (BA, Washington Bible College; ThM and PhD, Dallas Theological Seminary) served as provost and dean of education at Moody Bible Institute before becoming professor-at-large of Bible at Moody and host of *The Land and the Book* radio program. Charlie has traveled extensively throughout the Middle East for forty years, leading over a hundred trips, and is the author of numerous books, including *The Christian Traveler's Guide to the Holy Land*. Charlie and his wife, Kathy, have been married more than forty-five years and have two grown children.

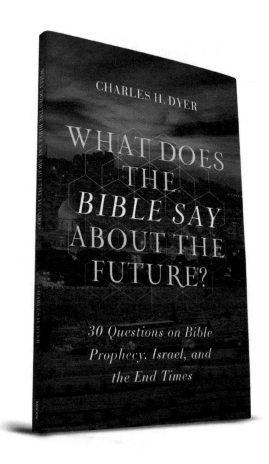